BLACK FREEDOM IN
THE AGE OF SLAVERY

THE CAROLINA LOWCOUNTRY AND THE ATLANTIC WORLD

Sponsored by the Program in the Carolina Lowcountry
and the Atlantic World of the College of Charleston

BLACK FREEDOM
IN THE
AGE OF SLAVERY

*Race, Status, and Identity
in the Urban Americas*

JOHN GARRISON MARKS

THE UNIVERSITY OF
SOUTH CAROLINA PRESS

Published by the University of South Carolina Press
Columbia, South Carolina 29208

www.uscpress.com

Manufactured in the United States of America

29 28 27 26 25 24 23 22 21
10 9 8 7 6 5 4

Library of Congress Cataloging-in-Publication Data
can be found at http://catalog.loc.gov/.

ISBN 978-1-64336-122-2 (hardback)
ISBN 978-1-64336-123-9 (paperback)
ISBN 978-1-64336-124-6 (ebook)

For my mom and dad

Contents

Tables and Illustrations

Acknowledgments

This book would not have been possible without the help and encouragement of some of the best advisers, colleagues, friends, and family anyone could ask for. My intellectual journey and development as a historian began late in high school. That was when I first learned I had a knack for history and writing, and I will be forever grateful to my teacher Bob Fenster for putting up with my attitude and encouraging me to cultivate my abilities and to take them more seriously. My development as a historian really began as an undergraduate at Lynchburg College. My undergraduate adviser, mentor, and friend, Kirt von Daacke, has helped me grow as a person and as a scholar for going on fifteen years now. Kirt introduced me to the process of primary research and historical writing, and his high standards and unwavering support helped mold me into the scholar I have become. Thanks as well to the rest of the LC History cohort—Nikki Sanders, Brian Crim, Ashley Schmidt, Charlotte Arbogast, and Jonathan Shipe—for their support and friendship (and for commiserating with me as we all dealt with Kirt).

Generous research and travel support from the Department of History at Rice University, as well as the university's Wagoner Foreign Study Scholarship, allowed me to take extended research trips to Bogotá and Cartagena, Colombia; Seville, Spain; and Columbia and Charleston, South Carolina. Rice's history department also generously funded conference travel and presentations, allowing me to gain feedback and insight that has surely improved this final project. I owe a huge debt of gratitude to everyone at Rice.

I have benefitted from an incredible adviser in Jim Sidbury. Jim came to Rice the year after I started in the doctoral program, a stroke of luck that probably shifted my scholarly trajectory. Jim has always been generous with his time, and his careful reading of my work has undoubtedly improved the final product. Thanks as well to other committee members and professors who read chapters or articles and worked with me during my time in Houston: Caleb McDaniel, Alida Metcalf, Jenifer Bratter, John Boles, Rebecca Goetz, David Dow, Randal Hall, Bethany Johnson, Ussama Makdisi, Carl Caldwell, Ed Cox, Kerry Ward, Lora Wildenthal, and John Zammitto. I owe a great deal of gratitude to all of these professors for helping a student fresh out of undergrad who thought he knew everything to mature as a scholar and professional.

I have been extremely fortunate that my graduate cohort led me to many lifelong friends. I continue to believe that the relationship among the history graduate students at Rice is both uncommon and one of the program's greatest strengths. Thanks to all of you, for everything: Sam Abramson, Lauren Brand, Blake Earle, Andrew Johnson, Wright Kennedy, Andy Lang, Joe Locke, Allison Madar, Keith McCall, Maria Montalvo, Carl Paulus, Sarah Paulus, David Ponton, Kelly Weber Stefonowich, Tim Stefonowich, Whitney Stewart, Jim Wainwright, and Ben Wright. I look back fondly to my time spent with all of you on the fifth floor of Fondren, at Valhalla, and all over Houston.

Other scholars, departments, and professionals around the country have been instrumental in bringing this book to life. I owe thanks to all of them. Jim Sweet offered excellent recommendations for writing and improving this book. Dan Richter and the 2016–17 cohort at the McNeil Center for Early American Studies welcomed an interloper who just happened to live in Philly into their midst and allowed me to join their intellectual community. Jane G. Landers facilitated my access to Cartagena's church records; chapter 5 would not have been possible without her help. Jane, along with Celso Castilho and others at Vanderbilt University, warmly welcomed me to Nashville when I moved here in 2017 and helped get me set up as a visiting scholar, providing me essential resources that allowed me to complete the book. The Department of History Universidad de los Andes welcomed me to Colombia and provided much-needed assistance when I was getting settled in Bogotá. Thanks to all of you.

Thank you as well to Ehren Foley and Richard Brown at University of South Carolina Press, to David Gleeson, Simon Lewis, and John White, editors of the Carolina Lowcountry and Atlantic World series, and to the anonymous peer reviewers who provided such constructive and encouraging feedback on the manuscript. Finally I will forever be indebted to the amazing archival staffs at all of the institutions where I researched, particularly at Archivo Nacional de la Nación (Colombia); Archivo General de Indias (Seville, Spain); and the South Carolina Department of Archives and History.

I also need to thank the #Twitterstorians community on Twitter. Being part of such a huge community of scholars has been incredibly helpful to me in getting through the intellectual and personal challenges of scholarly work. Particularly after I moved away from Houston, the #Twitterstorians helped me feel like I wasn't doing this work in total isolation. I surely wasted a great deal of time on Twitter while producing this work, and the platform has changed quite a bit since I began using it for scholarly purposes almost ten years ago, but I benefited immensely from the community of scholars there. I won't go so far as @ mentioning you in my acknowledgments, but thanks to all of you.

Thanks as well to my family: my brothers, Roger and George, and my parents, to whom this work is dedicated. My mom and dad have always been supportive of my scholarly pursuits and have helped me in innumerable ways over the last ten years. My mom always has had good advice, encouragement, and sympathy, even when I made things seem pretty bleak. I have a vivid early memory of my dad telling me when I was fairly young to just read everything I could get my hands on; that proved to be sage advice. So thanks, Mom and Dad, for always supporting and believing in me.

Most important, I need to thank my wife, Caroline, for all of her support during this process. She helped me get through many personal challenges and low points and has spent countless hours listening to me talk through research questions, reading my work, and offering me careful and critical feedback along the way. She has stuck with me through the ups and downs of living abroad, writer's block, the academic job market, and multiple moves across the country. Though she probably doesn't want to, she now knows this material as well as almost anyone. Thank you, Caroline, for being so supportive and loving throughout this process; I wouldn't have been able to finish it without you. And last but not least, thank you to my companion and furry research assistant, Ollie; you're a good boy.

I have been with this book in some way, shape, or form for nearly ten years now. It has morphed more times than I ever imagined, and it's bittersweet to see it go out into the world. These ideas have been with me from Houston to Bogotá to Philadelphia to Nashville. I hadn't yet met my wife when I started this project; I made my final revisions in the house we own together in the earliest hours of the morning during the year after the birth of our first child (hi!). It's impossible to finish a book without help, and I am very thankful to have had lots of it from some phenomenal people. While any mistakes and deficiencies that might remain in the following pages are mine alone, I can't stress enough how much I appreciate the support I've had from so many of you while I wrote this.

INTRODUCTION

In 1777 Manuel Herrera, a man of mixed African and European ancestry, lived and worked in Santo Toribio—an upper-class, racially mixed neighborhood inside the walled city of Cartagena de Indias, situated on the Caribbean coast of modern-day Colombia. A member of the city's voluntary *pardo* militia, Herrera was a shoemaker who operated a workshop with his two sons, Toribio and Julian Estevan. Herrera, his family, and dozens of others lived in a large house on the Calle de Nuestra Señora de los Reyes (Street of Our Lady of Kings). Fellow artisans of African descent—woodcarvers, silversmiths, carpenters—lived and worked on the house's first floor and basement, while a coterie of royal officials, Spanish merchants, and other prominent whites occupied the upper floors.[1] Twenty-one years later and some fifteen hundred miles northward across the Caribbean Sea, an enslaved man of mixed racial ancestry named Jehu Jones purchased his freedom in the city of Charleston, South Carolina. Initially trained as a tailor, Jones went on to become a prominent hotelier and a member of Charleston's elite Brown Fellowship Society and was recognized by blacks and whites alike as one of the city's most distinguished residents.[2] Through their rise to distinction, both of these men lived lives that challenged the ideological underpinnings of white authority in the early modern Atlantic world. Though surely neither knew of the other's existence, exploring stories such as theirs begins to reveal the shared dynamics of race, freedom, and identity in the urban Americas.

Investigating the individual lives of Manuel Herrera, Jehu Jones, and many others reveals detail and nuance about the social and cultural worlds of free people of color in the African Americas—broadly speaking, the areas of Latin America, the Caribbean, and the United States that became home to Africans and their descendants during the colonization of the Americas—between the wars for independence in the United States and in Spanish America. By delving deeply into the lived experiences of free people of color, *Black Freedom* investigates how they navigated daily life and negotiated the boundaries of racial difference in the urban Atlantic world through a focus on two crucial mainland American port cities: Cartagena, along the Caribbean coast of Colombia, and Charleston, situated in the heart of the South

Carolina lowcountry in the U.S. South.[3] Transnational and comparative in perspective, this work analyzes how free people of color leveraged institutions, laws, personal reputations, and carefully cultivated social networks to improve their individual circumstances as well as those of their families and communities. By examining racial and community dynamics in both Latin America and the United States, I argue that free people of color, in their efforts to achieve social distinction, earn money, and build lives for themselves and their families, challenged racial norms and subtly called into question the logic of white authority in the eighteenth- and nineteenth-century Americas.

Although free people of color throughout the Americas worked to improve their fortunes in ways that represented a challenge to white racial logic, their means of doing so could vary widely between Spanish America and the United States; while the ends free people of color sought to achieve may link the Americas together, the means were always adapted to local circumstances. The challenges and opportunities they confronted reveal complex parallels and differences in their lived experience. For example, while Manuel Herrera could utilize a public institution such as the voluntary militia to press claims for benefits and privileges directly with the Spanish crown, free people of color such as Jehu Jones instead had to establish independent organizations like the Brown Fellowship Society to push for social distinction and its attendant privileges. By deeply exploring these fine-grained distinctions, I argue that even when their efforts to improve their lives necessarily differed, efforts by free people of color to advance their individual circumstances challenged the logic of white racial ideologies and subtly questioned the legitimacy of American racial hierarchies. Claiming rights and privileges and forcing exceptions to otherwise impenetrable ideas about black capacities' for freedom revealed cracks in the foundations of whites' racial logic. Although free people of color often declined to confront directly the systems of white supremacy that undergirded American society, their effort to achieve social and economic uplift represented a critical step forward in African-descended people's struggle to achieve the full rights of citizenship and equality—a struggle that continues today throughout the Americas, from Boston to Buenos Aires, from Chile to Canada, and everywhere in between.

While comparisons of race relations and slave systems between North and South America have fascinated scholars for much of the past century, the life stories of Herrera, Jones, and the millions of other African-descended people who lived throughout the Americas in relative obscurity have rarely found a place within comparative scholarship, even as more localized scholarly focus on race and slavery in the Atlantic world has transformed our

understanding of the worlds of people of African descent. With a few no-
table exceptions, explicitly comparative studies of race and slavery have not
kept pace with scholarly interest in the Atlantic world as a field of historical
analysis. While historians have moved on from the early, field-defining work
of scholars such as Frank Tannenbaum, Herbert Klein, Stanley Elkins, and
Carl Degler, few comparative studies have emerged to take their place, even
as more detailed studies of particular locales—coupled with an improved understanding of the links between Atlantic world communities—have revealed
new questions ripe for comparative analysis.[4]

While recent comparative studies remain few and far between, some
recent works have begun to reexamine questions of race and slavery
between the Americas and thus have helped provide a model for this study.
For example historians Alejandro de la Fuente and Ariela Gross's work on
the dynamics of manumission in Virginia, Louisiana, and Cuba, has transformed the way we understand how legal codes that appear very different
may in practice operate in a similar fashion. De la Fuente and Gross offer
a far more nuanced picture of how the legal regimes of the Americas dealt
with racial difference and argue that in Anglo-America and Spanish America
alike, colonial authorities attempted to build discriminatory legal regimes
that equated African descent with slavery.[5] Mariana L. R. Dantas's innovative
Black Townsmen, through its study of the way free and enslaved people of
African descent transformed the cities of Baltimore, Maryland, and Sabará,
Minas Gerais (Brazil), remains one of the few recent comparative studies
to examine closely the local actions and experiences of African-descended
people in both Latin America and the United States.[6] Yet, as Dantas rightly
observes, because other scholars have often built comparisons of race and
slavery using a top-down approach largely grounded in the secondary literature, comparative studies often "fail to take advantage of the analytical
potential offered by a simultaneous in-depth study of different regional or
local histories."[7]

Much of the best recent scholarship has taken a detailed, local approach
to questions about the lives of African-descended people—but that approach
has yet to be utilized in service of a broader comparative project. Research
on communities in the United States, Latin America, and throughout the
Atlantic world has transformed our understanding of the social and cultural
worlds of African-descended people. By examining the local dynamics of
much larger processes and phenomena, scholars have used their detailed
analysis of particular regions, cities, and communities to improve our understanding of the lived experiences of free and enslaved people of African
descent across the Americas, providing a needed corrective to the generaliza-
tions so often found in much of the comparative literature. Yet by uncovering

and investigating new dimensions of the worlds of African-descended people, recent scholarship has also revealed the need for scholarship that more fully investigates how the lived experiences of free and enslaved people of African descent compared throughout the Americas.

Many recent studies on free people of color in the United States, for example, have revealed the ways various legal restrictions on black freedom belie the social and cultural worlds that free people of color created. Although Ira Berlin's *Slaves without Masters* remains the masterwork of southern whites' general views of black freedom, more recent scholarship has significantly complicated the paradigm presented there. Analyzing southern communities from Virginia to Texas, historians have considered how free people of color cultivated reputations for respectability, established strong and durable community ties, and carved out lives for themselves throughout the antebellum era. Examining the worlds of free people of color both North and South, scholars have revealed the ways they worked, worshipped, raised families, and built relationships alongside white neighbors, often in the face of substantial restrictions on the exercise of black freedom.[8] Additional scholarship—though rarely explicitly comparative in nature—has also revealed the impact on free black communities of access to the broader cultural and intellectual currents of the Atlantic world, examining how Atlantic ideas deeply affected the development of personal and collective identities of African-descended people.[9] Yet despite this much deeper understanding of the lives of free people of color in the United States, both these insights and this locally focused approach have for the most part remained outside the scope of comparative scholarship. Gestures to the U.S. case by scholars of Latin America often fall back on the *Slaves without Masters* paradigm.

Such a process of historiographical revision has happened in microcosm for the study of race and slavery in antebellum South Carolina. Marina Wikramanayake's *A World in Shadow* contended that free people of color who did not merely attempt to survive on the margins of South Carolina society were elite, mixed-race individuals who tried to mimic and break into the social world of whites. With a more careful reading of local sources, historians such as Michael P. Johnson and James L. Roark, Philip L. Morgan, Bernard Powers Jr., and Amrita Chakrabarti Myers have revealed the far more complicated story of race and freedom in South Carolina. Johnson and Roark, by analyzing the life of the remarkable William Ellison, demonstrated how a free man of color with considerable skills and determination could enter South Carolina's planter elite, however tenuous or exceptional such experiences may have been. Powers and Myers, meanwhile, have revealed that despite laws restricting manumission and in various ways limiting the exercise of black freedom, people of African descent in Charleston

negotiated the boundary between slavery and freedom and developed relationships and social institutions to support the lives of individuals, families,
and communities. They have revealed the ways free people of color carved
out meaningful lives for themselves in freedom in the face of a wide variety
of legal restrictions. Like for the United States more broadly, however, scholarship on Charleston, while acknowledging the city's Caribbean or Atlantic
character, has yet to explore how the lives of free African-descended people
there compare to those in other cities of the Americas.[10]

Scholarship on race and slavery in Latin America has followed a similar
historiographical trajectory, where recent advances in our understanding
of the social and cultural lives of African-descended people have yet to be
incorporated into the broader comparative literature. Historians have revealed the many ways white authorities throughout Latin America worked
to oppress and control African-descended populations from Spanish Florida
to Argentina—in contrast to earlier depictions of race relations and slavery
as milder in Latin America—and likewise have demonstrated how African-
descended people attempted to fight racial discrimination to achieve freedom, citizenship, and equality.[11] Alternately, in studies of communities
and regions in both mainland South America and the Spanish Caribbean,
scholars have revealed the ways enslaved and free people of African descent
challenged white authorities, established meaningful family and community
lives, and used a wide variety of means to attempt to improve their social
position and economic fortunes.[12] Although the findings of these locally
focused studies have yet to be integrated into a broader comparative framework, Latin Americanists, more so than their Americanist counterparts,
have begun to recognize the need for increased attention to how the lives of
African-descended people in Latin America compare to their counterparts
elsewhere in the hemisphere.[13]

Recent studies examining race and slavery in Caribbean Colombia in particular have revealed in great detail the social and cultural worlds of African-
descended people and have provided a necessary foundation for a broader
comparative analysis. English-language works by historians such as Pablo F.
Gómez, Jane Landers, and David Wheat have deepened our understanding
of how Africans in seventeenth-century Cartagena and Caribbean Colombia
constructed and reconstructed social lives and cultural practices despite the
trauma of enslavement.[14] Similarly recent scholarship by Aline Helg, Marixa Lasso, Jason P. McGraw, and James Sanders has revealed a great deal
about the social, cultural, and political lives of African-descended people in
eighteenth- and nineteenth-century Caribbean Colombia, particularly their
efforts to achieve racial equality and political representation in the late colonial era and during the early years of the Colombian republic.[15]

Additionally the work of Latin America–based scholars studying race and slavery in Colombia has further improved and transformed our understanding of the role of African-descended people there, particularly during the eighteenth and nineteenth centuries, though this scholarship often remains an additional degree removed from comparative studies. Alfonso Múnera merits particular attention, as his work has not only revealed in great detail the active role people of African descent played in the wars for independence and the creation of the Colombian nation but has likewise encouraged an increased focus on the lives and worlds of Afro-Colombians more broadly.[16] Work by other Latin American scholars—Luz Adriana Maya Restrepo, Maria Eugenia Chaves, Hugues Rafael Sanchez Mejia, Sergio Paulo Solano D., among others—has deepened our understanding of the world of Afro-Colombians from a wide variety of social and cultural perspectives.[17] By and large, however, the work of these Latin American scholars has struggled to gain readership beyond historians of Latin America and thus has exerted less influence than it should on English-language Atlantic world scholarship and on comparative studies of race and slavery in particular.

Thus even as our understanding of the lives of African-descended people in communities throughout the Atlantic world has improved thanks to an outpouring of scholarship that carefully considers local evidence and local circumstances, the stories of the everyday lives of free and enslaved people of color have yet to be framed within a broader comparative perspective. By analyzing the ways free people of color carved out lives for themselves and their families in Cartagena and Charleston—by placing the worlds of Manuel Herrera and Jehu Jones within a single analytical framework—*Black Freedom* explores and compares the daily lives of free people of color and reframes the debate about race and slavery in the Americas. By focusing on the local impact of more general ideologies, policies, and structures, this book reveals the social dynamics of racial difference in two distinct American communities, examining how free people of color attempted to achieve social and economic distinction and how the realities of racial difference across the Americas affected their daily lives. It argues that as free people of color engaged white authorities, claimed rights and privileges they were not typically afforded, and strived to improve their individual circumstances, they subtly challenged the logic of American racial hierarchies and confronted the structures of white authority that subsequent generations tackled more directly.[18]

Cartagena and Charleston are uniquely suited for an in-depth comparison. Both served as crucial mainland port cities that remained intimately and directly connected to the broader Caribbean and Atlantic world throughout the eighteenth and nineteenth centuries. While slavery was more central to

the economy of Charleston than it was to that of Cartagena, which functioned largely as a commercial entrepôt, both cities served as crucial sites of
disembarkation for enslaved Africans transported through the trans-Atlantic
slave trade. Though far fewer enslaved people remained in Cartagena than
in Charleston, and while the years of heaviest slave trading ended in Cartagena before they began in Charleston, African-descended people constituted
a majority of the population in both cities. Charleston and the surrounding
lowcountry were home to a massive slave majority with a very small community of free people of color, while Cartagena's population was made up
primarily of free people of color with a much smaller enslaved population
persisting throughout the first half of the nineteenth century.

Cartagena emerged as a significant locale within the Spanish circum-
Caribbean during the sixteenth century, and Africans and their descendants
played critical roles in the founding and development of the city. While mining in the Spanish colonies of New Spain and Peru may have provided the
primary impetus for Spain's imperial ventures in the New World, Cartagena
de Indias and other emergent cities of the sixteenth-century Spanish circum-
Caribbean served crucial defensive and administrative functions and played
a critical role in supporting both regional and transoceanic trade through
the production and processing of foodstuffs and other goods necessary to
support an expanding Spanish empire. By the late sixteenth century, Cartagena was already considered one of the principal cities of Spanish America,
and it was the first stop for European vessels trading in Spain's colonies.[19]
Because of its commercial, military, and administrative importance by the
early eighteenth century, the city became the center of the Viceroyalty of
New Granada (encompassing modern-day Colombia, Venezuela, Panama,
and Ecuador) when it was created in 1717. Cartagena's large, protected harbor
made it one of the best in the Americas and—as interimperial warfare in the
Caribbean increased during the late seventeenth and eighteenth centuries—
made the city an attractive target for attack by rival empires and a hotbed
for smuggling and illegal trade. Likewise the city's strategic and commercial
prominence made it central in New Granada's effort to achieve independence
from Spain during the late eighteenth and early nineteenth centuries.

Cartagena's rise to become one of the most prominent cities in Spain's
colonial empire occurred in no small part because of the activity of Africans
and their descendants. Historian David Wheat has revealed that the functions
described above, foundational to Spanish colonization of the Americas, were
carried out in large part by these inhabitants. From early in the city's history,
the majority of the city's residents were Africans or African-descended.[20]
Already by the early 1600s, one estimate determined, Cartagena and the
surrounding province were home to seven thousand enslaved Africans and

only three thousand Spaniards.[21] As Cartagena grew in importance during the seventeenth century, its position as a major site of disembarkation for enslaved Africans increased as well. During the late sixteenth and early seventeenth centuries, the city functioned as Spanish America's primary slaving port. Wheat's analysis reveals that there was "a minimum of 487 slave ships known to have arrived in Cartagena between 1573 and 1640, disembarking at least 78,453 enslaved Africans in the city and neighboring ports."[22] During these early years of slave trading, Africans disembarking in Cartagena came primarily from Upper Guinea and Angola, with the latter gradually replacing the former as the primary provenance zone later in the century. As historians such as Landers and Gómez have shown, seventeenth-century Cartagena was at least as much an African city as it was a Spanish one.

As Spanish slave trading shifted to other locales during the eighteenth century, the absence of extractive industry or plantation monoculture in Caribbean New Granada and the well-established routes to freedom for enslaved people that existed in Spanish America (discussed in greater detail in chapter 1) resulted in a growing population of free people of African descent; they constituted the majority of Cartagena's population by the early eighteenth century. The exigencies of urban life created opportunities for free *pardos, morenos,* and *negros* in the city that would have been recognizable in nearly any city in the Americas, particularly in the realm of associational life and labor. Other opportunities were unique to the city's strategic importance and status as a military outpost, like the establishment of voluntary militias to provide for the city's defense. Although Spaniards and whites never relinquished full control over the channels of authority and administration, Africans and their descendants shaped Cartagena from the beginning.

The centrality of Africans as active agents of Spanish colonization extended to the development of South Carolina as well. In 1526 a Spanish expedition from the West Indies brought the first Africans to the shore of what later became South Carolina.[23] While Africans took part to varying extents in abortive efforts by the French and Spanish to settle areas of the southeastern coast of North America during the seventeenth century, it was not until the migration of English settler-colonists from Barbados in the 1670s that Africans arrived more permanently in South Carolina.[24] Sugar cultivation in Barbados increased dramatically during the mid-seventeenth century, and with it so too did the importation of enslaved Africans—from almost none in 1630 to some thirty thousand in 1670. Competition among planters, the consolidation of land holdings, natural disaster, warfare, and a host of other considerations pushed many English in Barbados to pursue opportunities elsewhere. By the 1670s that "elsewhere" was the coast of South Carolina.

While the coast's unsuitability to sugar cultivation delayed the development of plantation monoculture in South Carolina, Peter Wood has estimated that "even in the earliest years, between one fourth and one third of the colony's newcomers were Negroes."[25] By the second generation in South Carolina, that number grew to more than half, and that black majority persisted through the Civil War. In the late seventeenth century, enslaved Africans in and around Charlestown tended livestock and supported farming efforts, with the colony supporting Barbados and other English sugar colonies in a manner similar to Cartagena during the same era. It was the introduction of rice cultivation, however—and English colonists' need for both African expertise and labor to produce it—that transformed the state from a minor colonial outpost into the slaving capital of North America. Though when rice was first introduced to South Carolina, planters attempted to grow it on dry land, they soon learned, through West African expertise, that the most productive way to cultivate the crop was in swamps, an arrangement that required an intensive investment of labor to clear land, dig canals and ditches, and engineer complex arrangements to irrigate, flood, and drain rice fields.[26] In South Carolina this work was done almost exclusively by enslaved Africans and their descendants. As Wood has noted, West Africans' familiarity with rice cultivation and their ability to withstand the punishing climate and disease environment of coastal swamps directly "contributed to the gradual evolution of their status as chattel slaves," pushing South Carolina's colonists to embrace African slavery and eschew any alternative forms of labor.[27]

Indeed the centrality of South Carolina, and of Charleston specifically, to the development of race and slavery in the United States cannot be understated, as whites in South Carolina, concentrated primarily in the Charleston area, embraced slavery and rice cultivation in ways that transformed the city, state, and nation. Sullivan's Island, just outside Charleston Harbor, where enslaved Africans were sometimes briefly quarantined prior to disembarkation in the city, has been described as "the Ellis Island of black Americans."[28] Fully 40 percent of the enslaved Africans who disembarked in North America did so in the port of Charleston. As historian Ryan A. Quintana has noted, black Carolinians quite literally created South Carolina, as the state put enslaved people to work "building roads and bridges, digging canals and cuts (small canals), erecting public buildings and towering causeways."[29] From the colonial era through the antebellum, people of African descent, the vast majority of whom were enslaved, built the state. Although most Americans, scholars included, may think of "King Cotton" when considering the history of U.S. slavery, William Dusinberre estimates that on the eve of the Civil War in 1860, "twelve of the perhaps seventeen largest slave masters in the United

States were rice planters; and three-fifths of the families holding the most South Carolina slaves—twenty-one out of the thirty-five families which each held at least five hundred Carolina bondspeople—planted rice rather than cotton."[30] Africans and their descendants built Charleston from the earliest days of colonial South Carolina and continued to form a majority of the population of the city, region, and state through the Civil War.

Though at first glance Cartagena and Charleston are quite different, they ultimately shared a number of important commonalities that suits them well for high-level comparison: their ties to the intellectual and cultural currents of the Atlantic, their status as two of the most important port cities for their respective continents, their centrality to the African slave trade, and the large populations of African descent who lived there, both voluntarily and not. Coupled with their differences—the greater ease of manumission in Cartagena and the city's expanded access to public institutions for people of African descent, along with its much earlier history of slave trading—Cartagena and Charleston are primed for an extended comparative analysis. Comparing the world of free people of color in these two cities, this story points toward new answers to old questions about race and slavery in the Americas, using local focus and comparative perspective to reveal the complicated racial dynamics of American communities.

Black Freedom offers a unique view of the way racial difference affected the daily lives of free people of color in two of the Atlantic world's most important port cities. By comparing the lived worlds of free people of color, it reveals both broad parallels and crucial differences in the way race and freedom operated throughout the African Americas. In the pages that follow, the free people of color in these communities only rarely mount any direct challenge to white authority. Yet in their efforts to achieve social distinction and economic stability for themselves and their families, they subtly defied the logic of the racial hierarchies that undergirded American society. By requesting special privileges from the Spanish crown, petitioning a state legislature for an exemption to various legal proscriptions, or crafting relationships through their work in a trade such as barbering or tailoring, free people of color engaged with white authorities and confronted the racial norms that characterized social life throughout the urban Atlantic world. In their efforts to improve their individual circumstances and to achieve social distinction, they confronted the boundaries of racial difference and challenged the logic of white authority.

Chapter 1

PATHS TO FREEDOM

For and in consideration of the sum of one thousand pounds . . . being the
earnings and gains arising from her labour and industry from time to time
by me allowed to carry on and transact . . . have enfranchised, manumized,
released, and set free . . . from the bondage of slavery the said Negroe
Woman Diana and her daughter . . . Susannah.

Charleston, 1777

[The free womb law of 1821] did not dictate suitable provisions to prepare
the manumitted for the enjoyment of their liberty. . . . The manumitted
turn to idleness, become unhappy, and turn into layabouts. Daily the
number of vices that threaten public order grows.

Colombia, 1842

On January 1, 1829, New Yorker Rensselaer Van Rensselaer wrote to his father
from Barranquilla about a manumission ceremony held in Cartagena's main
plaza a few days earlier, on Christmas. According to Rensselaer, Cartagena's
manumission board had bestowed liberty upon "thirty slaves of both sex
and all ages," and Rensselaer "followed the crowd" into the plaza to witness
the spectacle. Enslaved men and women wept as local magistrates presented
them with the "Cap of Freedom," as shouts of "Viva el Librator" [*sic*] and
"Viva la Republica" [*sic*] emerged from the crowd. "The delighted freed men
. . . paraded the streets," Renssalaer relayed, "with the most grotesque demon-
strations of joy. It was laughable to witness the ludicrous expression with a
broad grin on their comical faces and the spring halt sort of step with which
they skipped along receiving the congratulations of friends."[1]

For Rensselaer such a public celebration of manumission represented a
phenomenon unique to Latin America. And in some ways it was: although
the large number of enslaved people freed in this ceremony was unusual, between the mid-1820s and Colombia's abolition of slavery in 1851, these kinds
of public spectacles often accompanied the emancipation of slaves by Colombian *juntas de manumission* (manumission boards). This public celebration

of manumission helps illustrate the stark differences in white attitudes and policies relating to the emancipation of enslaved people between the United States and Latin America during the nineteenth century, particularly between the southern lowcountry and Caribbean Colombia, regions of their respective continents most heavily populated by people of African descent. Yet differences in policy and attitude bely underlying parallels that connected North and South America, namely a racial ideology among the dominant classes that doubted black people's fitness for freedom and the feasibility of a society in which both black people and white people enjoyed equally the rights of citizenship.

As white southerners in the United States reaffirmed their commitment to the institution of slavery after 1800, they attempted to curtail black freedom, enacting more restrictive policies toward manumission. The South's white authorities feared the ability of free black people to disturb supposedly contented enslaved populations and incite racial discord and violence. Thus in South Carolina, between 1800 and 1841, whites all but eliminated enslaved people's avenues for moving from slavery to freedom. Colombian policies, meanwhile, trended in the opposite direction, as avenues to freedom expanded during that same era rather than contracted. Support for the emancipation of enslaved people extended to the point of government boards using state funds to free enslaved individuals throughout the 1820s and 1830s, just as U.S. southerners began promulgating some of their most fervent defenses of slavery.

These differences in policy toward manumission reflect the very different nature and extent of slave owning in Caribbean Colombia and the South Carolina lowcountry, in addition to the political exigencies in both regions. First, the institution of slavery was far more central to the economy and social life of the South Carolina lowcountry than it ever was in Caribbean Colombia. As a slave city and the primary port for an area with one of the densest populations of enslaved people anywhere in the country, Charleston served as the point of export for rice and cotton produced through slave labor and the port of entry for a wide variety of manufactured goods and other products the region required. Cartagena, by contrast, was primarily a commercial entrepôt, one far less organically connected to the primary regions of slave activity in New Granada, including the mining and sugar production that occurred in the central and pacific regions of the country rather than along the Caribbean coast. While Cartagena still served as a significant port both for the introduction of enslaved people and the commercial needs of the country more broadly, slavery played nowhere near as important a role in the city and surrounding region as it did in Charleston. Likewise prominent whites in Cartagena were far less likely to be invested in plantation agriculture than their counterparts in Charleston. While many of the most prominent whites in Charleston, including many of its merchants, owned plantations that relied on slave labor, whites in Cartagena were far less likely to exhibit that kind of investment in plantation slavery.

Stemming from these economic conditions, political realities likewise affected white authorities' approaches toward manumission. While in Cartagena manumission allowed the patriot cause fighting for independence in the nineteenth century to juxtapose their policies with the colonial Spanish crown, in South Carolina, as elsewhere in the U.S. South, policies restricting black freedom coalesced white political support, even among yeomen and the working poor.

Further, white elites in these regions conceived of manumission's role in society and its relationship to slavery in fundamentally different ways. In Cartagena manumission during this era was considered a way to reduce the possibility of racial violence and, ultimately, to affect the gradual abolition of slavery, emancipating individual enslaved people as the institution of slavery slowly declined. As such much of the anxiety regarding manumission among whites was about the need to prepare enslaved people for freedom. No such effort existed in Charleston, where whites believed slavery would continue to exist as an institution in perpetuity. Rather than preparing enslaved people for freedom, whites occasionally manumitted enslaved people for faithful service, but more broadly they sought to limit and control the process of manumission. Between the American Revolution and the Civil War, South Carolina slowly shifted from an environment in which manumission was tolerated under carefully controlled conditions and in which black freedom was carefully regulated to one in which manumission represented too great a threat to the institution of slavery to allow at all. Yet while the distinction between the manumission policies of a slave society and of a society with slaves was clear, doubts and anxieties about slave emancipation and black freedom linked these two very different cities, as whites shared a racial ideology that denigrated people of African descent and revealed the shared challenge of African-descended people in the Atlantic world to forge paths to freedom.

POLICY AND LAW

Laws and policies governing manumission could differ significantly between Latin America and the United States. Spain's long history with slavery compared to elsewhere in Europe resulted in the development of formal policies toward manumission as early as the thirteenth century, with the organization of the early legal code the Siete Partidas. The Siete Partidas formalized the ability of slave owners to manumit their slaves and also laid out the rights and responsibilities of both enslavers and enslaved people. The Partidas allowed enslaved people to gain their freedom through formal denunciations of their masters for various misdeeds, and it established a legal basis by which the enslaved could purchase their own freedom as well. The tenets of the Siete Partidas were transferred to Spanish America both in law and in custom, and some aspects were later formalized in the Código Negro of 1789. Collectively Spanish traditions and customs, as historian Frank Tannenbaum once argued, were in some ways "biased in favor of freedom and opened the gates to manumission when slavery was transferred to the New World."[2] Such attitudes of course shifted and transformed as the Spanish established slave societies in the Americas and as individual colonizers adapted long-standing customs to new circumstances. Yet this long tradition of manumission established precedents that enslaved people could call upon in their efforts to gain freedom from slavery in the Americas.[3]

So while African slavery featured as part of the earliest efforts of Spanish colonial settlement in the Americas, so too did efforts of enslaved Africans to obtain their freedom. Viewed by the Catholic Church as having a moral personality and granted access to the Spanish legal system, church and state structures in Spanish America offered enslaved people opportunities for manumission that their North American counterparts found much more difficult to access. The legacy of the Siete Partidas in particular provided several bases on which enslaved people in Spanish America could be emancipated. As historian Ann Twinam notes, the Partidas provided enslavers "options to free slaves through 'good will,' 'for the price they receive,' or if 'the master by his will directed the heir . . . to emancipate.'"[4] The second of these, the right to self-purchase, known as *coartación,* came to represent a significant avenue by which people of African descent in Spanish America moved from slavery to freedom. Legislation as early as the mid-sixteenth century confirmed the official legal basis for self-purchase in Spanish America. Historian Alejandro de la Fuente has noted that in Cuba, the legal recognition of self-purchase emerged "as a pragmatic response to the frequent litigation initiated by slaves themselves."[5] Whether through self-purchase or other means, Spanish laws, cultural attitudes, and historical precedents created pathways to freedom that enslaved people used to their advantage.

For Caribbean Colombia and the city of Cartagena in particular, this relative accessibility of manumission throughout the colonial and early republican eras produced a majority free, African-descended population in the city and region for much of the eighteenth and nineteenth centuries. In comparison manumission likely proved more difficult to come by in areas of Colombia more heavily reliant on enslaved labor, particularly in the mining and sugar regions of the Cauca Valley and Pacific coast. Yet while avenues to freedom existed, even policies that outwardly favored the emancipation of slaves often derived from something less than a commitment to antislavery among whites, as authorities endeavored to prolong the institution of slavery and sought to reinforce the structures of white control in the region.

Much of Colombia's relative openness to manumission during the nineteenth century was dictated by the exigencies of the wars of independence from Spain between 1810 and 1820. The need for additional men to take up arms, and the nascent republic's need for international assistance and recognition encouraged the development of policies that favored manumission. Indeed some of the earliest modifications of official policy toward slave emancipation came as a result of Simón Bolívar's international posturing. As Great Britain increased pressure on states to cease their participation in the international slave trade, for example, Bolívar made promises to that effect in the early years of the war for independence. Bolívar hoped a declaration of New Granada's commitment to ending the international slave trade, coupled with Great Britain's existing animosity toward the Spanish, would encourage Britain to formally recognize New Granada and perhaps provide some form of assistance. As the Spanish reconquered much of the Caribbean region in 1814, Bolívar traveled to Jamaica to try to secure British support. Later he traveled to the new republic of Haiti to secure assistance from Pres. Alexandre Pétion as well.[6]

Haiti's recognition and support, however, came with the requirement that Bolívar make tangible commitments to abolish slavery. To that end Bolívar declared in 1816 the "absolute liberty of the slaves who have groaned under the Spanish yoke the past three centuries."[ ] Such emancipation, however, came with the condition that all "robust" enslaved men between fourteen and seventy years old present themselves for military service. The elderly, women, and children would be exempt, while any "new citizen that refuses to take up arms in order to carry out the sacred duty to defend their liberty" would remain enslaved.[7] Four years later, in 1820, as the war for independence neared its end, Bolívar yet again called upon the enslaved to serve the army of New Granada. As his military struggled to recruit able bodies willing to serve far from home, Bolívar ordered Gen. Francisco Paula de Santander to recruit five thousand enslaved people from the provinces of Antioquia, Chocó, and Popayán, where slavery predominated more than in the Caribbean region, declaring that he would "offer them freedom from the moment they leave their country, and two years after having entered into service, will give them absolute license to enjoy their plain liberty."[8]

Beyond this requirement for soldiers, denunciations of slavery served also as a way to bolster support for the patriot cause. The city of Cartagena and the Caribbean coast more broadly represented key regions in the fight for New Granada's independence, and African-descended people constituted the majority of that region's population. Patriot leaders during the war for independence began to tie the abolition of slavery and racial equality directly to their cause, contrasting their views with Spanish support for slavery and their unwillingness to provide representation to African-descended people at the courts of Cádiz, which passed a new Spanish constitution in 1812 following the invasion of Napoleon into Spain and the abdication of the royal family. By declaring racial equality and support for the abolition of slavery without being forced to demonstrate any tangible sign of their commitment or progress on those fronts, New Granadan patriots managed to garner the support of African-descended people in the Caribbean without being forced to reconcile the reality of manumission with their views about the supposed limited capacity of enslaved people to function in freedom or the political impact of free people of color's participation as citizens. Manumission and emancipation became inextricably linked to the cause of national independence during the 1810s, and demonstrating a commitment to manumission served as a way to bolster one's republican credentials.[9]

In 1820, following various declarations regarding slave emancipation, the Congress at Angostura, convened in 1819 to provide a constitution for the newly independent republic, declared it necessary to provide some structure to the emancipatory process in light of the "state of ignorance and moral degradation" in which the country's enslaved people could be found. They stated in January 1820 that the government needed to devise a way to open to former slaves "a vast field of their industry and activity, in order to provide against crimes and corruption, which everywhere follows misery and idleness." The Angostura congress feared that in the absence of slavery, the idleness into which people of African descent would fall could eventually lead to criminality. Thus they proposed that before slavery could be abolished in Colombia, the government needed to first "actively promote . . . the civilization of the slaves." They proposed that slave children should be taught to read and write, "giving to all in general some idea of social duties, inspiring love of work and of public virtues, and making the more or less prompt possession of their liberty dependent on the same." Already in 1820 the Angostura congress revealed the extent to which whites' views regarding both manumission and abolition were linked to their broader view of black capacity for functioning in freedom, seeing it as necessary to cultivate in them the characteristics of good citizens in order to overcome what they believed was black people's natural predilection toward vice. As the congress put it, they needed to implement measures designed "to make men before making citizens."[10]

In 1821, at the constitutional congress in Cúcuta, the newly formed Republic of New Granada formally declared their intention to begin supporting the manumission of slaves as a means of slowly ending the institution of slavery. The congress declared that the institution of slavery was at odds with the existence of a "truly just and philanthropic republican government" and sought measures to alleviate the "degraded and afflicted" population of enslaved people that remained in the country. Rather than immediately abolishing the institution, however, the congress passed gradual emancipation measures so as not to "[compromise] the public tranquility nor [violate] the rights of slaveowners." Thus, like elsewhere in the Americas during the mid-nineteenth century, they passed a "free womb law," declaring the children of enslaved mothers would be born free from that moment forward. Yet despite this free status, these nominally free children would be required to serve their mother's enslaver until they reached the age of eighteen as "recompense" for the costs incurred in their upbringing. Once they reached the age of eighteen, it was incumbent upon slave owners to deliver these free people to the local manumission junta, accompanied by a report on their conduct and character, so they could be placed in "useful jobs and professions."[11]

In addition to this plan for gradual emancipation, the Law of 21 July also banned the introduction of foreign slaves into Colombia as well as the sale of slave children outside of the province in which their parents resided and the sale of any slaves outside of the country. More important, the law established *juntas de manumisión* across the country. Using funds raised through the taxation of slave owners and slave property, the manumission juntas were charged with periodically purchasing the freedom of enslaved people deemed worthy by local officials, with the money raised going (as it did elsewhere in the Americas) to indemnify slave owners. Typically, elaborate celebrations accompanied these manumissions, and they often occurred on national holidays. The law stated specifically that on December 25–27, the manumission board would liberate "the most honest and industrious" enslaved people of the canton.[12]

These measures reveal a level of support for manumission that places Colombia in stark contrast with the U.S. South. For Colombia's Caribbean coast in particular, the lack of a reliance on enslaved labor, coupled with military and political necessity, made the prospect of manumission far more tenable than it was in the United States. Yet despite this greater support for manumission, these policies also indicate a real ambivalence toward black freedom among Colombian leaders, as they feared the impact of slave emancipation on enslaved people and the future of politics in the fledgling nation. For one thing, despite the "free womb" provisions of the 1821 law, requirements that children of enslaved mothers serve their mothers' owner until the age of eighteen meant that children born under this law would not receive full enjoyment of their freedom until 1839 at the earliest. The degree to which manumission juntas catered to slave owners, meanwhile, virtually assured that the boards would free few slaves. Indeed, as historian Jason McGraw has noted, the manumission boards were perpetually underfunded, lacked power, and were able to free few people over the course of their existence.[13]

In both the January 1820 declaration and the July 1821 law, the congresses revealed serious concern about the implications of emancipation on the social and political life of the new republic. The congress's 1820 declaration revealed the extent to which Colombian legislators by and large believed enslaved people (and likely people of African descent more broadly) to be unprepared for the demands of citizenship. Further, by favoring only the most "honest and industrious" slaves for manumission and couching the 1821 law in a commitment to preserve "public tranquility," coupled with the gradual emancipation of children born to enslaved mothers, the 1821 law promised freedom to African-descended people without actually delivering it. Representatives to the constitutional congress at Cúcuta catered to the wishes of prominent slave owners and revealed a degree of unease about the impact a more immediate emancipation of enslaved people or outright abolition might have on the stability of communities and the country more broadly. Even as Colombian officials in the 1820s advanced policies favorable to manumission, they did so in ways that reveal they doubted the ability of enslaved people to function in freedom and contribute to society. Time and again declarations of support for manumission were coupled with caveats and restrictions that undercut the impact of manumission policy, revealed apprehension about the impact of slave emancipation, and served to prolong slavery and white political rule in Colombia.

Over the course of the 1820s and 1830s, Colombia's official policies toward manumission remained more or less static. The children of enslaved mothers continued to be born free throughout this era, though they remained under the control of slave owners. The slave population of the Caribbean region declined during these decades, though it did so slowly and mostly thanks to the action of enslaved people themselves. While manumission juntas freed relatively few slaves, enslaved people used various formal and informal means of self-liberation to gain their freedom, including self-purchase and running away to coastal backlands. Despite a lack of new commitments to either individual emancipation or abolition in Colombia, the tide slowly continued to shift from slavery to freedom throughout the 1820s and 1830s.[14]

Though the exact number of enslaved people living in Cartagena during this era is difficult to pin down, some evidence suggests that the number of enslaved people in Caribbean Colombia indeed declined significantly as a result of self-liberation as well as the efforts of manumission boards. In the last major census of the colonial era, the city of Cartagena was home to 4,034 whites, 6,745 free people of color, and 2,584 enslaved people. Along with the small population of indigenous people and *ecclesiasticos,* the total population of the city was 13,690. Enslaved people comprised a considerably larger proportion of the population within the city, as compared to the province. For the province of Cartagena more broadly, which in the colonial era comprised much of the Caribbean coast of the Kingdom of New Granada, the numbers were of course much larger. In the province there were 13,426 whites, 75,490 free people of color, 9,622 slaves, 19,416 indigenous people, and 424 *ecclesiasticos* (table 1.1).

TABLE 1.1 **Population of city and province of Cartagena, 1777**

	Whites	Free People of Color	Slaves	Indigenous	*Ecclesiasticos*	Total
City	4,034	6,745	2,584	88	239	13,690
Province Total	13,426	75,490	9,622	19,416	424	118,378

SOURCE: Meisel Roca and Aguilera Díaz, "Cartagena de Indias en 1777," 234.

Later censuses of the Caribbean region reveal a steady decline in the number of enslaved people, both in their total numbers as well as in their proportion of the population. In 1825 the Caribbean coast was home to 7,120 enslaved people, comprising about 4 percent of the total population. By 1851, just a few years before the final abolition of slavery, that number had declined to 2,555, less than 1 percent (table 1.2).

TABLE 1.2 **Population of enslaved people in Caribbean Colombia**

Year	Slaves	Percent of Population (%)
1825	7,120	4
1843	4,507	1.8
1851	2,555	0.8

SOURCE: Fernándo Gómez, "Los Censos de Colombia," in *Compendio de estadísticas históricas de Colombia,* edited by Miguel Urrutia and Mario Arrubla (Bogotá: Universidad Nacional de Colombia, 1970). Tables reproduced in McGraw, *Work of Recognition,* 25.

As these numbers reveal, even as white officials may have expressed anxiety about the process of manumission in Colombia, the numbers of enslaved people steadily declined throughout the postindependence period. This decline in the number of enslaved people in the region suggests that even amid white ambivalence toward slave emancipation, self-purchase and private manumissions resulted in freedom for many during the first three decades of independence. During the 1840s, however, the activities of the manumission juntas largely ground to a halt.

Two decades after the wars for independence had ended, and despite growing antislavery sentiment, gradualist approaches to emancipation continued to prolong the institution of slavery in Colombia. In April 1842 the Congress of New Granada declared that the Law of 21 July—passed at the constitutional convention at Cúcuta in 1821, establishing manumission boards and declaring the children of slave mothers free—required revision, because while it provided freedom to some slaves, it did not sufficiently "prepare the manumitted for the possession of liberty." Just three years after the first children born to enslaved mothers under this law could have gained full possession of their freedom, Colombian authorities moved to change it. To the Congress of New Granada, formerly enslaved people's lack of preparedness for freedom saw them "[enter] into idleness, become unhappy, and [turn] into layabouts (vagos)." They added that "the number of vices that threaten the public order" was daily growing. The Congress called for the formation of a more precise slave census, enumerating exactly how many enslaved people still remained in Colombia. They called for separate censuses calculating enslaved people; children born free to slave mothers but still in the power of their mothers' enslavers; and a census of enslaved people considered runaways or fugitives, including a list of their "crimes committed" or "dominant public vice."[15]

Additionally the April 12, 1842, decree called for a study of the process of emancipation and apprenticeship in the British Caribbean. They ordered a "collection of legislative regulations that the English government has dictated to avoid the bad consequences of the manumission of slaves." Colombia's congress would attempt to impose a similar system of apprenticeship—a policy in which the formerly enslaved were required to continue a period of service, often to their former masters, during the gradual abolition of slavery—in their efforts to "improve the condition of slaves and manumitidos" and prevent them from turning into "pernicious members of society."[16] A law passed the following month dictated that once libertos born to slave mothers had reached the age of eighteen, they were to be presented by their mothers' enslaver to the local alcalde, so they could be set up in an "apprenticeship," often with said enslaver. This period of concertación in reality extended the servitude of nominally free individuals. These freeborn people received training in a "useful job, art, profession, or occupation," as the *alcalde* would arrange for them to serve their "former master or other respected person who could educate and instruct them" until they reached the age of twenty-five.[17]

In 1848 decrees by Pres. Tomás Cipriano de Mosquera once again altered the process of manumission in Colombia. After that time private manumissions—including self-purchase by the enslaved and private manumissions from slave owners—were outlawed. Though it seems doubtful these laws were fully recognized and obeyed, Mosquera declared that municipal councils would replace the manumission juntas as the only bodies legally able to manumit slaves.[18] Mosquera's 1848 decree yet again reiterated the preference among ruling whites for manumitting "honest and industrious" enslaved people, likely as a means of encouraging continued patience and service from those who remained enslaved. Furthermore Mosquera directed that in order to address questions about which slaves to manumit, preference should be given to "the youngest and most robust," overruling an earlier decree that gave preference to the eldest among honorable and industrious slaves. Though this process reopened manumission, at least in theory, it did so by reinforcing the notion that the state should use manumission boards to set an example for those still enslaved, emancipating those with enlightened characters and reinforcing prior negative views about the possibilities of black freedom. Though manumission became legally possible again, manumission policies continued to be coupled with declarations doubting the abilities of enslaved people to function as free workers, citizens, and people.

Throughout the postindependence era, white elites sought to limit and control the rate of manumission in Colombia as a means of maintaining white political dominance. Though the apprenticeship system was only implemented late in the process of ending slavery in Caribbean Colombia, concern at the national level for the rate at which slaves were gaining freedom is telling. Even despite the ineffectiveness of the manumission juntas in freeing large numbers of slaves, legislators in Colombia worried about the impact of enslaved people gaining their freedom too quickly and their potential to destabilize social life and local politics. Even though manumission had always been relatively accessible in Caribbean Colombia and despite the fact that few enslaved people remained in the region, at the national level concern still existed among whites about blacks' unpreparedness for the demands of freedom and citizenship, as slave owners and planters sought to prolong the survival of the institution. That freeborn individuals could have their servitude to a slave owner extended until they reached the age of twenty-five reveals the extent to which the 1821 law could often be a dead letter for those held legally or nominally in bondage. As historian Jason McGraw has noted, the

1821 law "raised expectations of freedom without providing it."[19] Colombian patriots could chastise the Spanish system of slavery, point to declarations of racial equality, manumission juntas, and the 1821 free womb law as overt signs of progress. But in reality racial discrimination persisted, the manumission juntas were perpetually underfunded and undercut and freed few slaves, and slave owners often dictated both the pace and nature of emancipations. Though the diminished need for slavery in the non-plantation zone on the Caribbean coast may have made manumission more accessible there than in Colombia's sugar and mining regions, the ability of enslaved people to move from slavery to freedom during the postindependence years never stemmed from whites' belief in racial equality.

While whites in Cartagena at times masked desires to prolong the institution of slavery and obscured their doubts about blacks' preparedness for the demands of freedom and citizenship, Charlestonians translated their doubts about slave emancipation more directly into law. Despite relatively relaxed attitudes toward manumission for much of the colonial and Revolutionary eras, South Carolina officials slowly eliminated the avenues enslaved people might use to gain their freedom beginning in 1800, amid a period in which the free black population rapidly grew. Through a series of laws passed by city and state officials, manumission became all but impossible in South Carolina by 1841, as white South Carolinians (and southerners more broadly) felt the institution of slavery coming under increasing scrutiny and pressure. While white authorities in both South Carolina and Caribbean Colombia expressed various concerns about slave emancipation and the problem of black freedom, the fears of whites in South Carolina were based not in concern about black citizenship but rather in concerns that the example of black freedom would destabilize the otherwise thriving institution of slavery.

In the colonial United States, manumission represented a possibility available in practice though rarely formally inscribed in law. When North American colonists began turning to African slavery in the seventeenth century, the boundary between slavery and freedom could still be crossed. In colonial North American and early U.S. societies with slaves, slavery represented just one possible labor arrangement; slave holdings tended to be relatively small, and enslavers sometimes worked alongside enslaved people. Laws restricting the lives of enslaved people tended to be fewer during this early era, and opportunities for achieving freedom—whether through self-purchase or private manumission—led to the emergence of communities of free black Americans throughout the United States, both North and South. This was particularly true during the era of the American Revolution, as enslavers across the country took the call for liberty in the nation's founding documents as impetus for emancipating enslaved people, sometimes immediately but more frequently after the enslaver's death. Yet over time some regions of the United States increased their dependency on enslaved labor and single cash crops, transforming societies with slaves into slave societies. As they grew more reliant on enslaved labor as the backbone of economic and social structures, white authorities in slave societies began severely restricting the ability of African-descended people to cross the boundary between slavery and freedom. And yet even as African slavery became the foundation of all economic and social relations in regions across the South and even as whites increasingly attempted to use the vise of enslavement to restrict the opportunities available to Africans and their descendants, the enslaved used creativity and ingenuity to find pathways to freedom.[20]

As early as the 1720s, South Carolina officials instituted legislation antithetical to black freedom. In 1722 the colony's general assembly passed a law requiring manumitted slaves to leave South Carolina within a year's time, or else their manumissions would be invalidated. An additional law passed in 1735 stipulated that any formerly enslaved people who returned to the colony within seven years would forfeit their freedom and be returned to slavery. Following the Stono Rebellion in 1739, the South Carolina assembly passed the more comprehensive "Act for the Better Ordering and Governing of Negroes and Other Slaves in This Province," commonly known as the "Negro Act." Among other restrictions on the movement and assembly of enslaved and free black people, the Negro Act stated that manumissions could only be delivered through a special act of the assembly.[21] These restrictions on manumission, however, do not appear to have been very carefully observed, perhaps because, for much of the colonial era, free black people constituted only a small fraction of the total black population. After 1740 private manumissions continued to take place but remained relatively rare: about thirty occurred during the 1740s, and even fewer in the 1750s.[22] It was not until the Revolutionary era that the frequency of manumissions began to increase, an uptick evident across the United States.

Between the American Revolution and 1800, relatively relaxed laws and white attitudes toward manumission enabled hundreds of enslaved people in South Carolina to find avenues to freedom—a relatively small number but still considerable when viewed within the broader context of the state's history. Despite this increase in manumission, South Carolina's legal and cultural scales were still tipped toward slavery, and slave emancipation there did not take place with the same frequency as it did in the U.S. North or much of Latin America. Whites in South Carolina never believed manumission would slowly lead to the end of slavery. Yet relative to the outsized importance of slavery to the region and the impossibility of manumission in later years, opportunities became more accessible for enslaved people during the early national era than at arguably any other time in the state's history as slave owners and enslaved people may both have taken inspiration from American rhetoric about liberty and equality during this era. Further, manumissions took place with considerably higher frequency in the Charleston District than elsewhere in South Carolina—and most of those manumissions occurred within the city of Charleston—owing both to the region's much larger population of enslaved people and to the advantages offered by Charleston's urban environment.

During the Revolutionary and early national eras, enslavers manumitted hundreds of enslaved people, many of whom received their freedom after the death of their owners. Still others gained manumission for financial considerations, either through self-purchase or purchase by a family member. In view of the large numbers of enslaved people gaining their freedom in the quarter century prior to the turn of the nineteenth century, coupled with concerns about slave rebellion that emerged during the 1790s, South Carolina implemented measures in 1800 to curb the flow of people from slavery to freedom.

In December 1800 the South Carolina General Assembly passed "An Act . . . to Impose Certain Restrictions on the Emancipation of Slaves."[23] In addition to outlawing private meetings of enslaved and free black people and prohibiting their assembly for education or religious instruction after dark, the law enacted a number of restrictions on the manner in which slave owners could free enslaved people. The law claimed that for many years, it had been a practice in South Carolina for slave owners to emancipate enslaved people "of bad or depraved character, or, from age or infirmity, incapable of gaining their livelihood by honest means." As such the general assembly declared that slave owners could no longer emancipate slaves by simply filing a deed of manumission. Rather they would be required to inform the local justice of the quorum, who would convene a panel of five freeholders to determine whether or not the manumission could take place. In particular the magistrates and freeholders would question the slave owner respecting "the character of the said slave or slaves" as well as the slave's "ability to gain a livelihood in an honest way." If a slave owner emancipated an enslaved person without such approval from the magistrates and freeholders, it would be lawful for "any person whosoever, to seize and convert to his or her own use, and to keep as his or her property" the illegally manumitted slave. The legislature was careful to state, however, that such measures were in no way intended to "deprive any free negro, Indian, mulatto or mestizo" from legal redress should they be illegally held in bondage.[24] After huge growth in South Carolina's free black population in preceding years, the state's legislature attempted to close avenues to freedom for enslaved people. The legislators doubted the ability of enslaved people to survive in freedom due to alleged character flaws and feared that old and infirm free black people would become a drain on state resources. Those who were illegally manumitted would be at risk of being reduced once more to a state of slavery.

The possibility of improperly manumitted slaves being returned to slavery was not entirely an idle matter. In December 1805 Rowland Lowndes Gervais of Charleston "did take, seize and keep possession of George, a mulatto boy who had been manumitted and enfranchised by Robert F. Turnbull . . . in manner contrary to the Act of the General Assembly of South Carolina dated the twentieth day of December" in the year 1800. Because the manumission had not been executed according to the restrictions laid out by the general assembly, Gervais deemed it "improper and illegal," and as such he took possession of George "as forfeited by the law, and retains him as his now legal property."[25] Though George's case may have been exceptional—it is the only case of an improperly manumitted slave being taken back into bondage I have found—it represents a reversal of fortune that would not have been possible just a few years prior. Word of the reenslavement of George or others like him likely would have spread throughout Charleston's free black community and struck fear into many of the city's free people of color, particularly those who possessed improperly executed manumission papers. Indeed the ability of whites to take possession of improperly manumitted free blacks speaks to an increasingly restrictive and distrustful racial climate in Charleston after 1800.

Ultimately the substantive effect of this restriction on manumissions in Charleston was mixed. Manumissions continued to be filed with the secretary of state's office in Charleston that made no reference to this change in the law. Others did. For example, in March 1801, shortly after the new law had taken effect, Jon Drayton manumitted a slave named Carlos. Drayton carefully stated that "a certificate has been lawfully obtained from five different freeholders" that certified Carlos was "not of bad character and is capable of gaining a livelihood by honest means." Having received such a certificate, Drayton manumitted Carlos in consideration of the sum of one hundred pounds and in recognition of Carlos's "honest behavior and faithful services."[26] Carlos's certificate from the freeholders reads verbatim according to the text of the law. While the motivation for manumitting Carlos was identical to that of earlier manumissions—claiming a record of faithful service in addition to money received from the would-be manumitted—the mechanism by which the manumission was executed changed. Carlos's manumission, however, is the only one I have identified that followed these new provisions so exactly. Because the records from the court of magistrates and freeholders no longer exist for the Charleston District, it is impossible to say how many manumissions took place there after 1800. Nevertheless the restrictions on manumission enacted in 1800 narrowed the avenues to freedom enslaved people in South Carolina could legally pursue, reflecting the antagonistic attitude toward black freedom in the state. Even though enslaved people continued to utilize creative means to achieve their freedom in the years after 1800, official attitudes and policy toward manumission trended toward greater restrictions, and the frequency of manumission began to decline.

Despite the restrictions enacted on the emancipation of enslaved people, the Charleston District's free black population increased significantly in the years after 1800. In that year the U.S. census counted a nonwhite free population of 1,153 persons, with 13,823 whites and 35,914 enslaved people. By 1810 the nonwhite free population grew to 1,783, while the white population grew to 16,011 and the enslaved population to 45,385. In 1820, in an inexplicable explosion of population growth, the free colored population had grown to 3,615, more than doubling over the course of a decade. The white and slave population continued to grow more steadily, increasing to 19,376 and 57,221 (table 1.3).[27]

TABLE 1.3 **Population of Charleston District, 1800–1830**

Year	Free People of Color	Whites	Slaves	Total
1800	1,153 (2.3%)	13,823 (27.2%)	35,914 (70.6%)	50,890
1810	1,783 (2.8%)	16,011 (25.3%)	45,385 (71.8%)	63,179
1820	3,615 (4.5%)	19,376 (24.2%)	57,221 (71.3%)	80,212
1830	3,594 (4.7%)	20,169 (26.4%)	52,522 (68.8%)	76,285

SOURCE: Historical Census Browser, University of Virginia, Geospatial Statistical and Data Center: http://mapserver.lib.virginia.edu.

The growth of the free black population between 1810 and 1820 was so large that it seems unlikely it could have come from any one individual source. It may be indicative of the ability of slave owners and enslaved people to skirt the general assembly's 1800 restrictions. It seems likely as well that many enslaved people who received promises of freedom during the Revolutionary era finally came into enjoyment of that freedom following their owners' deaths. Finally Charleston's status as one of the South's most prominent cities and seaports suggests that free blacks may have settled there from elsewhere in South or elsewhere in the Atlantic world. Ultimately, regardless of its source, this rapid population growth—not only in real numbers, which started at a relatively low baseline, but as a percentage of the total population—seemed to have sparked the legislature's 1820 decision to enact additional restrictions on manumission.

In that year the South Carolina General Assembly passed "An Act to Restrain the Emancipation of Slaves, and to Prevent Free Persons of Color from Entering into This State." Citing the "great and rapid increase of free negroes and mulattoes in this state, by migration and emancipation," the legislature enacted two new major restrictions. First, they declared that individual slaves could thereafter only be emancipated by an act of the state legislature. Second, they declared it unlawful for "any free negro or mulatto to migrate into this State." Those who did would be apprehended and directed to leave immediately; if a free person of color disobeyed those orders, they would be fined up to twenty dollars and possibly sold into slavery "for a term of time not to exceed five years." The legislature made exceptions for free blacks working as personal servants to whites and for those belonging to vessels who would thereafter depart.[28] They specified as well that free people of color born in South Carolina would not be affected by the new law, and natives of the state living outside it would have up to two years to return legally.

Though some slave owners still attempted to skirt these new restrictions and manumit slaves through traditional means or through sales in trust, petitions to the legislature suggest the 1820 manumission law held some weight. In 1823 William N. Mitchell petitioned the Senate of South Carolina requesting they emancipate an enslaved boy named James Powell. Mitchell reported that, in 1820, James's father, a free black resident of St. John's Berkley Parish in Charleston District, had recorded a last will and testament in which he assigned Mitchell to be James's "guardian and protector." Mitchell informed the legislature that James Powell Sr., the father, had served Mitchell's family as a free servant and that Powell held his son James Jr. in slavery. James Sr. had always intended to manumit his son, but legislative restrictions had prevented him from doing so. Mitchell urged "upon the sympathy of your honorable House the miserable state in which the subject of this petitions now remains," because James Sr. had died with no heirs yet appointed Mitchell as only guardian and protector of James Jr. Because of those circumstances, and because "of the unforeseen difficulty arising from the recent legislative restrictions upon manumissions," James Jr. was "altogether unprotected at a time when the public sentiment calls for vigilant supervision." James Jr. was in the unfortunate position of being "the slave of nobody and at the same time . . . not a free negro."[29]

The following month a committee ruled on Mitchell's petition. They noted that although the "principles of humanity" inclined them to sympathize with James Powell's position, the "peculiar situation of the country" led them to feel "constrained upon principle to report unfavorably to the prayer of the said petitioners." They further cited their belief that Powell would be introduced to a state of "vice, idleness . . . which experience has proved a state of freedom is afforded." Finally they worried about the precedent they would set if they agreed to free Powell.[30]

The circumstances surrounding James Powell's continued enslavement speak volumes about the restricted nature of manumission following the passage of the 1820 law, as well as to the more volatile racial climate of South Carolina in that era. First, the 1820 manumission law seems to have had its intended effect, as Mitchell felt his options sufficiently constrained that he petitioned directly to the legislature for James Powell's manumission, citing it as an "unforeseen difficulty." His petition and the response of the legislature point as well to the broader white attitudes toward slavery and black freedom in the early 1820s. Mitchell referred to the "public sentiment" as calling for the "vigilant supervision" of blacks in South Carolina, and the committee who responded to his petition noted that the "peculiar state of the country" prevented them from acceding to his wishes; both Mitchell and the committee surely were referring to the city's continued unease after the discovery and aftermath of the Denmark Vesey conspiracy from the year before. That the committee believed black freedom resulted in "vice, idleness" suggests as well that the tropes used by southern whites to bolster the system of slavery and diminish perceptions of black freedom in the late antebellum era were by the 1820s already given the force of law in South Carolina. Certainly the debate surrounding the Missouri Compromise and its eventual passage in 1820 made southern planters and white elites, perhaps South Carolinians in particular, acutely aware of the potential uncertainty in the future of slavery. Their desire to keep free people of color from entering the state and to restrain manumissions speaks to their efforts to maintain and strengthen the institution.

In 1836 Moses Irvin wrote to the state legislature in a similar vein, hoping they would provide special legislative permission for Irvin to emancipate his children. Unlike Mitchell, Irvin's petition revealed that some arguments, particularly religious appeals, could lead to success with the legislature. Irvin had been born enslaved and served Gen. Francis Marion "at various time during the war of the Revolution and particularly during the siege of Charleston." After "the fall of Charleston," Irvin was seized by the British and carried to the upstate. He later escaped and returned to "his master Mr. Irvin, who afterwards gave him his freedom as a reward for his faithful services." After the Revolution, Irvin married an enslaved woman, with whom he had two children. Irvin informed the legislature that "by the savings of his long labors, he has since purchased his wife and her two children." He noted that "he and his wife are far advanced in years and [he] is rendered very unhappy by the situation of his children . . . who are in danger of being sold after he is dead as vacant property and confiscated in the use of the State." Irvin hoped the legislature would "sanction his children's freedom by allowing [them] to follow the condition of their father."[31]

Anticipating the legislature's concerns about free blacks of bad character, as discussed in both the 1800 and 1820 manumission laws, Irvin included a testimonial signed by thirteen local whites in which they called attention not just to his virtuous character but also to his involvement with the local church. They testified that Irvin had "been a member of the Baptist Church in Charleston since the year 1790" and "that during a great part of that time he has been authorized by the Church to teach and instruct the coloured people." In his role in the church "as well as in every other . . . he has behaved himself with such propriety as to earn the confidence and esteem of the Church and of those who know him." The subscribers, including the pastor of the Baptist church, Basil Manly, as well as three deacons, added that "the salutary influence of the example of the leading coloured members of this church has been such" that during the Denmark Vesey conspiracy in 1822, "not one connected with the Baptist church was found in any degree implicated." Pastor Manly added in an addendum that Irvin was likely older than seventy-five years old. Finally Joseph Lynch, the grandson of Irvin's former owner, testified to the "excellence and goodness" of Irvin's character as well. He noted that since attaining his freedom about thirty years prior, Irvin's "conduct as a member of the community has been unimpeachable."[32]

For the whites who signed Irvin's testimonial, the most compelling reason he should receive special legislative permission to emancipate his children—or at the very least, the reason they felt the legislature would find most compelling—was not only Irvin's character but also his deep connection to Charleston's Baptist church. While at other times, and with other churches, a free person of color providing religious instruction to other black people was viewed as a threat (like with the African Church during the Vesey affair), for Irvin his commitment to the church was an outward sign of his respectability. Irvin's affiliation with the Baptist church proved to his white supporters that he did not fall prey to the vices they believed plagued so many other free blacks and demonstrated that his children should be emancipated. It proved it to the legislature as well.

A legislative committee approved Irvin's petition. They noted that for some years past it had "been considered to be against the policy [and] interests [of] the state to allow persons of colour to be emancipated and remain in the state," and although they "still entertain the same opinion," the petition of Moses Irvin "appears to be a marked exception to the general rule." Thus

"on a count of the very excellent character given of the petitioner by numerous and highly respectable citizens and in consideration of the faithfulness
and services of the petitioner during the Revolutionary War," the committee
recommended that "the children of the petitioner be allowed to follow his
condition" and declared them free.[33]

Moses Irvin capitalized on his reputation with members of his local church
and the family of his former owner, using personal bonds to strengthen his
petition to the legislature. Coupled with his service during the Revolutionary
War, his reputation as a respectable member of the church and Charleston
community convinced the legislature to look favorably on his request to free
his children. The committee who reported on the petition also felt the situation was rare enough that it would not establish a precedent for manumitting
slaves by legislative action. They stated plainly their belief in the propriety
of the law restricting manumissions, despite offering an exception to Irvin.
As the institution of slavery came under increasing scrutiny beginning in the
1820s, and amid concern about character of the state's free blacks, the South
Carolina legislature sought to prevent the growth, through migration and
emancipation, of the state's free black population. Few applied for legislative
relief to these new restrictions, and even fewer succeeded in convincing the
legislature to emancipate their slaves through legislative action. Nevertheless exceptional circumstances, reputations, and personal connections could
persuade the legislature.

After 1820 manumission became increasingly difficult in South Carolina.
Although some exceptional individuals managed to achieve manumission
through the legislature, others continued to skirt the law through sales in
trust. Through these arrangements, enslaved people continued to be held
in slavery only nominally, owned by individuals unable or unwilling to sell
them or make use of their labor. For example, a free black woman named
Charlotte Kreitner purchased an enslaved man named William Nero in trust
from P. M. Campbell for $393 in 1827.[34] Though few, these and other arrange-
ments became officially outlawed by the state general assembly in 1841. That
year the legislature passed yet another "act to prevent the emancipation of
slaves," extending the prohibitions outlined in the 1820 law. They carefully
stated that enslaved people sold by way of "trust or confidence, either secret
or expressed, that such slave or slaves shall be held in nominal servitude
only" were to be null and void. Any sales in trust "for the benefit of any
slave or slaves" were outlawed. As the future of slavery continued to look
ever more uncertain in the 1840s, South Carolina officials closed the final
routes to manumission altogether in 1841. Though free people of color could
continue to own family members, the state had eliminated the possibility of
emancipating spouses and children.

While the nature and prevalence of slaveholding and the particular legal cultures of Cartagena and Charleston led to the development of vastly different attitudes and policies toward manumission, a closer inspection of the development of manumission policies in the two cities reveals a more complicated picture in which white elites in both places conceived of slave emancipation and black freedom as problems that needed to be carefully controlled. Between 1800 and 1850 in Cartagena, manumission policies generally trended toward greater openness. Thousands of enslaved people gained their freedom during the wars for independence in the 1810s as a result of their active military participation. Private manumissions also continued during that era, as links between antislavery sentiment and republicanism grew stronger, a means of contrasting the patriot position with Spanish policies. At the first congresses of the new republic, national legislators affirmed their commitment to the gradual abolition of slavery in Colombia. They declared "free womb" laws, at least nominally providing freedom to the children of enslaved mothers. They prohibited the separation of enslaved families, the importation of enslaved people, and their sale outside of the country. And they established manumission juntas, tasking local officials with purchasing the freedom of enslaved people and linking manumission with prominent national holidays. Manumission became part of republican identity in early nineteenth-century Colombia.

Manumission in Charleston, on the other hand, became more restricted during the same period. Though South Carolina whites had long been opposed to the very notion of black freedom, attempting to regulate or outlaw it from the 1720s onward, these policies remained largely ineffective or unenforced until the Revolutionary era. Following huge growth in the number of manumissions, the state began to place the practice under greater restrictions beginning in 1800. When the requirement that manumissions receive approval from a court-appointed board failed to stem the tide of manumissions, the state's general assembly further restricted the practice in 1820, declaring that manumissions could only be executed through legislative action. Although the ingenuity of enslaved people and a small portion of slave owners continued to allow some to skirt these restrictions and find avenues to freedom, the legislature cut off remaining routes to manumission in 1841, effectively ending the possibility of enslaved people in South Carolina gaining their freedom through legal means.

Yet despite this stark contrast in official policy toward manumission, whites in both cities carefully attempted to control the process of manumission, viewing black freedom as a threat to social and political stability. In Cartagena white concern about manumission stemmed from their fear of disruptions to social order—vice and crime in addition to political participation;

white Charlestonians, meanwhile, restricted manumission because it represented a threat to *the* social order—the continued subjugation of tens of thousands of enslaved people to the authority of the white planter class. These anxieties about manumission and black freedom, coupled with some similarities in the urban environments of the Atlantic world, led enslaved people to seek avenues to freedom that paralleled one another in crucial ways.

PRACTICAL AVENUES TO ACHIEVING FREEDOM

Although the legal and political environments and the attitudes of white authorities could differ in important ways between Anglo and Spanish America, enslaved people throughout the Americas often relied on similar strategies to achieve freedom. First, throughout the African Americas, enslaved people purchased their own freedom or that of family members from enslavers. Exigencies of the urban environment made it possible for enslaved people to carve out a degree of functional autonomy from their owners, hire out their own time, and sometimes earn and save enough money to purchase their own freedom. Continuing such work in freedom, often in skilled trades and service occupations, formerly enslaved people used some of the money they earned to purchase the freedom of spouses, children, and other family members. Second, some of the reasoning for manumission provided by enslavers featured commonly in both North and South America, particularly the manumission of enslaved people for claimed political, religious, or moral considerations. Sometimes effective immediately and other times following their death, enslavers cited such considerations throughout the eighteenth and nineteenth century but did so most frequently during the Age of Revolution as a new discourse about individual liberty circulated throughout the Atlantic world.

Additional means of achieving freedom featured more prominently in one region or another. In Cartagena, for example, enslaved people possessed legal rights their North American counterparts did not and thus were able to denounce slave owners in court and could occasionally find relief from an abusive master either through sale to a new owner of their choosing or through outright manumission. Further, after the 1820s some enslaved people received their freedom through local manumission juntas and councils, formally organized institutions that used state funds to affect slave emancipation. Additionally, in part because plantation agriculture never fully developed in Caribbean Colombia, self-liberation in the form of running away represented a far more viable and more permanent means of achieving individual freedom in Cartagena than it did in Charleston. Alternatively more enslaved people in Charleston seem to have achieved freedom because of some type of sexual or familial relationship with their enslaver, as slave owners periodically emancipated enslaved sexual partners or the children borne from such relationships.

Caribbean Colombia's status as society with slaves, coupled with the more flexible legal status of enslaved people in Iberian America, made manumission in the region relatively accessible throughout the era of slavery there.[35] Enslaved people in and around Cartagena utilized methods both legal and extralegal to achieve freedom, though it is impossible to determine precisely exactly how many enslaved people gained freedom through which means. Extant documentation suggests legal manumission remained more accessible for women than for men throughout this period as economic opportunity and sexual exploitation opened avenues to freedom. Further, the wars for independence created opportunities for enslaved people to gain their freedom, both through direct participation in the war and through the link those wars established between patriotism and support for racial equality and black freedom. This support for manumission proved tenuous, however, as by the 1840s routes to manumission had been all but eliminated in most of Colombia as enslavers and legislators sought to prolong the institution of slavery. Nevertheless economic considerations, military necessity, and republican fervor opened avenues to freedom for enslaved people across Caribbean Colombia.

Unfortunately data on the rate and types of manumission for Cartagena is unavailable, making a direct comparison with Charleston difficult. However, using data collected for the city of Santa Marta—which, as one of the few cities of Caribbean New Granada that could rival Cartagena in size and importance, we can reasonably expect to share a large number of similarities with Cartagena—and for other Spanish American cities, it seems likely that patterns of manumission in Cartagena dovetailed neatly with those of other locales in the urban Spanish Atlantic.[36] For example, self-purchase constituted one of the primary ways that enslaved people in Caribbean Colombia gained their freedom. As discussed earlier in this chapter, this ability to purchase one's freedom from slavery, known as *coartación,* had long precedents in Spanish legal culture and was prevalent throughout Spanish America. During the final two decades of colonial rule in Santa Marta, which recorded a slave population of 571 in the late 1770s (much smaller than the more than 2,500 in Cartagena at the same time), 64 women, 32 men, and 16 children were manumitted. Of those 112 individuals manumitted, nearly 85 percent received their freedom through purchase; of those purchases roughly two-thirds achieved freedom through self-purchase, while many of the remaining people received their freedom thanks to the purchase by a family member, usually a mother.[37] The remaining 15 percent were freed through private manumission acts by their enslavers. Though Cartagena had a larger enslaved population during the same era, it seems likely that these patterns would have extended there, as they reflect trends not just applicable in Spanish America but throughout the Atlantic world more broadly.[38] Thus it seems likely that between 1790 and 1810, the vast majority of enslaved people who gained their freedom would have done so through self-purchase or family purchase, turning the particular conditions and economic possibilities of urban life to their advantage.

Despite the relative accessibility of manumission through self-purchase in Colombia, however, barriers still existed—along with a sense of unease among whites about the possibilities of black freedom. In 1783 a royal *cédula* stipulated that although enslaved women could acquire their freedom through self-purchase, their children would remain in slavery and would not be immune to being sold. While Spanish authorities may have tacitly condoned the process of self-purchase, such a treatment of slave children reveals they allowed it out of practical and economic considerations rather than moral ones. The relative accessibility of private manumission in Cartagena existed largely for considerations other than a commitment to antislavery, and whites rarely ceded control of the processes through which enslaved people gained their freedom.

In addition to those who gained their freedom through private manumissions, enslaved people in Cartagena used the legal system and the courts to their advantage in ways their counterparts in the United States could not. With the ability to take legal action against whites without a guardian or intermediary, some enslaved people in Cartagena used the courts to gain release from cruel or neglectful enslavers and sometimes to achieve their outright manumission. This ability to challenge the authority of slave owners directly represented a legal dynamic for achieving freedom that was simply not possible in the U.S. South. In 1781, for example, an enslaved woman named Getrudis Subisa sued her owner for extreme cruelty and abuse. In an exceptional outcome, Cartagena's governor ordered Subisa's enslaver not only to grant Subisa her freedom but also to pay her a small pension. This ability to challenge the authority of one's master in court in cases of abuse or neglect was recognized in Spain's 1789 Código Negro, and historian Aline Helg has argued that many enslaved people thereafter came to see this ability to challenge their masters in court as not just a privilege but also a legal right.[39]

In a case that transpired a few years before Getrudis Subisa obtained her freedom, in 1777 Pedro Regalado Cores of Cartagena filed a lawsuit for his freedom against the executors of the estate of his former master, a priest named Diego Rodriguez Bravo. According to Cores, his former master "did me the grace and mercy of giving me my liberty, for [the] good services, love, and fidelity" with which Cores served Bravo until his death. Unfortunately, according to Cores, his former master did not have the time to document properly in a will his wish to free Cores, though he expressed his dying wish to Fray Josef de la Pedrosa. As such Cores demanded that the executors of his former master's estate grant him documentation of his free status. Bravo's executors denied Cores's claims, arguing that in Bravo's final confession to Father Pedrosa, he did not express a wish to free Cores and, further, that such a confession would not constitute a legal emancipation. Thus, they argued, Cores remained the property of Bravo's estate. Through a protracted legal battle in which each side argued over whether Diego Bravo had indeed expressed a wish to free his slave Pedro and whether such a wish held legal weight if not recorded in writing, the court ultimately ordered the executors to free Pedro Regalado Cores.[40]

Next some enslaved people in Caribbean Colombia did receive their freedom from local manumission juntas. Using funds raised through taxation and private donations, these manumission juntas periodically freed enslaved people by indemnifying individual slave owners. Such grants of freedom were sometimes accompanied by elaborate ceremonies and often took place on national holidays both religious and secular, particularly November 11, the anniversary of Cartagena's independence, and December 25, Christmas. In 1829, as mentioned earlier, Rensselaer van Rensselaer relayed the story of large crowds in the city's main plaza accompanying a manumission ceremony that took place around Christmastime. He noted that the manumission junta had freed about thirty enslaved people to much public acclaim, and those who received their freedom paraded through the streets to cheers from friends and family. Two decades later emancipations from local manumission councils slowed, following a long period of inactivity. In 1849 Cartagena's manumission council reported that 178 men and 176 women still remained enslaved in the province. They declared that in the previous year, just 2 enslaved people had gained their freedom: a woman freed through the funds of the manumission junta and a man freed by "the generosity of his masters."" Additionally the province was home to 216 people born free to enslaved mothers who had yet to reach eighteen years of age.[41] The following year, despite just 2 enslaved people receiving their freedom through the manumission board in 1849, the Province of Cartagena was home to just 256 enslaved people, a decline of nearly 100 people.[42] Even at the cusp of the abolition of the institution in 1851, the vast majority of the province's enslaved people were under the age of forty, as shown in table 1.4.

TABLE 1.4 **Age of enslaved populations as reported by manumission boards, Cartagena, 1848–50**

	Under 40	40–50	50–60	Older than 60
1848–49	187	97	48	22
1849–50	142	70	22	22

SOURCE: AGN, República, Manumisión, t. 1, ff. 140–52, 282–98.

Thus even as manumission boards freed few enslaved people, the enslaved population of the region continued to diminish during the 1840s as enslaved people pursued a range of opportunities to gain their freedom and to work around the deliberately slow pace of manumission boards.

Finally, in 1850, just six months before Colombia's declaration of final abolition, Cartagena's manumission board emancipated two slaves in a ceremony on November 11, in celebration of the anniversary of Cartagena's declaration of independence. The board paid 150 pesos to Señor José Vicente Lopez for the freedom of an enslaved woman named Agustina Lopez. They also paid out 100 pesos for the freedom of María del Espiritu Santo Céspedes, purchasing her from her owner, Nicolasa Castillo de Franco.[43] That enslavers were willing to sell the freedom of enslaved people to the manumission boards amid a declining enslaved population suggests, perhaps, a recognition of slavery's limited future in the country, the diminishing value of slave ownership, and a culture in which social prestige could be gained not from slave ownership but from slave emancipation. Links between manumission and the virtues of republicanism in Spanish America seem to have inclined at least some slave owners to emancipate their slaves, particularly toward the end of this era when the final abolition of slavery was clearly imminent. Ultimately, despite the fact that manumission juntas sought to encourage patience and docility among those still enslaved, catered to the whims of slave owners, and typically rewarded enslaved people best able to assuage white fears about vice and idleness among freed people, they nevertheless represented a possible avenue to freedom for enslaved people in Caribbean Colombia.

Finally enslaved people in Cartagena also utilized extralegal methods for obtaining their freedom. Running away or absconding to nearby backlands areas represented a far more feasible, and more permanent, path to freedom for enslaved people in and near Cartagena than it was for those of the South Carolina lowcountry. Though slaves often made attempts at self-liberation in and around Charleston, the enslaved of Caribbean Colombia achieved more sustained success. Self-liberated enslaved people, free *pardos* and *mulattos,* and Indians established settlements outside the cities of Caribbean Colombia —as they did elsewhere in the greater Caribbean world—and some of these settlements developed into independent communities recognized by Spanish and later Colombian officials.[44]

One of the earliest established and most prominent of these communities established by fugitives from slavery, known in Spanish America as *palenques,* was San Basilio, located in Cartagena's nearby hinterlands. In 1781 a bishop taking stock of the parishes of the province of Cartagena observed what he described as the "deplorable state" of San Basilio and its church. The *palenque,* "whose inhabitants are all blacks," featured a church he deemed incapable of serving the spiritual needs of its members: walls made of sugar cane, a roof left in ruin, and an inability to provide the sacraments for the community's many inhabitants. He noted that many of San Basilio's residents lived in marriages unsanctioned by the church, as a consequence of their "poverty and absolute lack of the means to satisfy" the requirements of the sacrament of matrimony. The bishop also noted that the residents of San Basilio afforded "no subordination to the priest or royal justice." Rather they were "governed by a Captain, also black." He described San Basilio as being "a refuge for all freed blacks, who had escaped their masters." He advised that it would benefit that community greatly if there were "a white man as judge, with the necessary faculties to contain [the blacks] in their inebriation and other vices."[45]

Though concerned in particular with the religious life of San Basilio, this bishop's observations about the inhabitants and the governance of the community reveal the extent to which self-liberation represented a viable avenue to freedom for enslaved people in Caribbean Colombia. First San Basilio was well established enough that it was included in official church visits of the parishes of the provinces, despite the fact that the community was composed largely of fugitives from slavery and their descendants. Further the residents of this community were by and large self-sufficient. They had means of attending to the community's spiritual needs (though of course in a manner the Catholic Church deemed unacceptable), and they had governed themselves without the interference of local or Spanish authorities. They obeyed their "black captain" without accountability to the Crown or church. Finally this church official alluded to tropes about black freedom prevalent throughout the black Atlantic world, describing the "freed blacks" of San Basilio as addicted to vice and in desperate need of white oversight. Despite this church official's dim view of the state of San Basilio, however, his visit revealed the extent to which an independent, permanent black community could survive in the hinterlands of one of Spanish America's most important cities.[46]

In 1790 a crown representative relayed to the viceroy of New Granada information regarding other similar, if smaller, autonomous communities of self-liberated people. He informed the viceroy that dozens of individuals and families lived in the hills and mountains outside of the city of Cartagena. He noted that in the "dense mountains" of Cartagena Province there could be found "many people and entire families making an absolutely barbarous life" outside of the boundaries of "politics and Christianity." The inhabitants of these backland communities recognized the authority of neither the Crown nor the church, just as the inhabitants of San Basilio had been described. He lamented that "neither Judge nor Priest can care for their education and government." He continued to note that these autonomous mountain residents lived "devoted with appalling abandon to the most atrocious offenses" yet lamented that they "could not be extracted." Indeed the residents of the backlands of Cartagena lived outside of the boundaries of accepted religion and government "with the security that they could not be apprehended."[47]

The rivers and mountains of Cartagena's hinterland made this region very difficult to traverse, and the effect of this impenetrability of terrain was twofold. First it made the development of plantation agriculture in Caribbean Colombia more or less an impossibility, certainly preventing it from taking hold to the effect it did in other areas of the greater Caribbean and Atlantic world. Second, because of this lack of plantation agriculture, enslaved people could escape their enslavers with greater ease than elsewhere in the Atlantic world, achieving a state of freedom that was comparatively sustainable. In eighteenth- and early nineteenth-century Cartagena, running away to the backlands of the province represented a far more reliable and permanent method for achieving freedom than in Charleston, though it occurred throughout Latin America and the Caribbean, including most notably in Cuba, Suriname, and Brazil.

More broadly, enslaved people in Cartagena utilized a wide variety of methods, both legal and extralegal, to gain their freedom during the late eighteenth and early nineteenth centuries. Enslaved people throughout the Atlantic world, including in Charleston, used many of these same approaches.

In Charleston enslaved people often gained their freedom through private manumissions of various motivations. Some enslavers indicated the precise reasoning for their decision to free individual slaves—moved by sentiments of the American Revolution, affection toward particularly loyal or long-serving enslaved people, or suggestions of direct family links being the most common—while others offered no explanation at all. At other times, like in Cartagena, enslaved people purchased their own freedom from slave owners using money earned by hiring out their own time in a variety of skilled trades or domestic occupations. Still other manumission decrees seem to indicate either a sexual or familial relationship between slave owners and enslaved people.

Each of these motivations for executing a deed of manumission, broadly speaking, has a nearly direct corollary in Cartagena and elsewhere in the urban Atlantic world. In Charleston such motivations can be most precisely gleaned for manumissions executed prior to the restrictions enacted in 1800, when slave owners could manumit slaves through a simple deed. Following 1800, as the South Carolina legislature forced enslaved people and slave owners to jump through increasingly difficult administrative hoops to process manumissions, the motivations behind them became more difficult to discern.

The vast majority of manumissions processed in Charleston before 1800 were justified by enslavers' private considerations. Of the 268 manumissions I have identified between 1776 and 1800, more than half (142) of slave owners cite some kind of moral reason for emancipating individual slaves.[48] Often enslavers used a form of manumission boilerplate, simply citing "good causes and considerations" as their sole motivation, and left the details ambiguous; throughout the late eighteenth century, that phrase appeared on nearly all deeds of manumission, even when they also included additional details. Other times, enslavers explicitly outlined their motivation for manumitting individual enslaved people, claiming faithful service to them or their family. At least some instances that on their surface appear to be motivated by good will were likely motivated by a slave owners' desire to rid himself of old, infirm, or troublesome slaves, as the South Carolina General Assembly pointed out in 1800 when they restricted manumission, or perhaps granted as a way of encouraging continued service among other enslaved people they owned. Many of the enslaved people manumitted in this fashion received promises of freedom in the last will and testament of their enslaver, though others gained their freedom more immediately.

For example John Farquahar emancipated two slaves in June 1776, just a month before the United States declared its independence from Great Britain. On June 10 he "set free . . . from all slavery, bondage, and servitude" for "the many faithfull services done and performed" by his "Negro wench slave named Sarah." Three days later he cited similar reasons in a manumission for an enslaved man named Joe.[49] Dozens of other enslaved people received their freedom for similar considerations. In 1784 an enslaved man named William, who prior to his baptism was known as Prince, received his freedom for his "faithful and honest behavior."[50] William Luyten declared in 1790 that he had "no right to leave in bondage after my death" an enslaved man named Morey. For this consideration, coupled with Morey's "true and faithful" service, Luyten emancipated Morey on February 27, 1790.[51] In February 1796 Charles

Hill of Charleston manumitted four enslaved people, Sam, William, Mary Ann, and Amy, simply citing "good causes and considerations."[52] In 1800 Edgar Wells cited "the fidelity and services" of an enslaved woman named Hagar as his reason for freeing her.[53] Charleston butcher George Young freed an enslaved woman named Molly "as a reward and compensation for her faithful and constant attention."[54] Like slave owners of the Revolutionary era across the United States, Charleston enslavers cited this generic language of moral consideration and faithful service in the emancipation of individual enslaved people or small groups—though surely it sometimes masked less noble motivations—providing freedom to hundreds of enslaved people through private manumission.

Occasionally enslavers citing such language also attached a variety of restrictions to manumissions, providing freedom to enslaved people only after certain barriers had been cleared. Most often slave owners manumitted enslaved people but required they continue to serve the owner or his family for a set term. In 1798 Charleston merchant Joseph Winn Jr. manumitted his "Mestizo woman slave" Grace but stipulated "she should remain with him during his natural life, subject and obedient to his order and authority."[55] In 1799 Caleb Hughes "from the bond of slavery forever set free" four enslaved people: Patty, Jacob, James, and January. Hughes required that January serve an additional five years. Patty, Jacob, and James were each required to remain in bondage until they reached the age of twenty-two.[56] In November 1800, just a month before South Carolina changed their manumission law, Joshua Eden manumitted an enslaved man named William. Yet Eden stated that "the condition of the above manumission is that the said Negro William is to serve me faithfully and attentively during the remainder of my life."[57] In each of these instances, enslavers claimed to have been motivated by some sense of moral duty to reward their enslaved people for faithful service, though they still required continued service from enslaved people until the enslaver's death or the death of their spouse. In these instances, perhaps similar to enslaved people born under the free womb laws of the U.S. North, Spanish America, and elsewhere, enslaved people received their freedom in theory but remained bound to their enslavers for years afterward, sometimes for more than a decade. Many of the slave owners who extended promises of freedom were attempting to encourage the continued "faithful" service of the bondmen and -women they owned.

Another frequently used path to freedom for enslaved Charlestonians was self-purchase; about 20 percent of enslaved people manumitted between the 1776 and 1800 gained their freedom in that way.[58] This makes self-purchase less common than in Cartagena, where the process of *coartación* was more firmly established and accepted, but still it represented a well-worn path to freedom for enslaved Charlestonians. Like enslaved people throughout the urban Americas, Charleston enslaved people often had the ability to earn money for themselves through a variety of arrangements with slave owners. Most frequently enslaved people "hired out" their time, working independently of their master throughout the urban milieu, often as carpenters, seamstresses, tailors, laundresses, and a wide variety of other skilled and unskilled positions. Enslaved people hiring their own time typically agreed to return a set amount of money to their enslaver, whether daily, weekly, or monthly, and were able to save the rest and often function autonomously, living apart from the oversight of slave owners. While such arrangements offered considerable independence to many enslaved people living in urban environments all throughout the African Americas, it was not freedom. In the United States, there was little to no protection for self-hiring enslaved people or their earnings, and the relative privilege of hiring out could be always be rescinded.

Alexander Hewat explained clearly the process by which enslaved people managed to purchase their own freedom in his deed of manumission for an enslaved woman named Diana. In 1777 Hewat emancipated Diana in exchange for "one thousand pounds good and lawful money" he had received from his "negro woman slave." Diana had acquired this large sum "from her labour and industry from time to time by me allowed to carry on and transact during the term of her servitude."[59] Hewat permitted Diana to work and earn money independently, eventually allowing her to save the considerable sum required to purchase her own freedom.

Over the course of the Revolutionary era, dozens of enslaved people purchased their freedom in this way. In 1777 Jacob Valk of Charleston declared that he had received "from my Negro wench Lawry" a sum of £420. Valk stated that he had a previously agreed with Lawry "that on receiving such a sum of money she should be free."[60] In December 1779 an enslaved woman named Chloe had to pay £1,500 for the privilege of purchasing her freedom.[61] Three Charleston slaves purchased their own freedom in June 1796. Merchant Alexander James manumitted his "black slave called Maria" in exchange for $370.[62] An enslaved woman named Mary purchased her freedom from tavern keeper Christopher Martin for "ten pounds sterling."[63] Mariner Thomas Ross emancipated a slave named Pompey for the "sum of one hundred Guineas."[64] In January 1798 an enslaved man named Jehu Jones purchased his freedom from tailor Christopher Rogers for "one hundred pounds sterling."[65] Jones would go on to open a remarkably successful hotel and would become one of the most prominent leaders in Charleston's free black community. Each of these enslaved people almost certainly hired out their own time and saved money over a period of years to purchase their freedom outright.

Occasionally enslaved people developed arrangements with their owners to purchase their freedom over time rather than all at once. In 1797 an enslaved woman named Phoebe, "together with her husband and their son Isaac," was purchased at an estate sale by Isaac Teasdale and J. D. Vale "for the purpose of allowing them to work themselves free." For the ten months that followed, Phoebe worked for Henry William Desaussure "in the capacity of a servant, taking care of [his] children." In late June Phoebe "from her labour paid her proportion of the money," thus earning her freedom.[66] The fate of her husband and son remains unknown. This arrangement reveals the opportunities potentially available to enslaved people in Charleston. Presumably Phoebe and her family had some sort of previous relationship with Teasdale and Vale, such that the two were willing to purchase her after the death of her previous owner, John Creighton. Perhaps Phoebe had been hired out to them as a domestic servant at some point, or else they knew of her reputation as a hardworking, reliable woman. Once Teasdale and Vale purchased the family, sufficient opportunity existed within the city that Phoebe was able to earn the money to purchase her freedom in a relatively short time. Other slave women gained their freedom through similar arrangements.[67] Additionally in 1780 Thomas Bourke of Charleston sold Joseph Badger an enslaved man named Scipio, a cooper, for "the sum of fifty-nine pounds, sixteen shillings, and three pence." Just a few months later, Badger manumitted Scipio, citing the consideration of the exact same sum, "well and truly paid ... by Negro Scipio." Scipio surely earned the money to repay Bourke through his work as a cooper.[68]

Other enslaved people gained their freedom after a third party purchased it from a slave owner on their behalf. Occasionally a family member, close friend, or other individual either bought the enslaved person outright before manumitting them or paid the enslaver an agreed-upon sum in exchange for manumission. Sometimes this arrangement occurred between a slave owner and a philanthropically minded white person; often it occurred between a slave owner and either an enslaved or free family member of the person to be freed. While later in the antebellum period, free black people sometimes owned family members but were unable to free them—in addition to those who owned slaves not for egalitarian purposes—at least a few of those manumitted prior to 1800 achieved freedom through the financial assistance of family members.

In September 1778 Charleston merchant William Greenwood emancipated a mulatto woman named Charlotte and her daughter Diana Maria "in consideration of the sum of one thousand pounds . . . paid by Edward Legett Junior," also a merchant in Charleston.[69] In 1779 Louis Dutarque sold "a mulatto wench named Sarah and her child named Catey" to Cornelius Hinson for "the sum of twelve thousand pounds." A month later, Hinson manumitted Sarah and Catey.[70] In November 1787 George Haig freed an enslaved girl named Moll "about ten years of age" after receiving sixty pounds from a man named William Kennedy, though his relationship to either is unknown.[71] In the winter of 1800, Mary Magdalene Grimball freed a mulatto infant named Henry, just eleven months old, and the daughter of Phillida, an enslaved woman owned by Grimball, after receiving sixty dollars from Samuel Barnett.[72] In each of these cases and a number of others, the enslaver granted freedom to one or more slaves in consideration of money received from a third party.[73]

Many instances of these outside-purchase manumissions involved a family member of the enslaved, usually a parent or spouse, putting forth the money to secure their freedom. In 1779 a "freed Negro man" named Carolina manumitted his wife, Jane, for "the love and affection which I now have and bear" toward her. In Jane's manumission decree, Carolina noted that he had "lately purchased" Jane from a "Ms. Rachel Caw."[74] A free black woman named Kate paid William Blamyer and Stephen Drayton five hundred pounds in March 1780 to secure the manumission of her daughter, a "Mulatto girl named Nancy, aged about seven years."[75] Charleston baker Ulric Friend and his wife, Ann, manumitted an enslaved man named Jack, who they acquired following the death of Ann's father, after receiving "eighty-three Guineas . . . paid by Isabella, the slave of William Payne . . . & the wife of the fellow Jack."[76] Rather than purchasing her own freedom, Isabella purchased that of her husband, Jack. Because of her ability to earn money, and because she was owned by the same William Payne who emancipated an enslaved woman named Dolly Waters two years later, it seems likely that Isabella had acquired a degree of autonomy and independence perhaps not afforded to her husband and so prioritized his freedom over her own.

In 1797 Thomas Smith manumitted a "Negro or Mustizo" named Rachel, the daughter of his enslaved woman Sylvia. Smith had been paid twenty pounds to manumit Rachel by "George Lockey, on behalf of his Negro servant Cain."[77] Lucas Florin emancipated an enslaved boy named John, "eight months of age," after receiving thirty pounds from "Mary, his mother."[78] Similarly Joseph Clay of Savannah, Georgia, received seventy-five pounds from Susannah Hepburn, a free mulatto woman, of Charleston, for the purchase of a "Negro man named Evan." Hepburn manumitted Evan in Charleston the following month.[79] A free mulatto man named Claude Moran purchased his son Francois from Elias Pohl for the sum of eighty dollars in 1798.[80] In October 1800 Abigail, a "free mulatto woman," purchased her daughter Rosetta from Mary Elliott for eighty guineas. Thereafter she manumitted Rosetta, citing "the natural love and affection" she held toward her.[81]

In each of these cases, enslaved people gained their freedom for consideration of a sum of money paid to their owner. As slave owners received payments, either from enslaved people themselves, from family members, or from philanthropic whites, they occasionally agreed to free individual slaves. Those who purchased their own freedom would likely have been afforded some kind of functional autonomy for many years yet handed over considerable sums to purchase their freedom legally and outright. In other cases family members purchased the freedom of children and spouses, surely cognizant of how easily a family could be separated in slavery. Because some enslavers were willing to allow enslaved people to purchase themselves or were willing to sell others to family members, more enslaved people in Charleston found avenues to freedom than laws and attitudes toward black freedom might otherwise suggest.

Finally a number of manumissions during this period suggested a sexual relationship existed between an enslaver and an enslaved woman, motivating the emancipation of the woman and her (or often likely *their*) children. Though rarely explicit about the nature of the relationship or the parentage of the children, the tone of these manumissions sometimes differed from those in which enslavers simply expressed a desire to emancipate an enslaved person for private considerations such as long service or a commitment to liberty in the wake of the Revolution. In several such manumission decrees, enslavers declare a degree of concern about the future well-being and education of an enslaved child, distinguishing them from the hundreds of manumissions for which owners cited simply the "good causes and considerations" they found moving; such concern suggests that these were the children of white slave owners. Though enslaved people were often identified in official documents using the surname of their enslaver, this seems particularly pronounced where there are other indications that the enslaved person was fathered by their owner. Occasionally manumission documents declared a mother's race as "Negro" or "Black," while describing the children to be freed as mulattoes, strongly indicating that the slave owner filing the manumission was the father. I have identified nineteen such manumissions that took place between 1776 and the restriction of manumissions in 1800.[82]

In June 1778, for example, white Charlestonian Gabriel Powell manumitted an enslaved boy named Jeffrey Powell, "aged two years or thereabouts, the son of my mulatto woman named Nancy," citing "the good will & great regard which I have & bear unto, and for the future well being of" the said Jeffrey.[83] Joseph Creighton manumitted an enslaved child named James for similar considerations, declaring that he was motivated by "the good will and great regard which I have and bear unto and for the future well-being of my slave boy."[84] Charleston butcher John Freeman stated explicitly in 1789 that he was filing a manumission, for "my son John," classified as a "mustee" for his "good behavior" and "faithful services."[85] In 1790 Peter Bremar manumitted his "negro woman slave named Affee and her two mulatto children, named James and Rebecca."[86] Isaac Watson, for "the good will which I have and do bear" toward his "two mulatto children," Isaac Watson, aged three years, and William Watson, aged two months, manumitted them in 1793. Both the children of were born to "Phillis, a negro wench belonging to" Watson.[87] Both Bremar and Watson left unexplained the discrepancy between the racial designations of the enslaved mother and her children yet strongly suggested that the men were the fathers. Only one manumitted the mother of the children to whom they granted freedom.

Francis Bremar left a similar ambiguity in his manumission of Matilda, described as "my mulatto Child . . . the daughter of my mulatto slave Betsy."[88] Similarly John Hext manumitted his "Negro Child Slave Selina, daughter of my wench Phillis," directing that she was "to have a reasonable support at the direction of my executors until they think her able to provide for herself."[89] Indicating that the child was to continue receiving support from his estate was rare for Charleston manumissions, even for enslaved people likely born to white fathers.

Over the course of several months in 1799, a Charleston slave owner named John Lewis manumitted five enslaved people in three separate manumissions. In July he manumitted his "Negroe woman Lydia, and her two female mulatto children, named Mary and Ann." In September he separately manumitted his "mulatto girl named Hannah" and his "mulatto boy named Robert," both also children of Lydia.[90] Like Isaac Watson and Peter Bremar, the difference in racial designation between mother and children, coupled with their manumission, seems to suggest that Lewis fathered each of these children.

Finally some instances in which slave owners manumitted enslaved people in light of a sexual relationship and recognition of their status as the father of slave children seem to reflect the racial mores of the French Caribbean, where such relationships were more socially acceptable, or at least more common, than in the American South. Though the South Carolina lowcountry was home to a black majority through most of the eighteenth and nineteenth centuries, people of African descent constituted an even larger portion of the population in much of the sugar-producing Caribbean. This racial and gender imbalance led frequently to sexual relationships between white planters and women of African descent. Thus as refugees from Saint Domingue began arriving in Charleston during the 1790s after the outbreak of the Haitian Revolution, many arrived not only with enslaved people but with enslaved women with whom they had some sort of sexual relationship. In 1793, after the initial wave of refugees began arriving in the city (see chapter 2), Jerome Laval, "late of Port au Prince in the Island of St. Domingo," manumitted "an infant female Mulatto child . . . named Justine," who was the "daughter of my female slave named Caroline."[91] In 1797 James Drouillard, "late inhabitant of the Island of St. Domingo," granted freedom to "Louis, a Mulatoe [sic] boy born in the city about three years past."[92] Pierre Charles de Fournier manumitted an enslaved woman named Marie Louise in May 1797. He also granted freedom to Lucy, the daughter of Marie Louise, though with the caveat that "so long as I shall continue to be an inhabitant or resident of the United States of America," Lucy would "continue, be and remain under subject and liable to my care, directions, order, and control."[93] Jean Baptiste Marsenal, "planter of the Island of St. Domingo now residing in this City of Charleston," manumitted an enslaved woman and her four children in June 1797. In his manumission decree, he stated that he gave "freedom and absolute liberty to . . . Desireé a Negro woman and her four Mulatto children" named Marie Francoise, Jean Baptiste, Marie Louise, and Marie Adelaide, aged between three and fifteen years old.[94] In each of these instances, whites formerly of Saint Domingue manumitted enslaved children described as mulattoes and sometimes their enslaved mothers, indicating through complexional descriptions and the degree of affection or care for the recipient of manumission that they were likely the father of the enslaved children and sexual partner of their enslaved mother.

In Charleston enslaved people utilized a variety of legal avenues to gain their freedom. Like in Cartagena economic motives and private considerations from enslavers represented the two most common motivations for manumission in Charleston. In more than half of pre-1800 manumissions, enslavers expressed some kind of private, moral consideration, most often for faithful service though sometimes for reasons more explicitly tied to religious or political sentiment. Other enslaved people gained their freedom as a product of economic considerations, either purchasing their own freedom outright or having it purchased for them by a family member or acquaintance. Each of these motivations was present to varying extents in Cartagena as well. In Charleston more than in Cartagena, enslaved people received their freedom as a consequence of some kind of sexual relationship with slave owners, particularly if that relationship resulted in children. Even as South Carolina's legislature closed off avenues to freedom during the nineteenth century, enslaved people used creativity and ingenuity to find ways out of slavery.

CONCLUSION

The methods enslaved people used to gain freedom in eighteenth- and nineteenth-century Cartagena and Charleston offer a sense of the breadth of possibilities open to African-descended people in the urban Atlantic world. These two cities developed policies toward manumission that were in many ways opposites. In Cartagena, where slave ownership was less common and enslaved labor did not constitute a particularly important element of the region's labor force, manumission became more accessible over the course of the eighteenth and nineteenth centuries. In Charleston, by contrast, where slavery constituted the primary form of labor for the region's plantation agriculture and the foundation of social relations, whites restricted manumission to the point of impossibility for fear of the ways it could disrupt or destabilize the slave system. In Cartagena support for manumission became linked to republican virtue as Colombian leaders attempted to rally support against the Spanish and manumission boards drew on public coffers to emancipate enslaved people. In Charleston, South Carolina officials responded to growth in the free black population by restricting manumission time and again, seeing black freedom as destabilizing for the all-important institution of slavery. Each time slavery came under pressure, the South Carolina legislature responded by further restricting paths to freedom for the state's enslaved people—most of whom lived in the lowcountry.

Despite these differences, however, the white ruling class in both Cartagena and Charleston demonstrated a real apprehensiveness about the ways black freedom could destabilize communities, though the nature of their racial anxieties differed. Though outwardly supportive of manumission, in Cartagena at least some freeborn children of slave mothers were forced by law to continue to live under the control of their mothers' enslaver until they reached the age of eighteen. Further, even though the population of enslaved people in Caribbean Colombia steadily declined over the first half of the nineteenth century, the manumission boards established in 1821 actually freed few people, attempting to pacify enslaved people rather than actively advance freedom. In both Cartagena and Charleston, whites anticipated that once free, former slaves would descend into a life marked by vice and criminality and would fail to survive as free laborers. They also revealed a preference for manumitting only "honest and industrious" slaves, those they felt least susceptible to the aforementioned shortcomings. Though slavery was far less central to the economy of Cartagena, manumission laws both there and in Charleston often functioned to prolong the institution of slavery and reinforce the local authority of whites.

Furthermore in Cartagena white racial anxiety was rooted primarily in the fear that the formerly enslaved would fail to provide for themselves as free people and would not be able to fulfill the demands of citizenship in the nascent republic. Whites worked to limit the speed of manumissions and prolong the institution of slavery until they felt enslaved and formerly enslaved people could be properly trained and prepared to live as productive, free citizens. Because whites exerted their political control from a position as a racial minority in the region, they sought to dictate the terms of slave emancipation in ways that could reinforce existing structures of authority. In Charleston, meanwhile, the notion of preparing the enslaved for freedom never received consideration, due both to the size of the enslaved population and the centrality of enslaved labor to the region's economy, as well as because of the exclusion of black people from the state's formal politics. As white lawmakers and elites actively barred African Americans from the body politic throughout the South, they focused instead on the need to maintain and strengthen the institution of slavery—efforts they felt were hindered even by isolated examples of black freedom. More fundamentally whites in Cartagena, Charleston, and throughout the urban Americas viewed black freedom as a problem that threatened white authority. In different ways whites attempted through various means to control and dictate the process of manumission in ways that would reinforce white control over black populations.

Finally, despite white attitudes prejudicial toward black freedom, enslaved people in both Cartagena and Charleston accessed many of the same avenues to freedom. Throughout the African Americas, the exigencies of urban life opened opportunities for enslaved people to live independently from their enslavers, earn money, and sometimes purchase their own freedom—whether supported by formal legal structures or despite them. Occasionally these same benefits made it possible for African-descended people to purchase the freedom of their spouses and children as well. Further, enslavers privately manumitted enslaved people, frequently citing personally moving considerations. Whether they claimed it as a sign of Christian benevolence, republican virtue, or simply recompense for long and faithful service, the Age of Revolution saw many slave owners express a variety of seemingly moral considerations to explain their motivation for emancipating enslaved people. Though some avenues to freedom differed between the two cities, the vast majority of opportunities for enslaved people to gain their freedom were available in both Cartagena and in Charleston. These parallels in white conceptions of the problem of black freedom and in the paths to emancipation accessed by enslaved people reveal crucial links between the urban Americas throughout the age of slavery.

Chapter 2

THE HAITIAN REVOLUTION IN CARTAGENA AND CHARLESTON

"The slaves do not need much stimulus to conceive of ideas of liberty in view of the pernicious example of those of the French colonies."

Pedro Mendinueta, Viceroy of New Granada, November 19, 1800

"St. Domingo and Africa would come over and cut up the white people if we only made the motion here first."

Enslaved witness in the Denmark Vesey insurrection trial, Charleston, 1822

In late August 1791, the Atlantic world's largest and most successful rebellion of enslaved people began in Saint Domingue—the Caribbean's most profitable colony, the "pearl of the Antilles." In the French colony's northern province, enslaved people rose up in collective action, murdering enslavers and other whites and burning sugar plantations throughout the region. Over the next several years, self-liberated and freeborn people of African descent killed thousands of whites and destroyed hundreds of plantations, taking control of substantial portions of colonial Saint Domingue and forcing colonial leaders to abolish slavery on the island and grant political rights to men of African descent. Through a decade of military and political conflict, mostly under the leadership of the formerly enslaved Toussaint Louverture, African-descended people expelled whites from Saint Domingue, gained full control of the island, permanently abolished slavery, and established the Atlantic world's first black republic—Haiti—by declaring their independence from France. The dramatic and violent war waged by people of African descent in Haiti sent shockwaves through the Atlantic world.

In cities such as Cartagena and Charleston, blacks and whites both wrestled over the meaning of the revolution in Saint Domingue. As residents of port cities intimately tied to the Caribbean and Atlantic worlds, free and enslaved people of African descent often gained wind of events transpiring hundreds or thousands of miles away. Ships manned by both black and white crews regularly arrived in these cities to trade in enslaved Africans, agricultural staples, manufactured goods, and other commodities but also exchanged news and rumor of various sorts. Historian Julius Scott referred to this communication network among black sailors, free and enslaved port laborers, and the African-descended people of the Greater Caribbean as "the common wind."[1] As commercial activity and interimperial exchange increased during the second half of the eighteenth century, so too did black communication. As the height of economic success among Europe's colonial possessions in the Americas yielded to a tumultuous, turbulent Age of Revolution, these same communication networks became all the more crucial to Africans and their descendants; they also became of far greater concern for whites attempting to maintain authority and control amid an era of upheaval.

After the revolution began in Saint Domingue, white concerns about revolutionary discourses and racial violence in American port cities rose to a fever pitch. In Spanish, British, and U.S. ports, authorities attempted to quarantine French revolutionary ideology and prevent the people of African descent living in these cities from engaging with discourses of liberty and equality. Prohibiting French ships from landing and black sailors from coming ashore, white officials throughout the Caribbean and Atlantic world tried in vain to prevent what they saw as the ideological contamination of local populations of African descent.

In the South Carolina lowcountry, the ability and eagerness of African-descended people to engage wider Atlantic discourses emerged early in the region's history; so too did white attempts to stamp it out. In 1739 a group of enslaved people attempted one of the first organized slave revolts on the North American continent in what would come to be known as the Stono Rebellion. The following year South Carolina authorities passed the "Negro Act," dramatically restricting the activities of enslaved people. This tension between black efforts to grasp freedom and engage discourses beyond their local worlds, on the one hand, and white attempts to limit blacks' ability to participate in these revolutionary discussions and prevent Atlantic communication, on the other, only grew more fraught. Through the Age of Revolution, the abolition of the slave trade, and the era of emancipation, blacks and whites wrestled with the perils and possibilities of sharing a port city so deeply connected to the currents of the Atlantic.

On the Spanish American mainland at the opposite margin of the Greater Caribbean world, residents of Cartagena de Indias likewise struggled over communication and control. Established much earlier than Charleston as a commercial entrepôt and slaving port, the communication network connecting Africans and African-descended people in Cartagena was active long before the founding of South Carolina. In Caribbean Colombia, as elsewhere, Spanish and creole authorities worried during the Age of Revolution about the free and enslaved black majority in the region engaging ideas of liberty, equality, and revolution and exchanging news and rumor across imperial boundaries. For blacks and *pardos,* the opposite was true, as they relished the opportunity to gather news from abroad, eventually using it to challenge racial oppression and white authority.

The image of the Haitian Revolution proved to be both powerful and enduring in the minds of blacks and whites, if for different reasons. While the revolution bore on in Saint Domingue, people of African descent in Cartagena, Charleston, and port cities throughout the Atlantic did not just passively learn about the dramatic blow dealt to that colony's slave system and racial order; on occasion they also considered blazing their own paths toward liberty and equality through racial violence. White authorities, meanwhile, struggled to control the flow of information, news, and rumor during this turbulent time. As rumors of insurrection arose in these cities on more than one occasion, whites worked in vain to keep their ports open to commerce but closed to a radical ideology of racial equality.

A degree removed from the autonomy and cosmopolitanism of black sailors who physically traversed the Atlantic world, enslaved and free blacks living and laboring in port cities would have nevertheless benefitted from the experiences of these African-descended seafarers. These sailors transferred information of all kinds—including knowledge of the differences between the status of blacks in various European, West Indian, and American (both North and South) ports of call—to the far more numerous population of enslaved and free people of color working in and around these ports but never venturing to the deep sea. In this way, due to their deep ties to the Caribbean and the frequency with which free and enslaved black sailors would have come ashore or otherwise interacted with populations of African descent, free people of color in both Cartagena and Charleston would have been aware of the differences in the racial order of their respective continents and, increasingly, the parallels and similarities that tied the urban black Atlantic world together.

This chapter examines how blacks and whites in Cartagena and Charleston attempted alternately to harness and hinder the "common wind" of the Haitian Revolution. During the years of tumult on Saint Domingue, whites in both cities struggled to control the influx of news and rumor into their ports for fear that local black populations would rise up in racial violence. Blacks, for their part, demonstrated in various ways their knowledge of the ongoing revolution on Saint Domingue, sometimes laying their own plans for insurrection throughout the 1790s and well into the nineteenth century.[2] Nearly all of the rumored insurrection schemes of that era suggested links between American-, French-, and African-born blacks. Armed with knowledge of the condition of a shared experience of oppression for African-descended people throughout the Atlantic world, blacks and mulattoes in both Cartagena and Charleston began to find common cause with their racial counterparts elsewhere in the Atlantic world and to understand better the shared contours of black freedom in the African Americas.

CHARLESTON

Although white Charlestonians periodically worried about the local effect of the disturbances in Saint Domingue, commerce between Charleston and that colony continued throughout the 1790s and early 1800s. In addition to direct commercial ties to Saint Domingue, trade with the West Indies more generally constituted some of Charleston's most important commercial activity. This regular coming and going of vessels from Charleston to Saint Domingue and elsewhere in the Greater Caribbean resulted not just in the exchange of goods but also in a continuous flow of news, information, and rumor between the South Carolina lowcountry and the broader Atlantic world. Captains and others on American merchant vessels passed letters and messages to city and state officials in Charleston. The sailors, cooks, and other African-descended people who so frequently found work aboard such ships, along with the free and enslaved people of color working on the docks and wharves of Charleston, played a central role in feeding this news and rumor into black communication networks, connecting enslaved and free people of color in Charleston and the surrounding lowcountry to the informational and ideological currents of the Greater Caribbean and Atlantic worlds.[3]

Charleston newspapers featured regular updates about commercial interactions and opportunities with Saint Domingue, even as that colony erupted into revolution. Merchant vessels regularly arrived from and departed for ports in Saint Domingue and elsewhere in the Caribbean. Indeed after the American Revolution, commerce between the United States and Saint Domingue proved crucial in replacing the trade that had been lost between the United States and Jamaica and elsewhere in the British West Indies. Commercial agents such as Thomas Morris, Abraham Sasportas, and Joseph Vesey regularly advertised the sale of muscovado sugar, coffee, molasses, cotton, and a variety of other cargoes from Saint Domingue and elsewhere in the French West Indies throughout the 1790s and early 1800s.[4]

By the late 1790s, the continuing revolution in Saint Domingue and a series of insurrection scares closer to home led Charleston officials to proceed with an abundance of caution regarding the disembarkation of refugees from the French Caribbean. In 1798 "a Citizen," surely a Domingan refugee from earlier in the decade, objected to Charleston's denial of entry to Frenchmen. The Citizen observed, "At the moment when the ports of Saint Domingo and the French West-Indies are perhaps crouded [sic] with American vessels, and American merchants and passengers are daily arriving there, upon what grounds can you refuse a landing to French citizens?"[5] Such an observation not only reveals the continued public presence of the French in Charleston but also provides further acknowledgement of the frequency with which American merchants continued to trade with Saint Domingue, even through the tumult of revolution. Later that year, when the prospect of an independent Saint Domingue had become clearer, the *Charleston City Gazette & Daily Advertiser* observed that the development "is of immense importance to the mercantile interests of America" and that "however we may wish to avoid dabbling in revolutionary matters, this is a case in which our interest is so deeply involved, that secondary considerations ought to be disregarded."[6] A letter in January 1799 from a man in "St. Domingo" to a Charleston resident noted in the same breath that "the Brigands are determined to massacre all the whites, and have offered a free and unmolested commerce on their part, to all nations that will trade with them."[7] This disregard for the character of their trading partners went so far, according to one Charlestonian, that "if the Devil had an earthly empire, the merchants and manufacturers of Great Britain and America would gladly trade to it."[8] Even amid the disruption of racial violence and revolution, commerce between Charleston and Saint Domingue retained a central importance during this era.

As free and enslaved dockworkers and boatmen in Charleston interacted with African-descended sailors of various kinds who had recently arrived from elsewhere in the Caribbean world, they forged crucial links in a broader communication network connecting people of African descent throughout the lowcountry with news from Saint Domingue and elsewhere in the Atlantic. Charleston's commerce with Saint Domingue and the greater Caribbean played a crucial role in linking black Charlestonians to the revolutionary ideology of black freedom emerging in the Atlantic world.

While news and rumor of disturbances in Saint Domingue infiltrated the city through word of mouth, Charleston's newspapers also directly published excerpts from letters, diplomatic dispatches, and public comments on developments in that colony. From the earliest days of the slave uprising, Charleston periodicals took great interest in updating residents on developments there, publishing updates with varying frequency. Though rumors of insurrection closer to home occasionally sparked panic in Charleston, the city's newspapers seem to have published dispatches from Saint Domingue with little thought to their effect on local populations of African descent. Indeed, far from requiring furtive communication with black sailors, enslaved and free people of color in Charleston could learn of developments in Saint Domingue directly from Charleston newspapers.[9]

Some of the first accounts of the insurrection in Saint Domingue began appearing in Charleston's newspapers in late summer and fall of 1791. On August 4 the *State Gazette of South Carolina* reported "fresh disturbances in St. Domingo," as reported by a Captain Davis, who had arrived in Charleston from "Cape Francois" on the brig *Hetty*. The short article noted that the French national assembly "had passed a decree which gave to the free negroes and mulattoes in their colonies, equal rights with the other inhabitants." The publication of this information by the colonial governor of Saint Domingue resulted in "great disturbances" throughout the colony.[10] On September 12 the *City Gazette* learned of the racial violence in Saint Domingue from a Captain Newton, who had arrived at the port of Charleston on the sloop *Polly* two days prior. The paper reported that "a very alarming insurrection of the mulattoes and negroes took place in St. Domingo." It noted the "murder and devastation" caused by the uprising, including the destruction of the sugar works on sixty-four plantations. The article noted in closing that order had been restored on the island by white citizens and soldiers, "who indiscriminately put to death all the negroes who fell in their way."[11] Enslaved and free black Charlestonians surely began to take notice of these reports.

In the subsequent months, news from Saint Domingue continually found its way into the pages of the Charleston press. In January 1792 a Charleston newspaper report about decisions within the French national assembly reported that France's American colonies would have the ability to decide for themselves matters related to the "political state of slaves, of *Gens de Couleur* (mulattoes), and free negroes."[12] Reports continued to surface in the following weeks, noting the "unhappy insurrections" on the French part of Hispaniola. As ships continued to arrive from the Caribbean in Charleston's bustling port, accounts of the violence in Saint Domingue steadily streamed into the city and into the pages of Charleston newspapers.

In June 1793 an article reported that "the revolution at St. Domingo still continues," an apparent acknowledgement of the escalation of violence there from a mere insurrection.[13] Later that month the *City Gazette* published a letter from French civil commissioners Étienne Polverel and Léger-Félicité Sonthonax detailing the bombardment of Port-au-Prince.[14] In July a report from London revealed that the colony's governor had been put under arrest for "aristocratic conduct." It noted that, "fortunately for the governor's head," the vessel transporting him back to France had been intercepted by a British privateer and taken to Liverpool.[15] News from Saint Domingue seemed to flow so freely and regularly into Charleston that when a resident of Trinidad wrote to a friend in Charleston to update him on the activities of the French in the windward islands, he noted of the situation in Saint Domingue that Charlestonians were "better informed than we are."[16]

A letter in August 1793 described how the enslaved people near Port-au-Prince had been "put into a state of revolt" and effected a "massacre and conflagration there."[17] Months later, in October, the *City Gazette* lamented that "the calamity of St. Domingo is at its height," due to the actions of Polverel and Sonthonax. Their decision to "arm the Artizans [*sic*] to promote their tyranny" would soon, the paper presumed, leave "that wretched colony" as "nothing but a field of blood and desolation."[18] A November letter from the colony described the decision "to proclaim, only in the northern part, liberty (under some restrictions)" that the enslaved population "had enjoyed in fact for a year before."[19] Reports from elsewhere in the French Caribbean contrasted their situation with that of "the ill-fated island of St. Domingo." A letter from the governor of the French island of Guadeloupe noted that after some "sacrifices of prejudices," there existed there no "distinction between one free man and another, except that general demarcation which separates ranks and fortunes."[20] An October 1797 report claimed that civil commissioner Sonthonax had been recalled to France after making "a proposition to gen. Toussaint Louverture, to declare the colony of St. Domingo independent of France, and to butcher all the white inhabitants in the colony."[21] Throughout the decade Charleston newspapers published lurid descriptions of the revolution in Saint Domingue and frank acknowledgements of its effectiveness in advancing change, seemingly oblivious or indifferent to the effect such news may have had on the city's and region's African-descended population. Even when the city periodically threw itself into a panic over insurrection rumors, newspapers continued to publish stories about both racial violence and racial equality in the French Caribbean.

Charleston newspapers also regularly published updates referring to Toussaint Louverture, Saint Domingue's highest-ranking military and political leader between the emancipation of the colony's enslaved population in 1794 and the defeat of the French army and establishment of an independent Haiti in the early nineteenth century. On July 8, 1797, the *City Gazette* published a long excerpt from one of Louverture's military addresses, noting it was "not much in the modern style of military men," perhaps as a subtle jab against his leadership ability and military prowess. In attempting to inspire the military to expel the British from Saint Domingue, Louverture utilized religious language, arguing that they were fulfilling God's will by attempting "to restore men to the liberty which he gave them." Framing the violence in Saint Domingue as something of a holy crusade, he argued that God "employs Frenchmen to break the chains under the weight of which people of both hemispheres groan. It is through them he is to remove the obstacles which separate nations, and to unite mankind into a race of brothers."[22] Far from being perpetually uneasy about ideas from Saint Domingue making their way into Charleston and affecting the local enslaved population, the *City Gazette* published Louverture's words for any in the city to read. It seems likely that the connection Louverture drew between the struggle in Saint Domingue and the plight of enslaved people in "both hemispheres" would have been picked up on by enslaved people in Charleston. If enslaved people had not previously identified with their counterparts elsewhere in the Americas prior to the Haitian Revolution, access to such regular information about the disturbances in Saint Domingue, especially the words of Toussaint Louverture, may have pushed them down that path.

White Charlestonians seemed to have been either naive or willfully ignorant of the effect access to news about Saint Domingue may have had on Charleston's black population. In a later era, during the panic surrounding the Denmark Vesey conspiracy, one accused coconspirator told the court that during the lead-up to that alleged insurrection, Vesey was "in the habit of reading to me all the passages in the newspapers that related to St. Domingo."[23] Just as a portion of whites in Charleston may have in some ways identified with the plight of Domingan planters, so too black Charlestonians, particularly the enslaved, perhaps began to develop a sense of common identity with Saint Domingue's rebel slaves.

Charleston residents gained a more direct source of news from Saint Domingue when refugees from that colony began to arrive in the city. Not long after violence began in Saint Domingue, a wave of refugees from the colony streamed into Charleston and other North American port cities—New Orleans, Philadelphia, Norfolk, and a host of others. Domingan refugees, who sometimes arrived with enslaved people with whom they had managed to escape the island, arrived in South Carolina in two distinct waves—the first in the fall and early winter of 1793 following the outbreak of violence on the island and the second in late 1804 after Haiti had won its independence from France—though refugees arrived sporadically throughout the disturbances there. While the arrival of these French refugees concerned white Charlestonians, many of whom surely saw shades of their own worst fears in the stories of white planters narrowly escaping racial violence, the arrival en masse of this foreign population would have been unmistakable to people of African descent as well.

As a steady stream of refugees began to arrive in Charleston in late summer and early autumn 1793, the city's daily newspapers published numerous calls for aid. On September 28, for example, Charleston's *City Gazette* announced the first of what would become a series of charitable events. The paper gave notice that a "charity sermon" would be held the following day at St. Philip's Church—the parish of many of Charleston's wealthiest residents—for "the benefit of the unfortunate sufferers, who have arrived in this city from St. Domingo."[24] A few days later, the paper reported that the event had been a great success and hoped the example of St. Philip's would "be followed by the ministers of every congregation in this city." Thanks to the preacher and the charity of Charleston's residents, "a sum exceeding one hundred guineas was collected for our distressed fellow creatures from St. Domingo."[25] Charleston's Presbyterian, Independent, Methodist, and Roman Catholic churches all held charity sermons in late 1793, heeding the call from St. Philip's parishioners to follow their example.[26]

Calls for aid continued to appear throughout 1793 and into the subsequent years. The paper published a call for firewood "for the use of the distressed French from St. Domingo" almost weekly after September 1793.[27] A man residing along the Enoree River in the state's upcountry sent a shipment of wheat flour "as a present to the most necessitous sufferers from St. Domingo," delivered to Samuel Blakely but distributed by Capt. Joseph Vesey, treasurer of the "Committee for the Relief of Distressed Emigrants."[28] In March 1794 Charleston's St. Cecilia Society held a charity concert for the "worthy and unfortunate sufferers" from Saint Domingue.[29]

A number of refugees from Saint Domingue advertised their services for hire in Charleston's newspapers. Individuals offered instruction in such subjects as French language, art, and music.[30] In early November 1793, a "well informed French gentleman, from St. Domingo," advertised his services as an instructor of "French grammar, . . . music, mythology and history" to any "respectable family" in Charleston who wished to provide their children with a "genteel French education."[31] In late December 1793, a woman refugee from Saint Domingue advertised that she hoped "to resume the keeping of an English and French school," in which she would teach "all kinds of needlework, writing, reading, &c" to the children of Charleston.[32] In January 1794 a Mr. Robelot advertised in both French and English his services as a surgeon.[33] In August a "late inhabitant of St. Domingo" quite boldly advertised in Charleston's *City Gazette* that he was selling "an estate in that island, consisting of part of a plantation three miles distance from Port-au-Prince," noting that it was "susceptible of considerable improvement" and that "there belongs to it two hundred and thirty negroes."[34] It is unclear whether or not he succeeded. A refugee planter in 1795 offered to the "gentleman planters of South Carolina" his expertise in the cultivation of indigo.[35] In 1799 a fifteen-year resident of Saint Domingue, "well acquainted with the West Indies, where he has friends of the first respectability," offered his services as a translator.[36] A doctor forced to flee Saint Domingue in 1803 offered his services as a purveyor of various water cures.[37]

Beginning in 1804, a second distinct wave of refugees from Saint Domingue flooded into Charleston, accompanied by similar calls for aid and advertisements for employment. Like they had a decade prior, Charlestonians sponsored charity sermons and concerts to raise money for this new wave of refugees.[38] On January 6 the *City Gazette* reported that more than ten "distressed inhabitants of St. Domingo" had arrived in Charleston via Havana, Cuba, having likely first fled there after the outbreak of the revolution and then given up hope of returning to the island following the establishment of an independent Haiti.[39] Like during the earlier waves of refugees, one refugee advertised his services as an instructor of "the French language, mathematics, and the German flute."[40] In February 1805 the committee responsible for distributing aid to Domingan refugees declared that their funds were nearly exhausted and called for yet another charity concert to raise money, or else "helpless women and children would be reduced to the greatest distress."[41] As an expression of gratitude to the generous people of Charleston, in March 1805 a group of French refugees, "the French comedians," offered a show in Charleston's theater. They promised to "please by the variety of their performances, to charm by the beauties and the peculiarities of their music, to astonish by the quickness of their steps and dances, such will be the aim in their Plays, Operas, Pantomimes, and Ballets."[42]

As refugees from Saint Domingue fled the island and streamed into Atlantic ports like Charleston, they had an unmistakable effect on life in the city. The city developed a distinct French enclave among its white residents, and the level of support for French republicans at times even divided the city.[43] Less visible, but perhaps more important, refugees from Saint Domingue, some arriving with the enslaved people with whom they had managed to escape the island, brought news of the slave revolution happening there. In a city already receiving regular updates about developments in Saint Domingue through its commercial ties to the Caribbean world and publishing these updates in the local newspapers, the black and white refugee population that arrived in Charleston between 1793 and 1805 would have provided an incomparable level of detail. For both black and white Charlestonians, refugees from Saint Domingue came bearing news of great interest. While whites at times publicly expressed a sense of solidarity with the "unfortunate" and "distressed" Domingan planters, news and rumor about slaves and free people of color in Saint Domingue cooperating to overthrow the planter class surely reverberated with Charleston and the lowcountry's African-descended population.

Despite the sporadic efforts of South Carolina officials to quarantine the state from Saint Domingue's revolutionary ideas about freedom and equality, a number of refugees from the island arrived in Charleston with enslaved people. Although it is impossible to determine how many slaves from Saint Domingue arrived in Charleston over the course of the 1790s, runaway slave advertisements reveal that French slaves not only arrived in Charleston but attempted to find freedom. In 1796 a young enslaved sailor from Saint Domingue named Thomas escaped from his enslaver. Thomas, "a Portuguese Congo . . . about 15 or 16 years old," had been on a ship from Leogane, west of Port-au-Prince, destined for Charleston in May 1795. Thomas had "been used to the sea about two years" and, according to the advertiser, "was desirous of returning to his master, Samuel W. Linwood, in Jamaica."[44] Though this advertisement leaves unclear if Thomas ever settled in Charleston, or for how long, it suggests that enslaved people not liberated by the revolution in Saint Domingue used the anonymity provided by ocean commerce and port cities to find at least temporary freedom elsewhere in the Atlantic world.

In January 1798 a "mulatto boy, named John Pierre," ran away from his enslaver, John P. Sargeant. According to Sargeant, Pierre was "a native of St. Domingo," who spoke "tolerably good English" and often went by "Joe." He warned ship captains to be careful not to carry him off.[45] Two years later an unnamed male, sixteen years old, "supposed formerly of St. Domingo," escaped from Elizabeth Colleton. Colleton presumed that "as he was purchased from a Frenchman, he may speak French," but noted that "he stutters and stammers" in speaking English. It seems possible he had some kind of experience as a sailor or militia member, as Colleton stated he "beats well upon the drum." Like other advertisements for runaway slaves in a bustling port city such as Charleston, the subscriber warned "all captains of vessels not to carry him off."[46]

In the summer of 1802, Robert Giles offered a one-hundred-dollar reward for the return of John Baptize, an enslaved man "about twenty years of age" who "was born in St. Domingo, and brought out here at the time of the disturbance there." After being brought to Charleston, Baptize was sold to a "Vendue-Master" named Stewart, who thereafter sold Baptize to a Charlestonian named Captain Morrison. Morrison brought Baptize with him on "two voyages to the West-Indies," but Baptize eventually ran away in Charleston. Giles warned readers that Baptize, described as "well known in town," with experience at sea and likely comfortable throughout the port cities of the greater Caribbean, would "strive to go aboard some vessel."[47] Similarly in 1803 James Robinson sought information regarding the whereabouts of a "French mulatto girl named Josephine," who also went by Mary. Josephine was eighteen years old and of dark complexion and spoke English well. Prior to Robinson she had belonged to a "Madam La Casagne," perhaps a refugee from Saint Domingue or elsewhere in the French Caribbean. Robinson, like the other advertisers, warned ship captains not to carry her off and offered forgiveness if she returned of her own accord.[48] Another enslaved woman, "a NEGRO WENCH, named Sanite," ran away in 1805. Sanite was seventeen, was "brought up in St. Domingo," and spoke "but little or no English." J. Talvande, who placed the advertisement looking for her, added that "she is supposed to be harboured by a French sailor, who arrived here lately, as she has been seen in company with him."[49] In May 1805 Pierre La Boussay advertised his search for Lazard, "a young NEGRO FELLOW . . . between 16 and 17 years of age." Lazard was "a creole of the island of St. Domingo," and La Boussay warned "masters of vessels" not to carry him off or harbor him.[50]

Though enslaved people from Saint Domingue who ran away in Charleston represented only a small portion of fugitive slave advertisements placed in Charleston newspapers during the era of the Haitian Revolution, the advertisements suggest that, despite the best efforts of Charleston and South Carolina officials, whites were not able entirely to control the movements and activities of enslaved people from Saint Domingue who had arrived in the South Carolina lowcountry. Whether inspired by their experience with the slave revolution in the French Caribbean or simply taking advantage of the anonymity and possibility of a port city such as Charleston, some enslaved people from the French Caribbean achieved at least temporary freedom for themselves in the city. These "French" enslaved people would have interacted with the city's existing enslaved population, sharing stories of their experiences in Saint Domingue and introducing new conceptions of black freedom to Charleston and the lowcountry. While the number of enslaved people who were transported from Saint Domingue to Charleston is unclear (and perhaps unknowable) along with the uncertainty as to their final destination (whether on plantations or along with their enslavers in the city itself), the presence of advertisements for Saint Domingan runaways in Charleston reveals that at least some enslaved people from the colony ended up in Charleston and the surrounding region.[51]

While some enslaved people used their arrival in Charleston as opportunity to escape, a small number of slave owners who fled Saint Domingue manumitted their enslaved people voluntarily shortly after their arrival in Charleston. Often filing their manumissions in French, these slave owners frequently cited the service and loyalty of their slaves during the upheaval in Saint Domingue as motive for their manumissions. Perhaps feeling lucky to have escaped with their lives, they emancipated slaves who had direct exposure and experience with the tumult of the Haitian Revolution. In May 1797 Theodore Gaugin emancipated the "*negresse*" Eleanore "to recognize the good services rendered me."[52] In March 1798 Anne Margaret Frere "late of the Island of St. Domingo, but at present residing" in Charleston, manumitted an enslaved mulatto woman named Suzette, "in consideration of" her "faithful services."[53] In May fifty-year-old Agathe received her freedom from Saint Domingue refugee Lewis John Baptiste Grand.[54] Marie Louisa Caradeus Chateublond of Saint Domingue "manumitted, released, and from the yoke of slavery discharged" an enslaved woman named Manor in July 1798.[55] In 1811 Gerard Bastre de Lacomb, a planter from Saint Domingue, declared that "in 1798, at the time of his departure from Port au Prince," he manumitted two enslaved people, Veronique and Pierre, "in consideration of [their] faithful services," particularly that they "never abandoned him in the different revolutions of that island." He filed manumissions for both with the notary of Port-au-Prince prior to his departure from Saint Domingue. He had managed to secure a copy of Pierre's, but Veronique had been "lost in the derangements of that island," and thus he personally provided verification of her free status to the justice of the quorum.[56]

In November 1800 Saint Domingue refugee Marie Joseph Adelaide freed eleven enslaved people, including a number of infants and children, in recognition of their "good and faithful service."[57] Though former residents of Saint Domingue primarily emancipated enslaved people born on that island, some of those freed were natives of West Africa—a reflection of the greater frequency with which slaving vessels delivered enslaved cargo to destinations in the Caribbean compared to the United States. In 1799 Feuilloley Ceurion manumitted an enslaved woman named Louise "of the Arada nation" for the "good services" she had rendered "during the revolution of St. Domingo."[58] In September 1800 Maria Jeanne Destres emancipated a Cité, "of the Congo nation."[59] Angelique, an Ibo slave, received her freedom from a French planter in March 1801.[60] Coming from across the Caribbean and Atlantic worlds, foreign-born free people of color—in addition to the likely hundreds if not thousands of foreign-born enslaved people who did not gain their freedom during this era—represented an unmistakable presence in black Charleston.

While most manumissions of enslaved people from the French Caribbean occurred in light of their loyalty during the outbreak of revolution, other Saint Domingue planters manumitted enslaved people upon their arrival in the lowcountry in light of sexual relationships. Through these manumissions, coupled with the arrival of French free people of color and the escape from slavery of French Caribbean–born enslaved people, people of African descent with intimate knowledge of the Haitian Revolution not only arrived in South Carolina, but they also did so in ways that allowed—and at times required—them to interact with their U.S.-born counterparts. As free and enslaved people in the United States gained greater familiarity with the racial violence of the French Caribbean, they increasingly, if temporarily, saw revolution as a path to freedom.

Indeed throughout the era evidence periodically emerged that enslaved and free people of African descent in South Carolina had developed plans for insurrection, with some indications that they had been inspired by the example of Saint Domingue. In Charleston whites faced rumors of insurrection conspiracies on three separate occasions in the 1790s: in 1793, 1797, and 1799. Although the boundary between reality and white paranoia in these alleged conspiracies is blurry—as it always is when analyzing evidence of alleged slave revolts—a broad reading of the available evidence reveals how both blacks and whites engaged with the language and ideas of the Haitian Revolution during the 1790s and early 1800s. White Charlestonians nearly always linked insurrection rumors with outside influences rather than a more fundamental revolt against the slave system. Confronted with rumors of insurrection, South Carolina officials took care to reevaluate if and how people of African descent from Saint Domingue and elsewhere in the French Caribbean were finding their way into Charleston and to attempt to quarantine lowcountry blacks from revolutionary ideas. In this way white responses to insurrection rumors reveal how anxiety about racial violence could punctuate otherwise long periods of calm, even as a revolution raged in Saint Domingue. These insurrection conspiracies also reveal black Charlestonians' engagement with the Haitian Revolution and the radical political ideas circulating the Atlantic world at the end of the eighteenth century. In each of the rumored conspiracies in Charleston during the 1790s, whites accused enslaved people from Charleston and the surrounding lowcountry of planning not only to revolt against the slave system and massacre whites but also to do so by cooperating with slaves and free people of color elsewhere along the Atlantic coast and with those who had arrived from Saint Domingue. While the extent to which United States–born blacks cooperated with those born elsewhere in the Caribbean and Atlantic worlds in these alleged conspiracies remains unclear, the evidence surrounding them strongly suggests that during the Age of Revolution, free and enslaved people of African descent engaged with ideas from throughout the circum-Caribbean and Atlantic world as they confronted their continued subjugation at the hands of white authorities.

White Charlestonians had long feared outside influences on populations of African descent in the region, particularly those that may have offered impetus for revolt and insurrection. In 1791 a Charleston grand jury expressed concern to South Carolina's legislature about unusual gatherings of people of African descent. Months before the outset of violence in Saint Domingue, Charlestonians worried that white outsiders had begun encouraging "the free negroes and slaves within the city to assemble privately in great numbers under pretense of being initiated in the mysteries of freemasonry."[61] The legislative committee discussing the matter suggested a need to revise the state's "Negro Laws," enacted in 1740 in the wake of the Stono Rebellion. Surely cognizant of the overlap between the ideology of freemasonry and that of the American and French Revolutions, white Charlestonians expressed an early fear of what kind of effect a discourse concerning freedom and equality could have on the black population of their city.

In 1793 Charleston faced the first of three conspiracies that appeared influenced by the events in Saint Domingue. In what historians have come to refer to as the "Secret Keeper" conspiracy, a large number of enslaved people in South Carolina and Virginia allegedly planned to put a massive insurrection scheme into action. According to white officials in both states, key leaders in Richmond, Norfolk, and Charleston communicated throughout the summer and fall of 1793 to organize thousands of enslaved people in a planned uprising. With alleged support, both material and ideological, from Saint Domingue, French slaves, and the West Indies, the Secret Keeper conspiracy suggests in its reported details how the discourse of black freedom circulated the greater Caribbean during the 1790s and how African-descended people's conception of themselves and their worlds extended beyond their local communities and immediate circumstances.

In August a white Virginian discovered a letter from the "secret keeper" in Richmond to the "secret keeper" in Norfolk, dropped by a free black itinerant preacher named Gowan Pamphlet. This letter revealed details of a planned insurrection conspiracy connecting slaves across the southern U.S. Atlantic Coast. The Richmond secret keeper explained that the "great secret" long held by people of "our own color has come nearly to a head." He revealed that Richmond slaves possessed "about five hundred Guns" and ammunition but lacked gunpowder. The Richmond keeper also reported in his letter that he had been in conversation with "our friend in Charleston," who had enlisted the support of "near six thousand men" to support the insurrection and had identified a source of gunpowder in that city. The apparent leader of the insurrection scheme, the Richmond keeper informed the Norfolk keeper that he would write again "when I hear from Charleston." They planned to "kill all before us," and the interstate conspiracy would "begin in every town in one nite." The Richmond keeper predicted the slave conspirators would "be in full possession of the hole [sic] country in a few weeks."[62]

Not only did the 1793 conspiracy link African-descended people throughout the U.S. South, but it also appeared to receive inspiration and support from Saint Domingue. White Richmond residents reported overhearing a conversation between two enslaved men around this time, perhaps connected to the Secret Keeper conspiracy, in which one urged the other that the insurrection could succeed and reminding his interlocutor "how the blacks *has* kill'd the whites in the French island." In Charleston it seems those involved in the conspiracy were to be provided "by a person from the West Indies with arms and ammunition."[63] In the packet of letters sent to South Carolina governor William Moultrie by Virginia's lieutenant governor, James Wood, Thomas Newton, commander of Norfolk's militia, argued that "two hundred or more Negroes brought from Cape Francois" by the Saint Domingue refugees residing in Norfolk would surely "be ready to operate against us with the others."[64] In early October—just weeks before the alleged insurrection was to take place, at least according to some reports—an anonymous free black in Charleston, apparently in on the "secret," warned Moultrie that he should not be deceived in allowing his "attention be directed to frenchmen alone," alleging that the city also had "enemies to the Northward."[65] If enslaved people from Saint Domingue who had arrived with refugees to Norfolk were to take part in the conspiracy, it seems at least plausible that those in Charleston, with its much larger population of Domingan refugees, might take part as well.

While the extent of either interaction or planning between Charleston and Saint Domingue blacks is impossible to determine, Charleston's city council and the South Carolina legislature certainly drew some of kind causal connection between the Secret Keeper conspiracy and the arrival of blacks from the French West Indies. On October 8, 1793, at the height of insurrection panic, the citizens of Charleston met to discuss the growing need to quarantine their port from undesirable arrivals. Citizens of Charleston expressed their growing concern with the arrival of people of African descent from Saint Domingue. In particular they requested that the governor take "immediate measures, that the two vessels which arrived in this harbour last week, from St. Domingo, and are now lying under the guns of fort Johnston, with their crews, passengers, free negroes and people of color, do quit the harbor and state immediately."[66] These citizens contended that the state needed to quarantine itself from French blacks and from contagious ideas about revolution and black freedom. Though perhaps a coincidence that these slaves and free people of color from Saint Domingue had arrived outside Charleston amid the anxiety about the Secret Keeper conspiracy, Charleston's city council wanted to proceed with an abundance of caution. Further the council's explicit concern with the arrival of "free negroes and people of color" suggests that they feared not just the insurrectionary activity of French slaves but also the example of freedom and equality that free people of African descent from Saint Domingue could represent.

The citizens at this meeting continued, passing a measure stating that any future vessels that "may arrive from St. Domingo with passengers, negroes, or people of color" shall be forced to remain at Fort Johnston until those aboard deemed "improper to admit," along with any "negroes and people of color," could be sent from the state. Lest they be misunderstood, the citizens stated plainly that people of African descent would "be, on no account, suffered to land in any part of the state." The meeting went further, passing a measure stating that these conditions be extended to "all vessels, from any part of the world, bringing negroes and people of colour." Finally these citizens required that all "free negroes, and free people of colour, which have arrived from St. Domingo, or which have arrived within twelve months from any other place," be sent out of the state immediately.[67]

Elsewhere along the South Carolina coast, a citizens' committee in Georgetown passed similar measures in light of the "suspicions [that] have arisen, and appear to be too well founded" regarding possible disturbances in Charleston, surely alluding to the Secret Keeper conspiracy. On October 11 citizens of Georgetown passed resolutions forbidding the landing of vessels from either Philadelphia or Saint Domingue. Like Charleston the Georgetown committee also passed resolutions forbidding "negroes and people of color" from Saint Domingue or elsewhere in the Atlantic world from disembarking in their city and demanding that all "free people of color and free negroes" who had arrived from Saint Domingue quit the state.[68]

Governor Moultrie acted on the requests of the Charleston and Georgetown meetings just a week later. Between the disturbing information he had received from Virginia and Charleston's citizens committee's resolutions regarding French blacks, Moultrie acted quickly. On October 16 he officially declared unwelcome all people of African descent who had arrived in the state from the French Caribbean in the preceding twelve months. Observing that many "free negroes and people of color" from Saint Domingue had recently arrived in South Carolina and pronouncing them "dangerous to the welfare and peace of the state," Governor Moultrie declared that all people of African descent who had arrived in Charleston from Saint Domingue or elsewhere in the French Caribbean would have to leave the state within ten days. He expressly declared that this measure was enacted "to prevent any designs taking place, that may be formed to interrupt the quiet we now enjoy."[69] Decades before the state instituted the Negro Seamen Acts, South Carolina attempted to quarantine "pernicious" ideas by prohibiting blacks from the French Caribbean from arriving or staying in South Carolina, disrupting their ability to spread their influence among the lowcountry's black majority.

Following the flurry of panicked activity in October 1793, including resolutions by Charleston's city council and the governor's proclamation, South Carolina's legislature ordered in December of that year that measures be taken "to amend the several acts of assembly for regulation of slaves, free negroes, mulattoes, and mustizoes." Further the governor, after receiving a number of letters from concerned citizens in the autumn and winter of 1793, many of which surely related to the Secret Keeper conspiracy, recommended to the legislature that they enact "a revision of the negro law."[70]

The Secret Keeper affair reveals a great deal about the way black and white Charlestonians wove together notions of race, identity, and freedom during the era of the Haitian Revolution. Despite the regular arrival since 1791 of ships from throughout the Caribbean bearing news about the disturbances in Saint Domingue and amid a series of articles published in Charleston newspapers about the nature of violence there, white Charlestonians seemed far less concerned about the influence of this news on local enslaved people and far more concerned with the presence and conduct of French blacks in the city. Amid reports that an insurrection conspiracy was at hand, they directed their ire toward the arrival of French blacks, both free and enslaved, suspecting a far more direct involvement and line of influence on the lowcountry's African-descended population. After years of disregard for the ways enslaved and free people of African descent might access news of the revolution for black freedom emerging in Saint Domingue, white racial panic was strong and swift but fleeting.

Viewed from the opposite perspective, the Secret Keeper conspiracy offers a tantalizing glimpse into the worlds of people of African descent in South Carolina during the 1790s. Even without more concrete evidence, the letters between Governor Wood and Governor Moultrie, petitions and letters from Charleston citizens, and the continued arrival of both refugees and ships from Saint Domingue strongly suggest there was interaction between black Charlestonians and free and enslaved people of color from Saint Domingue. The communication and cooperation between the "keepers" in Charleston, Richmond, and Norfolk suggest that enslaved people in the southern states—particularly in port cities—who had access to news from throughout the United States and Atlantic world viewed their circumstances as connected during the era of the Haitian Revolution. That the "secret," according to the Richmond keeper, had been kept among people of "our colour," not just those in his community, city, or even state, reveals the way black conceptions of their worlds during this era began to stretch across both real and imagined boundaries. Further that Charleston slaves looked to "a person from the West Indies" to provide necessary supplies suggests not just the resources available to enslaved residents of a port city as cosmopolitan as Charleston, but also that slaves in the city felt they had reason to believe that their efforts would find support from others in the greater Caribbean world. Finally the response of Charleston officials lends at least some credence to the notion that enslaved people from Saint Domingue in Charleston, who likely witnessed the beginning of the slave revolution on that island, may have cooperated directly with South Carolina and American-born slaves in Charleston. Such cooperation would suggest that enslaved people from Saint Domingue and the U.S. South engaged some sense of racial identification, however temporarily or fluidly, seeing their identities and their future prospects as connected.

In May 1794, though the panic of insurrection seemed to have faded, concern over the arrival of blacks from Saint Domingue persisted. That month Charleston's *City Gazette* reported that a ship had recently attempted to import sixty-five enslaved and free blacks from Saint Domingue into the state. The *Montagne* attempted to introduce "a considerable number of negroes . . . mostly from the island of St. Domingo and of bad character." Of the sixty-five brought into the state, seven were "free Spanish negroes, serving as sailors," who had "made their escape." Another six had already been sent on to Augusta, Georgia. The ship's commander promised to carry these men back out of the state.[71] In 1795 the city of Savannah passed resolutions similar to those passed by Charleston's city council two years prior, preventing any "seasoned negroes or people of colour" from entering the state, for fear of the "evils that may arise from suffering people of this description, under any pretence whatever, from being introduced amongst us."[72] A 1796 report, again from Savannah, described "10 or 12 brigand negroes . . . part of those people employed by the Spaniards in St. Domingo against the French republicans," who had become stranded at Cumberland Island. These men, "under the command of the black general John Francois in St. Augustine," had murdered their ship's captain while en route to Havana and become stranded on Cumberland Island off the Georgia coast.[73] A November 1796 report revealed that "a number of Frenchman" had been jailed in Charleston, suspected of "setting fire to the city."[74]

Four years later, after the initial wave of refugees had arrived in Charleston and the momentary anxiety produced by insurrection fears had subsided, Charleston once again faced the prospect of slave revolt and the specter of Saint Domingue. In 1797 some of the "French negroes" who had presumably arrived in the state with white Domingan refugees in the preceding years allegedly planned an insurrection. A report in Charleston's *City Gazette* claimed that in late November, about "ten or fifteen" such persons designed a conspiracy "to fire the city, and to act here as they had formerly done at St. Domingo." Unable to wait until "their plan should be more matured, and their guilt more clearly ascertained," Charleston officials arrested and charged four enslaved men, Figaro, Jean Louis, Figaro "the younger," and Capelle, as the leaders of the conspiracy, all of whom appear to have been enslaved by refugees from the French Caribbean then residing in Charleston. According to the *City Gazette*, all of the accused denied knowledge of the conspiracy, but Figaro the younger "after some time, made a partial confession"—strongly suggesting coercion or outright torture. After a trial the court condemned Figaro the elder and Jean Louis to death by hanging, while Figaro the younger and Capelle were to be transported from the state. After the court handed down its sentence, Jean Louis allegedly (according to the newspaper account) addressed both Figaros and said, "I do not blame the whites, though I suffer; they have done right, but it is you who have brought me to this trouble." The state executed Jean Louis and Figaro the elder on November 21.[75]

Unlike the 1793 conspiracy, the alleged insurrection in 1797 seems to have been confined to enslaved people born in Saint Domingue and transported to Charleston earlier in the decade. Ultimately, however, corroborating evidence for this affair falls far short of the kind of evidence that is available for the Secret Keeper conspiracy. The records for Charleston's court of magistrates and freeholders in which the alleged conspirators would have been tried no longer exist, thus making it difficult to discern where white paranoia ended and where insurrectionary intention on the part of enslaved and free blacks began. Although there may not be much evidence regarding the specifics of blacks' alleged insurrection plans, significant evidence exists revealing that whites truly *believed* that an insurrection inspired by blacks from the French West Indies was afoot in late 1797.

In December 1797, just weeks after the alleged insurrection was to have taken place, an officer of Charleston's militia wrote a message to the governor requesting a larger force to protect the magazine and gunpowder in Charleston Neck, though he did not state why the increase in protection was necessary.[76] The message, however, came at precisely the same time other Charlestonians began petitioning the legislature to express their apprehension that the city was at continued risk of racial violence. On December 11, 1797, these petitioners requested new, more effective measures to control the free and enslaved black population of the state and to mitigate the influence of foreign blacks, particularly those from the French Caribbean; in so doing they referred directly to the recently discovered conspiracy. While the port's continued commercial activity virtually assured the regular arrival of news from Saint Domingue and elsewhere in the Caribbean, white Charlestonians sought, at the very least, to limit direct contact between the slaves and free blacks arriving from the French Caribbean and the lowcountry's black majority. The petitioners noted that "the dangerous designs and machinations of certain French West India negroes in this city for which they lately suffered consign punishment" had been "of such public notoriety" that further detail was not required. Though the plot had been "rendered entirely abortive by timely detection," the episode had "excited the most devious alarms and apprehensions in ours and the mind of our fellow citizens" so that they felt compelled to petition the legislature to request more effective means of control.[77]

One of the principal concerns of these petitioners was that existing prohibitions on the importation of foreign blacks had become ineffective, allowing a large number of "French" blacks access to the city and opportunities to spread their pernicious ideas about black freedom. For one thing, foreign-born enslaved people regularly disembarked in neighboring Georgia, making their transport thereafter to South Carolina relatively simple; for another, the city had little ability to enforce existing restrictions on the arrival of people of African descent. The petitioners complained that "many negroes of . . . the most desperate and dangerous dispositions and characters are continually smuggled from the French and other West India islands" into the city in violation of the law. The presence of such a dangerous population prompted the petitioners to request stronger policies from the state. The petitioners called for all French-born slaves and free people of color who arrived in the state after January 1, 1790, who they described as being of "nefarious and pernicious nature," to be required to depart from South Carolina. In light of rumors that French slaves had planned to set fire to the city, white Charlestonians sought to head off future insurrectionary designs by deporting all French-born people of African descent residing in the city.[78]

The authors of the 1797 petition also spoke to the dangers unique to the port cities of the Greater Caribbean, as they contended that "improper assemblies and conspiracies of negroes may be formed with more speed and facility and with less probability of timely discovery in Charleston than in in the other parts of the state" and that Charleston's blacks "by fire and other means" could enact "more complicated evils and disasters in a short time" than were possible in more rural environs.[79] For Charleston's whites the potential of French or Caribbean blacks to influence their city's free and enslaved black populations and spread ideas about liberty, equality, and racial violence was simply too great to risk. These petitioners sought in vain to prevent interaction between blacks from the French West Indies and the enslaved and free blacks of the South Carolina lowcountry.

Governor Charles Pinckney addressed these concerns in a message to the South Carolina House of Representatives early in 1798. He noted the "danger of suffering on any pretence either free persons of colour or slaves to be introduced from" the French West Indies "is so extremely great that I would recommend it to you immediately to pass a law making it a capital offence for any owner or master of a vessel hereafter to import any slaves of person of colour from any island in which an insurrection has taken place."

Likewise Pinckney had begun defensive preparation along the coast in light of the "official intelligence" that in some French Caribbean islands, "hostile designs were conceived to exist against the southern states."[80]

These fears of French influence in Charleston persisted, as local whites expressed their anxiety at the continual influx of refugees, both white and black, from Saint Domingue. One Charlestonian addressed South Carolina governor Charles Pinckney in 1798, imploring him to prohibit not just French people of African descent but whites as well. Calling attention to what he called the "delicate, nay, trembling state" of South Carolina at that juncture, the anonymous author asked the governor, and the Charleston public, if the French refugees then flooding into the city could be trusted, or rather if they should be considered "dangerous intruders." The author worried that after their treacherous actions toward both the French and the English, "they have been tampered with, and probably gained over by Toussaint." South Carolina's decision to allow "the whites to land, the colored to go off" was a "vain and useless distinction," he argued, as these white refugees from the French Caribbean would still seek to disrupt the state's social order. Though resettled in the United States, these Frenchmen would undoubtedly, he contended, "find ways . . . of procuring others to accomplish their designs."[81]

Although the details of the 1797 conspiracy appear only in the newspaper, thus making it more suspect than the better-substantiated Secret Keeper conspiracy, it is unlikely that the episode was entirely a product of white paranoia. Just as they had in 1793, white Charlestonians petitioned the governor and legislature requesting more effective restrictions on the arrival and activities of free and enslaved blacks from the French Caribbean, for fear of the influence they could have on the local black population. Though it is impossible to verify the extent to which the details of the *City Gazette* article were true, the events surrounding it suggest that throughout the 1790s, strong links existed between people of African descent in Charleston of all backgrounds, origins, and statuses.

Finally, in the spring of 1799, white Charlestonians again felt they had narrowly avoided a slave uprising in the city. Despite earlier directives that all French people of African descent were to be sent out of the state, city officials in Charleston and Wilmington, North Carolina, received a letter in April alerting them of a planned slave conspiracy. The letter claimed that "two packages covered with oil cloth" had arrived and were then being examined by "the governor and general Pinckney." According to the letter, "The emigrants from St. Domingo were much depended on, it seems, for the execution of the diabolical projects of firing our city, and attempting an insurrection." It continued that Charleston was "quite a community of soldiers" and thus well-prepared to counter insurrectionary activity, though "it is difficult to devise preventative measures against the plots of incendiaries." Finally the letter commented on the gravity of the situation, claiming that "if it had not been for the vigilance of our administration, my last letter to you might have been the last you would have received of mine—'ere this, our throats might have been cut; carnage and devastation roaming thro' our land, and our city one pile of ruins."[82]

Frustratingly few details exist about this 1799 conspiracy. It remains unclear whether the "emigrants from St. Domingo" referred to in the letter were people of African descent or, like a citizen worried the year before, radical white Frenchmen in the city who had been "gained over by Toussaint." Nevertheless the fact that these Saint Domingue emigrants "were much depended on" reveals how southern whites continued to fear that individuals both American-born and French-born were cooperating to effect a large-scale insurrection. Unlike the 1793 and 1797 conspiracies, the alleged 1799 plot lacks corroborating evidence, in particular any reference to the letters in the papers of Governor Pinckney. Though the detailed nature of the 1799 report lends some credence to its veracity, this lack of other corresponding evidence suggests it should be treated with greater skepticism than the other alleged conspiracies. Yet when considered in conjunction with the decade's other alleged plots in which lowcountry free and enslaved blacks were linked with their racial counterparts from the French West Indies, we can gain a broader sense of just how closely Charleston was linked with other port cities throughout the Greater Caribbean world.

Long after the immediate era of the Haitian Revolution, the image of the uprising in Saint Domingue and the establishment of the Atlantic world's first black republic continued to resonate with African-descended people in Charleston. A generation after the conspiracies of the 1790s, the city's most well-known insurrection scare—that of Denmark Vesey in 1822—also featured strong links to Haiti and the French Caribbean and reveals how durable the image of Haitian independence was for black Charlestonians. Although some scholars still doubt the reality of the Vesey conspiracy, considering it more likely to have been the tragic product of white racial paranoia, most historians believe that a group of enslaved and free black people in Charleston were plotting an organized revolt in the summer of 1822, prior to the plan's discovery. Whites accused Vesey of orchestrating a plot to collaborate with enslaved people from the plantations surrounding Charleston to murder whites, set fire to plantations and the city, and overthrow slavery in the lowcountry. While the evidence surrounding the episode is incomplete and problematic—like all evidence of insurrectionary activity, filtered through the lens of white racial anxieties and the imbalanced power dynamics of southern courtrooms—it suggests that the Haitian Revolution still held meaning for black Charlestonians into the 1820s.

Denmark Vesey, also known as Telemaque, was born sometime during the 1760s, either in the Caribbean or the Gold Coast of West Africa. He was purchased as a slave by Joseph Vesey, a ship captain and merchant, and settled with him in Charleston during the early 1780s. Prior to Denmark Vesey winning a Charleston city lottery and purchasing his freedom in 1799, he would have gained experience of the Caribbean world generally and of Saint Domingue specifically.[83] Captain Vesey frequently advertised in Charleston newspapers the sale of coffee and sugar from Saint Domingue and served as an officer of Charleston's "Committee for the Relief of Distressed Emigrants" from Saint Domingue during the 1790s.[84] Joseph Vesey's deep connection with Saint Domingue and regular interaction with emigrants from that island, in addition to Denmark Vesey's experience aboard ships and in the Caribbean, suggests it is plausible that Denmark would have had familiarity with the revolution in Saint Domingue that was transpiring at precisely the time he gained his own freedom.

Whether introduced by Vesey or otherwise, evidence produced during the prosecution of the alleged conspirators reveals that Haiti held a prominent place in black Charlestonians' understanding of the insurrection.[85] In many interrogations accused coconspirators invoked the image of the Haitian Revolution in one of several ways. Most frequently alleged participants expressed a belief that residents of Haiti would provide direct aid, either by reinforcing the effort and helping to advance the revolt or by providing transport to Haiti and safe haven there after the participants had gained control over the lowcountry.

An early witness to the court of magistrates and freeholders responsible for hearing the case in June 1822 claimed that an enslaved man named Rolla, one of the accused coconspirators, had intimated to him that supporters from "St. Domingo and Africa would come over and cut up the white people if we only made the motion here first."[86] A witness against Vesey likewise claimed that it was Vesey who told him that "a large army from St. Domingo and Africa were coming to help us."[87] Another claimed that they would receive support from the English, who would thereafter "carry them off to St. Domingo."[88] Though we do not have a clear understanding of what white court officials asked these individuals, they each suggested that "St. Domingo" would play a role in an insurrection.

An enslaved man named Jesse, in his confession to the court, invoked the image of Saint Domingue in a different manner, stating that "it was high time for us to seek for our rights, and that we were fully able to conquer the whites, if we were only unanimous and courageous, as the St. Domingo people were."[89] In another confession accused coconspirator Monday Gell told the court that Vesey attempted to "open a correspondence with Port-au-Prince, in St. Domingo, to ascertain whether the inhabitants there would assist us."[90] According to Gell, Vesey drafted a letter to Haitian president Jean-Pierre Boyer (mentioning him by name in his confession) and advanced plans to have the letter delivered by the cook on a merchant schooner then being repaired in Charleston.

Correspondence among whites and additional newspaper accounts of the affair repeated the claim that the would-be rebels expected or tried to recruit assistance from Haiti or otherwise anticipated they would flee to that island after they had executed their plans.[91] In November 1822 prominent South Carolina statesman and white Charlestonian Thomas Pinckney, in his reflections on the Vesey affair, noted that "nothing effectual can be done by us to obviate the influence of the example of St. Domingo, so long as it retains its condition. It would be difficult also to prevent encouragement being offered from thence, because we cannot cut off the direct communication."[92] Nevertheless the year after the Vesey affair, the South Carolina legislature passed the "Negro Seaman Act," prohibiting black seamen and sailors from coming ashore in Charleston, in an effort to diminish just this kind of communication, both from the Caribbean and from northern states.[93]

Though intriguing, confessions and testimonies stemming from the Vesey conspiracy are also fraught with problems. The power dynamics of courtroom prosecutions greatly affect the historical evidence produced there, exponentially more so when the magistrates were white and the defendants were black and particularly when they were enslaved. We simply do not know when accused coconspirators were lying and when they were telling the truth, when their testimony was delivered in an effort to simply save their own lives or please enslavers and white officials. Without knowledge of the questions asked or the circumstances under which the accused delivered confessions or testimony, their reliability as evidence remains deeply problematic.

Yet, as historian James Sidbury has argued, defendants in these trials would have, even if they felt compelled to lie, sought to tell plausible stories. Although courtroom dynamics created "ambiguous incentives for truth-telling," the insistence of white magistrates for details about a planned insurrection established "powerful incentives to tell stories that will be believed."[94] Even if an insurrection was not being planned in the summer of 1822, the evidence produced during the Vesey affair still reveals a great deal about the lives and worldviews of black Charlestonians. If accused coconspirators and other witnesses invented testimony to appease white court officials seeking only such information that confirmed the conspiracy (and rejecting denials), the testimony these interrogations produced reveals how enslaved and free black residents of Charleston and the lowcountry imagined such an event would look. As such the insistence that reinforcements from Africa or the French Caribbean would arrive, that the insurrection's leaders had written to Haitian president Boyer, or that the participants could sail to Haiti after they had completed their designs reveals the extent to which black Charlestonians remained engaged with the idea of Saint Domingue and Haiti, even a genera-tion after the revolution there began. Considered alongside the earlier insur-rection rumors from the 1790s, these episodes reveal how African-descended people in Charleston understood their lives and world as connected to the wider Atlantic. That such episodes nearly always included both free and enslaved people of African descent suggests as well how people of different geographical origins, colors, and statuses could be linked in a common proj-ect to overthrow white authority.

CARTAGENA

Like Charleston, Cartagena de Indias faced the possibility of racial violence inspired by the slave revolution in Saint Domingue during the 1790s and early 1800s. Farther away from Saint Domingue, Cartagena did not receive the same influx of refugees from that island. Nevertheless the more direct conflict between the Spanish and French on Hispaniola meant that news from Saint Domingue regularly arrived along the Caribbean coast of New Granada as well, likely with the same frequency as in Charleston.[95] As black and white residents processed the news and rumors about a war for black freedom and equality in the Caribbean's most profitable colony, different concerns and reactions emerged. Like in Charleston, white officials in Ca-ribbean New Granada worried about the example and influence of Saint Domingue as they attempted to maintain their authority over the region's free and enslaved African-descended majority. Black costeños, meanwhile, found meaning and inspiration in the struggle of blacks in Saint Domingue, as insurrection conspiracy rumors emerged in the 1790s, connecting many of Caribbean New Granada's principal cities.

Responses to the Haitian Revolution in and around Cartagena parallel neatly those of Charleston and the South Carolina lowcountry. Whites feared that French blacks would influence what they believed were otherwise con-tented local populations of African descent to revolt, violently using their demographic advantages to take over state power, as in Saint Domingue. Though most of Cartagena's African-descended population had already attained freedom by birth or manumission by the 1790s, white officials nev-ertheless worried the example of Saint Domingue would lead to violence against whites, arson, and a forceful challenge to white rule. Blacks and *pardos*, meanwhile, collectively derived influence from the image and idea of the Haitian Revolution and may have begun to identify common cause with the revolutionary former slaves and free people of color in Saint Domingue. During the 1790s insurrection conspiracies in Cartagena and throughout Caribbean New Granada reveal the extent to which African-descended people there understood their circumstances as connected to Saint Domingue and the wider Caribbean and Atlantic worlds.

As a commercial entrepôt, Cartagena's port featured the same kind of coming and going of commercial vessels from throughout the Greater Caribbean and Atlantic worlds as did Charleston. Cartagena's close links to other major Spanish Caribbean ports—particularly Havana and Caracas—allowed official and unofficial news to arrive regularly into the city. Along with those cities, Cartagena was one of the most important port cities, commercial centers, and military outposts in Spain's American empire and was the site of frequent intercourse between people from across the Atlantic world. Sailors and other ship workers had the opportunity to interact and exchange news and information with the permanent and transient residents of Cartagena, most of whom were people of African descent. Working as sailors, dockworkers, innkeepers, and hawkers, in addition to those employed in better-respected professions such as shoemakers, tailors, and barbers, Cartagena's African-descended population interacted regularly with people from across the globe, providing them access to a wide variety of news and information. Cartagena's position as a central commercial and administrative port in Spain's American empire connected the city's African-descended population to black communities across the Atlantic world, crossing national, imperial, cultural, and linguistic boundaries.[96]

Caribbean New Granada's robust legitimate trade at the end of the eighteenth century, along with a long history of smuggling, allowed ample opportunities for French revolutionary ideas to arrive in the city. It was during this era that Spanish officials began to express their anxiety that enslaved and free people of African descent along the Caribbean coast of Spanish America had begun to discuss the possibility of following the example of Saint Domingue. Especially as Spain became directly involved in the revolution in Saint Domingue as a consequence of their efforts to take over the French part of Hispaniola, news and rumor from Saint Domingue became even easier to access throughout the Spanish Greater Caribbean world for people of all classes and racial designations. Indeed Julius Scott has documented how the arrival of French prisoners in Venezuela from Saint Domingue, many of them blacks and mulattoes, aroused great interest from slaves and free people of color in La Guajira, Caracas, as well as in more remote parts of that colony.[97]

Enslaved people in Venezuela began to discuss their possibilities for freedom, framed in the context of the slave revolution occurring in Saint Domingue. The strong links between Caracas and Cartagena, the arrival of merchant vessels of all nationalities, facilitated by *comercio libre,* and New Granada's long history of smuggling virtually ensured that the revolutionary news and rumor of such great interest to and influence on the blacks of Venezuela would have arrived in Cartagena as well.

As slave revolts erupted in the French Caribbean, authorities in New Granada revealed that news of Saint Domingue arrived in Spanish American colonies and also revealed the extent of white racial fears, as officials nervously viewed the possibility of becoming the next Saint Domingue.[98] In 1794 the first Spanish translation of the Declaration of the Rights of Man began to appear in Spanish America.[99] Although it is impossible to verify whether or not this document arrived in Cartagena or what its impact might have been, Cartagena's strong links to the greater Caribbean and Atlantic worlds makes it seem likely that news of the declaration arrived in the city at some point during the 1790s.

The specter of Saint Domingue and the possibility of French influence continued to worry white authorities in Caribbean Colombia throughout the decade. In 1795 colonial authorities became alarmed after French privateers arrived off the coast of Caribbean New Granada, flying the French tricolor from a ship named *La Fantasía de un Mulato.*[100] Years later in 1803 government officials expressed concern after learning that three French commissioners from Saint Domingue and Martinique—Guillermo Pasqual, Eugenio Boyer, and Luis Delpech—displayed the tricolor flag outside their residence in the lower-class neighborhood of Getsemaní, home to a large portion of Cartagena's enslaved and free people of color. Colonial officials expressed anxiety that "day and night" these colonial officials insisted on "raising the flag of their nation" in the house they occupied. The situation was made all the more alarming by the fact that these officials resided in a neighborhood occupied almost entirely by people of African descent, including much of the city's enslaved population. It is a near certainty that in 1804 these commissioners from Saint Domingue would have been of African descent as well, and Spanish colonial officials worried about the impact such a brazen flying of the French "tricolor flag" might have on people of color in the neighborhood and city.[101]

Throughout the era of the Haitian Revolution, free and enslaved black sailors would have had contact with African-descended people in Cartagena, providing firsthand accounts of the war for freedom and equality occurring in the French Caribbean. While Spanish American "patriots" viewed the American and French Revolutions as models for voicing their rising discontent with Bourbon Spain, white officials in New Granada feared the destabilizing potential of the revolution in Saint Domingue in similar ways as American officials some 1,500 miles to the north. These fears of racial violence came to a head in 1799 and early 1800, as a series of insurrection conspiracy rumors emerged across the Caribbean coast of New Granada and Venezuela, in what some Spanish authorities believed to be a linked, cooperative effort connecting free and enslaved French, African, and creole blacks in an effort to overthrow white rule through violence inspired by the example of Saint Domingue.

On April 2, 1799, Spanish officials discovered a plot among a group of people of African descent described variously as "black French slaves and other creoles" and "black French slaves and other Africans" to take of the city's most important fortress, the Castillo de San Felipe de Barajas, which sat atop the hill of the Pie de la Popa, and clear its garrison. Following their takeover of the fort, these blacks would descend into the city "to kill the whites" and "plunder the King's fortunes and possessions." These conspirators were to be joined and supported by a man named Jorge Guzman, a black sergeant of one of Cartagena's artillery units. Just one day before the plan was to be put into effect, the conspiracy was betrayed to white authorities by Manuel Yturen, a captain of the city's voluntary *pardo* militia. Yturen learned of the plan when a "black creole slave," in conjunction with a number of French slaves, attempted to recruit Yturen and his militia unit into the conspiracy. According to Yturen, the enslaved men who attempted to recruit his unit believed they would be easy to sway "because of the conveniences that liberty brings." Though most of the culprits were swiftly arrested, two enslaved people evaded capture and later set fire to two haciendas just outside the city, lending at least some credence to the reality of the plan.[102]

The following month the governors of Santa Marta and Maracaibo, Venezuela, also discovered insurrection plots in their cities, and they feared connections with those "certain French blacks and mulattoes" who had developed the prior insurrection conspiracy in Cartagena.[103] On the night of May 19, a local *pardo* militia captain discovered a plan for an uprising, which was to take place that same night, among "the captains and crews of color of two French corsairs who had entered this port . . . from *Puerto Principe*" and planned to "rise up against [its] quiet and good order." Viceroy Pedro Mendinueta learned with great concern of the "uprising and sack planned" in Maracaibo "by the French blacks and mulattoes."[104] Officials reported that free and enslaved blacks and mulattoes of French, African, and creole origin—along with assistance from the indigenous people of the Guajira peninsula—had planned to take control of the city and kill all the whites.[105] According to Spanish authorities, these would-be rebels were also to receive material support from the French consul of Curaçao. These blacks from Saint Domingue planned to introduce into Maracaibo "the same system of freedom and equality that has reduced to total ruin" the French part of Hispaniola. Like in North America, Spanish officials feared that existing prohibitions against the introduction of foreign blacks into their cities, particularly from the French Caribbean, were not strong enough to halt the flow of unwanted ideas and people.[106]

The following year, when commenting on the transfer of prisoners convicted in the Maracaibo conspiracy from Venezuela to Cartagena and Panama, New Granada's viceroy, Pedro Mendinueta, discussed some of the troubles of introducing incendiary characters such as these into the city. For one thing, Mendinueta noted that in Cartagena there resided "an abundance of black slaves, for the most part foreigners, and people of color who are fond and partial to them." Though most of the enslaved people then residing in Cartagena were in fact creoles born in Spanish America, the viceroy feared the ways people of different nationalities and statuses might find common cause. He continued to discuss the city's enslaved population, noting that slaves in Cartagena did not "need much stimulus to conceive of ideas of liberty in view of the pernicious example of those from the French colonies." For Mendinueta the introduction of formerly enslaved individuals from Saint Domingue represented a serious threat given the affinity he had observed between creole and foreign-born people of African descent, both free and en-slaved, and the seemingly high likelihood of revolt among enslaved people. Mendinueta commented directly on the facility of communication among people of African descent in urban environments as well, noting that even when held in jail, it would be "difficult to maintain the culprits without com-munication with outside people."[107]

The concerns of Mendinueta reveal a great deal about the development of racial identity among people of African descent on New Granada's Carib-bean coast and speak directly to developments elsewhere in the urban At-lantic world. In Mendinueta's estimation blacks and mulattoes in Cartagena of various backgrounds—creole, French, African—both free and enslaved felt some affinity toward one another, an affinity he deemed so close as to be dangerous. He spoke as well to the ability and interest of people of African descent in engaging Atlantic discourses about liberty and equality. Mendinu-eta identified danger in the "pernicious example" of Saint Domingue, fearing the effect it could have on New Granada's enslaved population. The effective-ness of communication among blacks and mulattoes could easily penetrate the city's jails.

Taken broadly, the 1799 and 1800 insurrection conspiracies in Cartagena and along the Caribbean coast of New Granada reveal the complex interplay of race, identity, and status. First, we can see the extent to which Spanish officials feared the influence of Saint Domingue. They panicked at the appearance of French flags in the city, and they struggled to maintain authority over the black population of the region. They frequently made concessions to black militia members, on whom they relied heavily for the region's safety and security, understanding that in light of the revolution in Saint Domingue, it was as important as ever to maintain the allegiance of free people of color.[108] More broadly, these insurrection conspiracies reveal that during the era of the Haitian Revolution, both enslaved and free blacks in Cartagena and Caribbean Colombia seem to have engaged and internalized ideas about black freedom and equality and attempted to forge their own challenges to white authority.

Finally, like in Charleston, the image of the Haitian Revolution proved to be a durable one in the minds of both black and white residents of Cartagena, with references to Haiti and racial violence persisting into the 1820s and 1830s. During the 1810s Haitian sailors and corsairs became regular sights in the city.[109] Historian Marixa Lasso has documented several instances of blacks and *pardos* in Caribbean Colombia invoking the image of Haiti as an alternative to white rule during the early years of Colombia's independence. For example in 1823—just a year after the Denmark Vesey conspiracy in Charleston—a wealthy *pardo* named Remigio Marquez was appointed the general commander of Mompox, a strategically important city situated along the Magdalena River between the Caribbean coast and the highland interior. Marquez's policies, like the restriction of smuggling and other illicit activities, led to significant conflict between local whites, who accused him not only of overstepping his political authority but also of attempting to sow racial divisions between the city's white and African-descended residents. In the political conflict that followed, a publicly posted broadside in support of Marquez threatened white residents, stating, "In the end you will all be screwed because blood will run like in Saint Domingue."[110] In a complex conflict over race and local political authority in the new Colombian republic, the image and example of the Haitian Revolution still in the 1820s held an important place in the popular political imaginary of the city's black residents. Other historians have demonstrated similar patterns elsewhere in Spain's Caribbean and American possessions, most notably in Cuba, where fear of slave revolt inspired by the Haitian Revolution (and other insurrections) persisted into the 1840s.[111]

Though insurrection conspiracies and rumors of race war represent just short moments in the region's history, they offer a glimpse into the ways people of African descent in Caribbean New Granada conceived of race and authority and viewed the challenges they confronted within a broad, hemispheric lens. That the 1799 conspiracies in Cartagena, Maracaibo, and elsewhere along the Caribbean coast involved cooperation between French, creoles, and *bozales* both of full and partial African descent reveals how black identity during the era of the Haitian Revolution could extend beyond the borders of cities, colonies, and empires.[112] That Cartagena's "people of color" would be "fond and partial" to foreign slaves and free people of color suggests the era of the Haitian Revolution had a profound impact on the way people of African descent in Spanish America conceived of themselves and the development of a collective racial identity. Yet the fact that the conspiracy was betrayed to Spanish colonial authorities by an officer in the *pardo* militia reveals as well the many barriers that existed to the construction of racial identity throughout the Atlantic world, as African-descended people occupied different statuses and social strata that hindered collective identification.

CONCLUSION

The Haitian Revolution transformed the way people of African descent living in urban spaces across the Atlantic world conceived of their worlds. While scholars such as Jane Landers and Martha Jones have demonstrated that the exceptional "Atlantic Creoles" who physically traversed the Atlantic during the eighteenth and nineteenth centuries developed a more expansive sense of their personal and racial identities, the era was equally transformative for those people of African descent who largely stayed put.[113] Indeed their residence in cosmopolitan port cities such as Cartagena and Charleston ensured they need not go far at all to gain access to the informational and ideological currents of the Atlantic world. Rather the news came to them. Regular access to ideas from across the Atlantic world and frequent interactions with black seafarers who served as go-betweens connecting African-descended people from Boston to Buenos Aires expanded the worlds of blacks and mulattoes residing in Atlantic port cities. This knowledge of the Atlantic world, particularly during the tumultuous era of the Haitian Revolution, encouraged some African-descended people to think more broadly about race, status, and identity.

Throughout the urban Atlantic world, free people of color viewed the era of the Haitian Revolution as a moment of radical possibility. News of African-descended people in the Atlantic world's most profitable colony cooperating in a violent effort to overthrow white colonial rule and abolish slavery inspired free and enslaved blacks and mulattoes in Cartagena, Charleston, and port cities throughout the African Americas to begin considering similar paths. Of diverse geographic origins, linguistic backgrounds, and class statuses, African-descended people both free and enslaved expressed a more expansive sense of themselves and their standing in the world during the era of the Haitian Revolution. Despite the differences in slavery and racial difference between the Americas, there was at least a moment during the late eighteenth and early nineteenth centuries when African-descended people of different backgrounds and statuses viewed their histories and futures as linked, as they considered opportunities for racial violence and the overthrow of white rule.

Yet just as a collective identity and purpose could be constructed, it could be deconstructed. As African-descended people in the urban Atlantic were informed about the onset of racial violence in Saint Domingue, so too would they have been informed about the challenges of maintaining this solidarity among African-descended people, as freeborn and formerly enslaved blacks and mulattoes increasingly saw their visions for the new nation come into conflict. Even as the image of the Haitian Revolution retained its salience for African-descended people well into the nineteenth century, free people of color in Cartagena, Charleston, and throughout the urban African Americas increasingly sought to distance themselves from enslaved people and to emphasize class divisions as they attempted to solidify their status and social standing amid increasing external pressures. The era of the Haitian Revolution represented a fleeting moment—in both Latin America and the United States—where African-descended people used their shared engagement with the ideas of the Age of Revolution to pursue a radical, violent, collective strategy for racial advancement, seeing the fates of blacks throughout the Atlantic world as intertwined.

Chapter 3

ARTISANS AND LABOR

[Jehu and Abigail Jones] are honest, industrious, and decent
people, and have always sustained that reputation.

Petition to the South Carolina General Assembly, 1827

We have in the master Pedro Romero and his son Stephen . . . two
intelligent men that the force of their genius . . . has elevated to a
degree of perfection and delicacy that is truly admirable.

Description of Pedro Romero, Cartagena, 1810

Throughout the urban Americas, people of African descent flourished as
artisans. As barbers and tailors, stonemasons and shoemakers, free and enslaved people of color dominated many skilled trades in the urban centers of
North America, South America, and the Caribbean. This status was central
to their social lives and identities, particularly in the port cities of the greater
Caribbean—where people of African ancestry both free and enslaved often
comprised the majority of the population—as skilled black workers played
important roles in the local economy, providing goods and services crucial
to the well-being of urban residents, empires, and nations.

The importance of skilled occupations and artisan work in the lives
of free people of African ancestry constituted one of the central elements of
black freedom in the urban Atlantic world. Skilled labor allowed a segment of
the free colored population to distinguish themselves from the black popular
classes, including not only the enslaved people laboring on the plantations
and haciendas in the hinterlands of urban centers but also free and enslaved
people of color engaging in unskilled or marginally skilled work throughout port cities of the Atlantic world. By publicly demonstrating their skills,
industry, and public worth, free people of color gained distinct economic
advantages, boosted their social profiles, staked claims to respectability, and
more fully integrated themselves into the social worlds of their local communities. Such distinction, however, frequently came at the expense of racial

solidarity or a broader push for racial reforms. Free artisans of color used their elevated social profile and reputations as respectable to gain greater inclusion in a community life that included prominent whites as well as fellow artisans.

While enslaved people often used their skills to find avenues to freedom, a certain segment of the free colored population used the social and economic advantages of skilled labor to establish a measure of stability for themselves and their families in freedom. Free artisans of color maintained respectable urban residences and family lives. Through their engagement with well-respected occupations, they interacted frequently with other prominent free people of African descent as well as with wealthy whites, affording them the chance to develop or strengthen social ties and demonstrate their engagement with shared cultural values such as thrift, industry, and sobriety. Their skills and relative wealth sometimes allowed them as well to secure educations and apprenticeships for their children and arrange advantageous marriages for them with other members of the black artisan class. Artisan labor also afforded some free people of color the opportunity to develop patterns of public consumption that matched their class status, including, for some, slave ownership. Through interactions with their neighbors both black and white, artisans of African descent gained a measure of social prestige that extended beyond their more immediate client base, becoming a part of social life in their communities and distinguishing themselves from the black lower classes.

In the urban United States, African Americans did a wide variety of skilled work. Whether as enslaved people hiring their own time or as free workers, people of African descent found employment in a wide variety of artisan trades, often constituting the majority of such workers in a given city. From Boston to Cincinnati to New Orleans to Charleston, people of African descent found work in skilled trades. The population densities of urban centers created occupational opportunity—houses to be built and repaired, clothes to be tailored and laundered, and all manner of niche demands satisfied—and people of African descent took advantage with varying levels of success depending on particular locale. A statistical portrait of free black employment in the mid-nineteenth-century United States by historian Leonard P. Curry reveals "urban black artisan employment at its highest level in the Lower South," with opportunities diminishing in the Upper South and northern cities.[1] In the urban North, free blacks faced legal hurdles, societal restrictions, and competition from foreign-born whites, making success in artisan trades hard to come by. Outside of southern cities, free artisans of color "depended almost exclusively on a black clientele for support, and suffered all of the difficulties that such dependence entailed."[2] Similarly historian Patrick Rael has shown that while black freedom was more rare in southern states, free people of color there encountered greater economic opportunity. In northern cities, by contrast, "policy and informal practice subjected blacks in toto to degradations shared by elite and popular alike," a shared encounter with white racism that helped forge collective identity and action.[3]

In the South's urban centers, by contrast, free people of color encountered more opportunities for skilled work and the social and economic advancement that came with it. White southerners often eschewed particular service-oriented jobs because of their historical link to blackness, and of blackness to slavery, thus creating significant areas of opportunity for people of African descent. As Rael notes, the South's planation system "fostered the socioeconomic conditions necessary to form highly stratified free African American populations," with a free colored elite emerging as highly skilled craftsmen in cities throughout the Lower South.[4] Ira Berlin has shown that white disdain for occupations like barbering that were connected with African Americans—particularly in the Lower South, where slavery was most firmly entrenched—allowed free blacks to pursue skilled work "not merely to support themselves and their families but to bolster their self-esteem."[5] While Upper South cities did not typically develop the mixed-race, artisan elite that Lower South cities such as Charleston and New Orleans did, free people of color there still found work as artisans. In the city of Petersburg, Virginia, during the 1860s, for example, while most free blacks labored in unskilled jobs, "the most common skilled occupations were barber, blacksmith, boatman, bricklayer, carpenter, cooper, and shoemaker," occupations common in Charleston and throughout the urban Atlantic.[6] Though Upper South cities did not provide the same kinds of opportunities as the Lower South, historian L. Diane Barnes as shown that free people of color there "found more opportunities to participate in skilled occupations than did blacks living in northern cities before the Civil War."[7]

Similarly in the cities of Spanish America, people of African descent regularly engaged skilled labor as a means of improving their social and economic circumstances. Like in the United States, people of African descent took advantage of opportunities unique to urban life and knowledge of a skilled trade—often in niche sectors of the economy or in service-oriented roles generally eschewed by their white neighbors—to strengthen their social status and build wealth. Throughout Latin America free people of color "could be found in every skilled occupation," and there existed "entire occupations traditionally dominated by both free coloreds and slave artisans."[8] In Buenos Aires, Lima, Mexico City, Havana, and beyond, free people of African descent found opportunities for social and economic advancement through skilled work.[9]

Historian Ann Twinam, in her examination of whiteness petitions from colonial Latin America, has noted that for *pardos* such status could depend "on a range of moving variables, including appearance, clothing, occupation, wealth, and friends, rather than strictly genealogy or ancestry."[10] Such characteristics were inextricably linked, as one's clothing, wealth, and social contacts often depended in large part on one's occupation. Likewise Michele Reid-Vazquez's research on nineteenth-century Cuba reveals how, like elsewhere in Latin America and port cities of the Atlantic, people of African descent were barred from professional fields and thus "gravitated to opportunities as skilled laborers." Throughout Cuba free men of color "embraced a range of positions disdained by Spaniards and creoles and converted them into avenues for profit, self-esteem, and self-respect," occupations that could provide African-descended people and their families a "privileged economic and social position."[11] She reveals that free women of color pursued similar strategies, citing how those who worked as midwives "combined their work and reputations within the black, creole, and elite communities to further their own social and economic advancement and that of their families."[12] Similarly, in her work on barbers of African descent in Brazil and the wider Atlantic world, Mariza de Carvalho Soares has shown that barbering (and, in Brazil, its associated bleeder-surgeon function) provided an opportunity for "skilled men to climb up social ranks that had previously been more restricted," particularly in Brazil, where *barbeiros* served an essential role treating victims of the slave trade well into the mid-nineteenth century.[13] Throughout eighteenth- and nineteenth-century Latin America and the wider Atlantic world, people of African descent took advantage of skilled labor to build social connections and to boost their wealth and reputation.

These general racial-occupational trends extended to Charleston and Cartagena in particular. In both cities free people of African descent dominated many skilled trades and pursued similar occupational opportunities. As inhabitants of a growing port city, enslaved and free blacks in Charleston not only labored on and near the city's docks and wharves but also plied a wide variety of skilled trades to help drive the city's growth and provided services to the city's permanent and transient populations. As bricklayers and barbers, carpenters and cooks, tailors and tradesmen of a variety of other kinds, people of African descent found ample opportunity for skilled labor during the early national and antebellum eras.[14] Likewise Cartagena's status as a commercial entrepôt and Spanish American administrative center opened many similar opportunities for the city's free majority of African descent. In both Cartagena and Charleston, free artisans of color used their labor to gain a measure of social distinction, maintaining residences and workshops in desirable, relatively wealthy, and racially mixed neighborhoods of their cities. Through their work, free artisans of African descent throughout the urban Atlantic world gained the opportunity to cultivate client and patronage networks among the city's elite; to maintain social ties to other artisans matching their racial, economic, and social profiles; to bend Spanish and Anglo cultural values to their specific needs; and ultimately to cultivate reputations as hardworking, respectable members of their local communities. Artisans of African descent crafted lives that stood as refutation to a white racial ideology present throughout the Atlantic world that viewed blacks as unprepared or unwilling to work in freedom. Through the economic benefits of skilled labor and the social links it allowed them to cultivate, free artisans of color demonstrated an engagement with Spanish and Anglo cultural norms, subtly transforming those norms as they pursued individual improvement.

Yet differences in the legal and social circumstances of Spanish America and the United States also informed the decisions of free artisans of color in important ways. In Charleston the region's massive enslaved population and the centrality of slavery to the economy inclined free people of color to use their role as artisans to help erect and maintain a dividing line between slavery and freedom, establishing reputations not just as free people but also as respectable, industrious, and financially self-sufficient ones. Ultimately, however, as free artisans of color were forced to compete with both whites and enslaved people in a number of different occupations, skilled labor became just a necessary precondition to respectable social status, not alone a sufficient distinction. Many free black artisans continued to scrape by, living hand to mouth and holding more in common with enslaved people than they did with the black artisan elite. For Cartagena, a city also home to a black majority but one in which most African-descended people were born free, distinctions from what can be viewed broadly as the black lower class were based far more on class and economic status rather than legal status. Free people of color dominated skilled work in Cartagena to a far greater extent than in Charleston, and thus free artisans of color seem to have used the advantage of their skills to distinguish themselves from the unskilled or marginally skilled blacks and mulattoes. In Cartagena free people of color's utility in the eyes of the Crown represented a public dynamic that did not exist in Charleston, where free people of color depended far more on maintaining respectable reputations with prominent local whites. Thus while free artisans of color in Cartagena could use artisan labor to join the city's voluntary militia and to demonstrate their usefulness to the Crown, their counterparts in Charleston frequently used the economic benefits of artisan work to signal shared interests and values with the city's white elite, especially through slave ownership. While free people of color in Cartagena surely were concerned with their reputation among their neighbors, the ability and willingness of the Crown to confer tangible benefits onto artisans of African descent represented a public avenue to social prestige and economic stability that was never present for free people of color in Charleston, who focused far more heavily on cultivating the approbation of wealthy whites.

JEHU JONES AND PEDRO ROMERO

These racial-occupational patterns can be seen clearly in the life stories of two prominent mixed-race artisans living and working at the same time at opposite margins of the greater Caribbean world: Jehu Jones of Charleston and Pedro Romero of Cartagena. The similarities and differences in the opportunities available to these free men of color help reveal relationships between race, labor, and status evident throughout the African Americas.

Black Charlestonian Jehu Jones exemplifies the kinds of possibilities available to the luckiest and most enterprising free black artisans in the urban Lower South. Though born into slavery, Jones used his skills as a tailor to acquire sufficient funds to purchase his own freedom. In freedom he continued to ply his trade as a tailor, saving money and training his children in his craft. Through his work he expanded his circle of social contacts among blacks and whites alike. He used membership in St. Philip's Episcopal Church and organizations such as the Brown Fellowship Society to cultivate links with other prominent free blacks, formalizing them through marriages and baptisms. He expanded his social ties with whites as well, using his reputation for hard work and respectability to develop a social network capable of supporting him in times of need. Jones eventually saved enough money to leave the tailoring trade (though his children continued on) and open a prominent hotel and catering service in the city. Jones, through the advantages conferred by skilled labor, gained economic security, maintained a family residence in the heart of Charleston among prominent white neighbors, developed social links to prominent free blacks and whites in his neighborhood, and used his contacts in the community to carve out a reputation for himself as a respectable individual.

Jones, of mixed racial ancestry, was born into slavery in the late eighteenth century to a tailor named Christopher Rodgers, from whom he likely learned the trade. Like many skilled enslaved people in the urban South, he was afforded the opportunity to earn money independently from his enslaver by hiring out. As a result of this arrangement, Jones purchased his freedom on January 22, 1798, for "one hundred Pounds Sterling . . . well and truly paid" to Rodgers.[15] Jones seems to have made the most of his independence while enslaved, establishing a reputation as industrious, skilled, and respectable, because the same year in which he purchased his freedom he also gained membership in Charleston's exclusive Brown Fellowship Society, a mutual aid and benevolent society whose membership comprised the city's mulatto elite.

In the years that followed, Jones continued to work as a tailor and began to acquire property throughout the city. In 1809 he purchased a lot on Broad Street, and six years later he acquired the adjacent property as well, establishing what became "Jones's Long Room" and later the Jones Hotel. This hotel eventually became regarded as "unquestionably the best in the city."[16] Though Jones's role as a caterer and hotel proprietor replaced his tailoring, he must have trained his son in the trade, as Jehu Jr. is listed as a tailor in the city's 1831 directory. For Jehu Jones skilled labor not only provided for his freedom but also allowed him to amass a personal estate that could provide for him and his family.[17]

Jones also used his occupation in service-oriented jobs to cultivate a broader social network, establishing relationships with prominent whites and solidifying his reputation as respectable. In 1823, for example, he marshaled the support of a number of prominent white Charlestonians to gain an exemption to the state's restrictions on the movement of free blacks across state lines that were passed in the wake of the Denmark Vesey insurrection scare. Jones wished to visit his wife and daughter, who had some years prior relocated to New York, and so secured the assistance of a white man named John L. Wilson to petition the legislature. Wilson reported that Jones was "a man of good moral character, attached to the laws and government of this state." In another petition four years later, ninety prominent Charlestonians certified that Jones and his wife, Abigail, possessed a "genial and good character" and were both "honest, industrious, and decent people, and have always sustained that reputation." Jones was sure, should the legislature require it, that "satisfactory testimonials" could be provided from "many respectable citizens of this place." Many of these supporters were likely people he came to know through his work. His work serving white Charlestonians helped him establish helpful social connections within the community, develop a reputation as respectable and industrious, and—when it mattered—secure the support of nearly a hundred prominent whites to support his petition to the legislature.[18] While Jones's experiences are in many ways exceptional—the success and acclaim he encountered were undoubtedly uncommon—his story reflects broader trends and possibilities among free people of color in the nineteenth-century U.S. South.

Meanwhile in Cartagena the world of skilled *pardo* blacksmith Pedro Romero reveals parallels in experience for enterprising skilled laborers of African descent in the urban Atlantic world. Born in Matanzas, Cuba, Romero was of mixed European and African descent. Though we know little about his early life, at some point prior to the 1780s he gained his freedom and moved to Cartagena, where he worked as a blacksmith. In 1780 he was listed as operating a blacksmith shop in the neighborhood of Santa Catalina, home to most of the city's religious and civil buildings and one of the preferred places of residence for wealthy whites. Sometime after, Romero became a master blacksmith in the city's arsenal and later operated his own foundry at the entrance to the neighborhood of Getsemaní. His move from Santa Catalina to near Getsemaní was likely a response to a city ordinance that attempted to push noisy and dangerous trades outside the walled city.[19]

Through his work Romero became highly respected in the city by both blacks and whites alike and likely amassed considerable wealth, at least for an artisan. Colombian merchant and intellectual José Ignacio de Pombo described Romero in 1810 by stating, "We have in the master Pedro Romero and his son Stephen two intelligent artists in this profession [blacksmithing], or better yet, two intelligent men that the force of their genius . . . has elevated to a degree of perfection and delicacy that is truly admirable."[20] Romero cultivated a reputation for respectability and industry among prominent whites in Cartagena, using his skills as a blacksmith to support his efforts to gain social distinction. He distinguished himself as well within the city through his service as an officer in the city's *pardo* militia (see chapter 4). Romero and his family were able capitalize on their social prominence and reputation for respectability in very tangible ways: several of his daughters married well-to-do whites, and he was able to petition the king for permission for his son to pursue university studies, a privilege normally exclusive to whites, "excusing his condition of mulatto."[21] Indeed, as Ann Twinam has so carefully demonstrated, people of African descent such as Romero throughout Spanish America could appeal to the Spanish Crown for such exemptions, purchasing the privilege of whiteness. Though such a privilege was in theory open to all African-descended people, someone of light complexion who served the Crown in such crucial, tangible ways was certainly in a better position to make such an appeal. In turn, through the distinction of military service and, in exceptional circumstances, the ability to purchase whiteness, free people of color in Cartagena could in very direct ways have respectability conferred on them by the Crown.

In 1810, as the impulse to forge an independent Cartagena grew, local cabildo member José María Garcia de Toledo likely took Romero's reputation as a well-respected, influential, and honorable *pardo* into account when he enlisted his help in rallying Cartagena's black population against Spanish governor Francisco Montes. Garcia de Toledo called on Romero to enlist a militia of free people of color "of worth and resolution" from Getsemaní, as he wanted to be sure he had the support of the city's popular classes before any attempt to depose Governor Montes.[22] At a time when the city's white elite still worried greatly about the possibility Cartagena could become the next Haiti, it seems likely that Romero's social prominence and respectability among both white and black residents played a crucial role in Garcia de Toledo's trusting him to rally Cartagena's popular classes of African descent. Considered a different way, it was precisely Romero's efforts to distance himself from the popular classes that made a member of the white elite confident in his ability to command them.

More broadly Romero's status as a respectable, skilled worker afforded him a number of economic and social advantages in late eighteenth- and early nineteenth-century Cartagena. He owned a successful business and for a time maintained a residence in one of the city's most prominent neighborhoods. Through his industry and relative wealth, he cultivated ties to some of Cartagena's most prominent white leaders and claimed social advantages not available to most African-descended people. His work as an artisan and the economic advantages it afforded him offered opportunities to gain further distinctions, including membership in the city's voluntary militia and the opportunity to petition the Crown for other tangible privileges for his children. Skilled labor afforded Romero a level of access to public institutions and to the ears of Crown and local officials that were both unattainable by poorer people of African descent and instrumental in his efforts to improve the lives and condition of his family.

Though both Romero and Jehu Jones achieved uncommon success, their stories help to illustrate broader trends among free people of color in the urban Americas: the centrality of skilled labor to their lives and the economic and social advantages such work conferred. Through analysis of data from city directories, census records, and other sources, we can see the extent to which the prominence of particular trades in Charleston and Cartagena mirrored one another during the late eighteenth and early nineteenth centuries.

RACIAL-OCCUPATIONAL PATTERNS

For Charleston exact data on the extent to which free people of color engaged any particular occupation is difficult to discern for much of the early national and antebellum eras, due in large part to the fact that the U.S. decennial census did not record occupational information until 1850. Yet a combined look at city directories, legislative petitions, and census returns illustrates clearly the centrality of skilled labor to the lives of free people of color in Charleston. For example the 1831 *Directory and Stranger's Guide to the City of Charleston* reveals the degree to which prominent free people of color found work as artisans and provides insight into the most common occupations for people of African descent. The directory lists names, addresses, and occupations for a small number of free people of color in the city, individuals who composed the wealthiest of Charleston's free black population.[23] It is significant, then, that among this group nearly every individual recorded with occupational information engaged in some kind of skilled or artisan labor.[24] Though free people of African descent never constituted a large proportion of the population of Charleston District, they played an outsize role in the city's artisan occupations.[25]

For free men of color recorded in the 1831 directory, barber, carpenter, shoemaker, and tailor were by far the most popular occupations.[26] Other free men of color found employment in jobs that required both greater skill and greater capital. Jehu Jones ran his boardinghouse on Broad Street. A free black man named John Brown worked as a cabinetmaker on King Street. Among free women of color recorded with occupational information in the 1831 directory, most are recorded as seamstresses. Seventeen could be generally classified as such, though six of them are recorded specifically as mantua makers. Eight more women are recorded as pastry cooks; still others have more specialized occupations, like confectionary or nurse.[27]

The city's 1848 census further illustrates the degree to which barber, carpenter, shoemaker, and tailor represented areas of significant opportunity for free people of color. Although in 1848 free people of color made up less than 6 percent of the total population of the city of Charleston, they comprised nearly 78 percent of its barbers, 48 percent of its shoemakers, 30 percent of its tailors, and 11 percent of its carpenters (see table 3.1).[28] Barred by custom and law from most professional occupations, free people of color in Charleston turned to these types of skilled occupations as the highest positions to which they could aspire. Their significant overrepresentation relative to their proportion of the population demonstrates the desirability of these occupations for free black Charlestonians, the success of free blacks entering into these trades, and the centrality of skilled work to a particular segment of the city's free black population.

TABLE 3.1 **Racial classifications of most popular artisan occupations for men in Charleston, 1848**

	Whites		Free Blacks		Slaves		
	Number	Percent	Number	Percent	Number	Percent	Total
Barber	0	0%	14	78%	4	22%	18
Carpenter	117	46%	27	11%	110	43%	254
Shoemaker	13	45%	14	48%	2	7%	29
Tailor	68	47%	42	29%	36	25%	146
Total	198	44%	97	22%	152	34%	447

SOURCE: *Census of the City of Charleston, South Carolina, for the year 1848, exhibiting the condition and prospects of the city* (Charleston: J. B. Nixon, 1849), 29–35.

However, as table 3.1 illustrates, free artisans of color in Charleston faced significant competition in some of these trades from whites and from enslaved people. For example while forty-two free blacks worked in Charleston as tailors, making it the most popular occupation among that class, sixty-eight whites and thirty-six enslaved people are represented within that occupation as well. Likewise while many free people of color worked as carpenters (the second most popular occupation), they were far outnumbered in that profession by both whites (117) and enslaved people (110). In barbering, by contrast, free people of color seem to have had the arena to themselves.[29] While antebellum whites' perception of barbering as servile turned them away from the trade, it likewise made it an area of significant opportunity for free people of color.[30] Though free blacks were more likely than other demographic groups to be engaged in skilled work and were overrepresented among artisans relative to their proportion of the population, they were forced to compete with both white and enslaved laborers in a number of different trades.

Data culled by historians Leonard Curry and Ira Berlin suggests that these occupational patterns among free people of color persisted throughout the antebellum era. For example, using other Charleston city directories, Curry calculated that between 1845 and 1855, slightly more than 50 percent of free black men in the city engaged artisan trades, compared with just 16 percent of the free population generally.[31] Berlin calculated that fully 75 percent of free black Charlestonians performed some type of skilled labor in

1860. Though they only made up about 5 percent of the total population, free blacks constituted about 25 percent of Charleston's carpenters, nearly 40 percent of the city's tailors, and 75 percent of its millwrights in 1850. According to Berlin, Charleston's free blacks "enjoyed a level of occupational skill which surpassed that of most whites."[32] When compared with other urban centers, Charleston in 1850 had a far lower proportion of free blacks working in low-skill occupations than other antebellum cities; further, though only about one-sixth of all free males in Charleston worked as artisans, more than half of free men of color engaged in such occupations.[33] For much of the eighteenth and nineteenth centuries, free people of color in Charleston tended to possess greater skills than the population more broadly, were more likely than any other demographic group to be engaged in artisan work, and constituted a much larger portion of the artisan workforce than their proportion of the population would otherwise predict. The frequency with which free people of color engaged in skilled labor of this kind suggests several likely (and mutually reinforcing) possibilities: that the advantages conferred by such work were perhaps more important to free people of color than they were for other groups; that people of African descent who had the opportunity to develop skills in a useful trade were more likely to achieve freedom; and that freedom afforded African-descended people greater opportunity to develop and pursue these skills.

Free black skilled workers in Charleston had for many years used their relative privilege and wealth to push back against racial discrimination in the city. Thomas Cole, Peter Matthews, and Matthew Webb—a bricklayer and two butchers—petitioned South Carolina's legislature in 1791, requesting they be granted the rights of citizens and an exemption from the state's 1740 Negro Act. Their inability to seek legal redress against whites for damages and debts, they contended, interfered with their ability to support themselves and their families. They argued that as loyal, taxpaying, free people, they deserved the enjoyment of "the rights and immunities of citizens." Ever careful not to challenge the existing racial order too forcefully, however, these men added that they did "not presume to hope that they shall be put on an equal footing" with white citizens.[34] More secure both financially and socially, skilled workers such as Cole, Matthews, and Webb attempted to push (ever so slightly) for broader reforms. Though these reforms never arrived, the political concerns of these men reveal the unique position of free black laborers to push for greater inclusion in the social and civic life of early national Charleston.

People of African descent so dominated skilled labor in Charleston that white workers occasionally complained about their inability to compete. On a number of occasions, groups of white Charlestonians petitioned South

Carolina's state legislature to restrict the activities of black artisans.[35] In 1783 a group of more than thirty white bricklayers and carpenters in Charleston requested that the legislature prohibit free blacks and enslaved people from working in those trades in the city. These white laborers explained that they had struggled to obtain "sufficient employment to support their families, owing, they apprehend, in great measure, to a number of jobbing Negro Tradesmen who undervalue work by undertaking it for very little more than the materials would cost." The ability to offer their services so cheaply, these men contended, was evidence in itself that black tradesmen acquired their materials through theft or other dishonest means. Forced to compete with the numerous free and enslaved black skilled workers in the city, white craftsmen were "thereby deprived of the means of gaining a livelihood by their industry."[36]

Years later, in the early 1820s, more than one hundred "sundry mechanics of Charleston" also requested that the legislature protect them from being undercut by black artisans in the city. These men likewise complained that "the competition of negro and colored workmen, whether bond or free," undercut the value of their work, made their occupations less than prosperous, and disinclined a younger generation toward artisan trades. They bemoaned the fact that

> almost all the trades, but especially those of carpenters, bricklayers, plasterers, wheelwrights, house painters, shoemakers, &c., are beginning to be engrossed by black & colored workers; that these are multiplying in a prodigious ratio, and that Charleston, already swarming with a population of free blacks and of slaves, more licentious than if they were free, must, in a very short time, be in the condition of a West India Town.[37]

Not only did these white tradesmen desire state protection from black artisans they felt were undervaluing skilled work, but they also feared that as whites fled Charleston for locales where they could more easily ply their trades, the city would be home to an even greater black majority. South Carolina leader Edward Laurens echoed this sentiment in 1835, contending "that we first degrade the occupation by employing colored persons, and are then surprised that our young men . . . will not enter the arena with them."[38]

Though spaced nearly forty years apart, these petitions reveal both the extent to which people of African descent dominated Charleston's artisan trades and white anxieties about the ubiquity of black labor. White Charlestonians felt so unable to compete with black artisans that they petitioned the state legislature to prohibit people of African descent from participating in certain skilled trades. Many of the specific occupations these petitioners called to the legislature's attention as in need of regulation were precisely those that city directories and census returns reveal as most likely to be engaged in by free people of color, particularly carpenters, wheelwrights, and shoemakers.

As late as 1858, white tradesmen in Charleston (represented at that point by the South Carolina Mechanics Association) continued to petition the legislature complaining of the "baneful evil" that plagued the city, referring to "the hiring of slaves of their own time." Fully acknowledging that all restrictions on labor undertaken by both free and enslaved black Charlestonians had "become a dead letter," these men requested that a new ban and fine be imposed on slaves hiring their own time. Further they urged the legislature to "take into consideration the class of negroes known amongst us as free negroes and that a tax be imposed upon them or that some other remedy be made that shall at least place us in such a position that we may be able to compete with them, if they are to be on an equality with us."[39] Seventy-five years after the first time skilled white laborers petitioned the legislature for protection from black artisans, free people of color and enslaved people continued to dominate these trades in the city.

In an entirely different spirit, a group of 129 white Charlestonians petitioned South Carolina's legislature two years later in 1860, testifying to the ubiquity of free black skilled labor. As the southern slave system came under increasing scrutiny in the late 1850s, South Carolina proposed a bill devised to drive free people of color (long believed to be a threat to the stability of slavery) from the state. A large group of Charleston whites sent a petition to the legislature to protest the bill, contending they could "find no reason for such severity." Despite a generally paternalistic tone stressing the need to protect free blacks, these men acknowledged that many free blacks "are good citizens" who exhibit "patterns of industry, sobriety, and irreproachable conduct." More important, they pointed to the fact that free blacks in the city held property valued at "more than half a million dollars" and that "their labour is indispensable to us in this neighborhood." According to the petitioners, the people of Charleston could not "build or repair a house . . . without the aid of the coloured carpenter or bricklayer."[40] Even at the height of the sectional crisis, whites in Charleston continued to vouch for the essential work provided by the city's black artisans, revealing not only the extent to which blacks and mulattoes dominated artisan trades but also, perhaps, the relationships they developed with prominent whites as well.

From the eighteenth century through the eve of the Civil War, white artisans and skilled laborers in Charleston complained regularly about the competition they faced from black workers, particularly "the class known . . . as free negroes."[41] While data from the 1850 and 1860 federal censuses confirm the ubiquity of black labor in Charleston, these earlier concerns about the extent to which free people of color dominated skilled trades certainly suggest that such an occupational pattern persisted for much of the early national and antebellum periods. Throughout late eighteenth- and nineteenth-century Charleston, skilled work was central to the lives and identities of free people of color. Through their work in service oriented, skilled occupations, free people of color could establish reputations for themselves as talented, hardworking members of the community, cultivating social contacts both with prominent whites and other members of the black artisan class.

For Cartagena, meanwhile, quantitative analysis drawn from some of the city's late eighteenth-century censuses allows us to reconstruct a similar racial-occupational profile. For Cartagena's 1777 census, returns are available for four of the city's five barrios, though only three of those four contain information regarding race. Free people of color constituted just below 50 percent and enslaved people just below 20 percent of Cartagena's 13,690 total inhabitants in 1777, making people of African descent a majority in the city. Cartagena also had a relatively large population classified as white, just under 30 percent, as compared with only 11 percent in the province as a whole, including many Spaniards and members of the merchant class.[42]

Cartagena's 1777 census recorded occupational information for only 1,171 adult men, but this data reveals interesting relationships between racial classifications and employment. For example, of the 391 free people of color in Cartagena for whom occupational information was recorded, fully 241 (about 83 percent) were employed as artisans of some kind, with tailors, shoemakers, carpenters, and masons constituting the most popular form of artisanal employment. In addition 70 free people of color were employed by the military in some capacity, and as we will see later, a close association persisted between artisan employment and militia service in Cartagena.[43] The much larger number of free people of color for whom no occupational information was recorded likely worked as day laborers or in other unskilled professions. It seems likely that census administrators only recorded occupational information for individuals of higher economic status; that a substantial proportion of occupations recorded among free people of color were for artisans suggests a strong link between skilled labor and economic opportunity in Cartagena.

The 1777 census is also interesting for its use of the titles *Don* and *Doña*, reflections of a level of social respectability in colonial Spanish America. Though the honorific *Don* was traditionally an honor reserved for the Spanish and creole white elite, in Spanish American urban centers with significant populations of African descent, it could extend to prominent free people of color as well. In total 241 free people of color received the honorific title in the 1777 census, serving as a reflection of an individual's class status. For instance in the neighborhood of Getsemaní, noted for being home to much of the city's African-descended popular classes, only about 1.5 percent of the population received the title. In the neighborhood of Santo Toribio, the city's most populous and racially diverse neighborhood, however, 238 free people of color are listed with honorific titles.[44] The vast majority of the free people of color who received these honorific titles worked as artisans or as militia members, two categories with a significant degree of overlap: though not all artisans served in the militia, nearly all militia volunteers were also artisans.[45]

The census of artisans in Cartagena taken a few years later in 1780 further confirms the extent to which free people of color dominated skilled trades in the city. Of the 230 artisans enumerated in the neighborhood of Santo Toribio in 1780, only 22 were white, along with 182 *pardos*, 24 *negros*, and 2 *zambos*. Whites also did not constitute a significant portion of any individual trade in the neighborhood, with only barber and scribe having more than 3 individuals classified as *blancos*.[46] People of African descent held the vast majority of the neighborhood's most common artisan occupations. Tailor, shoemaker, carpenter, barber, and stonemason represented the five most popular trades in Santo Toribio, accounting for 136 of the 230 artisans recorded there. Of those 136 artisans, 80 percent (109) were classified as *pardos*, 14 percent (19) as *negros*, and just 6 percent (8) as *blancos*, with whites having no representation at all among carpenters and shoemakers (table 3.2).[47]

TABLE 3.2 **Racial classifications of artisan occupations in Santo Toribio, Cartagena, 1780**

	Pardo		Negro		Blanco		
	Number	Percent	Number	Percent	Number	Percent	Total
Tailor	37	95%	0	0%	2	5%	39
Shoemaker	24	73%	9	27%	0	0%	33
Carpenter	22	71%	9	29%	0	0%	31
Barber	14	74%	0	0%	5	26%	19
Mason	12	86%	1	7%	1	7%	14
Total	109	80%	19	14%	8	6%	136

SOURCE: 1780 Artisan Census, Santo Toribio.

Further the vast majority of these artisans of color also served in the city's *pardo* militias, offering them an additional level of social distinction. Of the 230 artisans recorded, only 50 did not also serve in the militia, 11 of whom were exempt. Though the role of the voluntary militia in the social lives of free people of color will be explored in greater depth in chapter 4, it seems worth noting that such a close correlation existed between artisan work and militia membership that it seems this may have been part of the reason for recording the artisan census at all. The census's omission of both enslaved people and women—individuals who surely engaged in some kind of artisan occupations during this era—seems to suggest that the Crown was only concerned with artisans who would have an impact on the voluntary militia. The omission of these other groups likewise reveals the gendered dynamic of respectability in Cartagena and the direct involvement of the Crown. At the very least, the 1780 artisan census reveals plainly the overlap between artisans and militia members and suggests how access to public institutions and labor collectively influenced the ability of free people of color to gain social distinction.

Artisan censuses in the city's other neighborhoods reveal similar patterns. According to the 1777 general census, the neighborhood of Las Mercedes was home to twenty-nine tailors, nineteen carpenters, twelve shopkeepers, eight writers or scribes, and six shoemakers, these occupations constituting Las Mercedes's most popular occupations. Though the numbers differ slightly, the 1780 artisan census of the same neighborhood reflects the same pattern, recording eighteen tailors, sixteen carpenters, seven scribes, and six each of shoemakers, barbers, and tobacconists. Of those for whom a racial designation is also listed, nearly all are of at least partial African descent, including all of the barbers, carpenters, tailors and shoemakers (table 3.3). Of the sixty-six total artisans recorded in Las Mercedes with a racial designation, fifty-four (82 percent) were listed as *pardo*, 9 (14 percent) as *negro*, and just 3 (5 percent), two scribes and a tobacconist, as *blanco*.[48]

TABLE 3.3 **Racial classifications of artisan occupations in Las Mercedes, Cartagena, 1780**

	Pardo		Negro		Blanco		
	Number	Percent	Number	Percent	Number	Percent	Total
Tailor	14	82%	3	18%	0	0%	17
Carpenter	11	92%	1	8%	0	0%	12
Barber	6	100%	0	0%	0	0%	6
Scribe	3	60%	0	0%	2	40%	5
Tobacconist	4	80%	0	0%	1	20%	5

Table 3.3 continued

	Pardo		Negro		Blanco		
	Number	Percent	Number	Percent	Number	Percent	Total
Shoemaker	2	50%	2	50%	0	0%	4
Total	40	82%	6	12%	3	6%	49

SOURCE: 1780 Artisan Census, Las Mercedes.

These trends continue in the neighborhood of Santa Catalina, likely Cartagena's wealthiest neighborhood. There people of African descent constituted about 77 percent of artisans recorded in the 1780 census, with 168 *pardos* and 26 *negros* (table 3.4). Fifty-six whites are recorded as artisans there, the highest of any neighborhood recorded by the 1780 artisan census. Of those 56, just under half were classified as *pulperos,* a shopkeeper or grocer. If *pulperos* are set aside and only the most popular trades from the city's other neighborhoods are counted, *pardos* and blacks constituted fully 81 percent of artisans in Santa Catalina. Like in the city's other neighborhoods, people of African descent—particularly people of mixed racial ancestry—dominated the artisan trades in Santa Catalina.[49] Unlike in Charleston, where free artisans of color competed regularly with whites and enslaved people, free people of color entirely dominated artisan work in late eighteenth-century Cartagena.

TABLE 3.4 **Racial classifications of artisan occupations in Santa Catalina, Cartagena, 1780**

	Pardo		Negro		Blanco		
	Number	Percent	Number	Percent	Number	Percent	Total
Tailor	53	85%	7	11%	2	3%	62
Carpenter	33	87%	5	13%	0	0%	38
Shoemaker	23	74%	5	16%	3	10%	31
Barber	18	95%	0	0%	1	5%	19
Mason	4	40%	1	10%	5	50%	10
Total	131	81%	20	12%	11	7%	162

SOURCE: 1780 Artisan Census, Santa Catalina.

The 1780 artisan census did not extend to the neighborhood of Getsemaní, and the 1777 general census for Getsemaní does not include racial classifications for the neighborhood, though it was populated almost exclusively by people of African descent during this era. This population included a number of the city's poorer people of African descent, certainly far more than in the neighborhoods within the walled city, though it was home to many artisans as well. As a result, for those individuals in Getsemaní enumerated with an occupation (only about 10 percent of the total entries), few held the types of skilled positions so common in wealthier, more racially mixed neighborhoods. Of the 400 individuals for whom jobs were recorded, 114 (29 percent) are listed simply as "*de la mar*," likely implying they worked as small-time mariners, boatmen, or otherwise were engaged in a variety of jobs at or near the city's port. The census also lists 32 fishermen, 24 shopkeepers, 20 "laborers," 10 caulkers, and 10 boatmen, meaning that fully 44 percent of the Getsemaní residents listed with jobs in 1777 engaged in some manner of marginally skilled work, most related broadly to the sea or shipping. Carpenter, shoemaker (a job primarily occupied by men classified as *negros* in the city's other neighborhoods), stonemason, and tailor constituted the only skilled jobs in Getsemaní for which more than 10 individuals are recorded. Despite lower total numbers, the patterns that emerged in Cartagena's other neighborhoods extend to Getsemaní as well, as people of African descent in Getsemaní frequently labored in occupations that combined skill and a reasonably low cost of entry. African-descended people dominated artisan work, though in Getsemaní free people of color tended to gravitate toward occupations more often engaged by *negros* in the city's other neighborhoods.[50]

While people of African descent dominated nearly every artisan trade in the city, three occupations were far and away the most prominent: tailor, carpenter, and shoemaker. Of the 926 men listed in the artisan censuses of 1780 (along with the 1777 census for Getsemaní, including only those recorded with skilled occupations), fully 44 percent of them were employed in one of those three occupations: 160 tailors (17 percent), 128 carpenters (14 percent), and 121 shoemakers (13 percent).[51] Additionally, while people of African descent dominated most of these trades, *pardos* constituted about 80 percent of artisans in nearly all of the city's neighborhoods. It seems likely, then, that people of mixed racial ancestry or lighter complexions would have tended to be better off economically than those wholly of African ancestry. While it may not be possible to determine causation, it seems plausible that a circular pattern of mutual reinforcement existed in which money "whitened" people of African descent in the eyes of census takers and people of mixed racial ancestry derived economic advantage from their complexion and background. This complexional distinction represents a link with Charleston, where such divisions clearly existed within the free colored population. In both Cartagena and Charleston, it seems artisan work was to some extent organized as a "pigmentrocracy"—to borrow a term from sociologist Edward

Telles—where individuals of African descent with lighter complexions tended to monopolize the most profitable artisan trades.[52]

For artisans of color in Cartagena, like elsewhere in Spanish America, skilled labor crucially supported efforts to achieve both economic and social mobility. In his study of the colored militia in colonial Mexico, Ben Vinson III found that, like in Cartagena, tailor and shoemaker constituted two of the most popular occupations engaged in by people of African descent. Vinson argues that "tailoring was considered to be among the most desirable jobs within the textile industry," where large numbers of blacks and *pardos* found work, and that "it would be erroneous to assume that because there were a large number of free-coloreds involved in tailoring, it was necessarily an artisan trade of lower status.[53] Michele Reid-Vazquez finds similar patterns in colonial Cuba, acknowledging how such work as barbering and carpentry allowed some free people of color to achieve "a privileged economic and social position."[54]

Vinson's and Reid-Vazquez's portraits of occupational trends in colonial Mexico and Cuba dovetail neatly with the racial-occupational profile of artisans in Cartagena. Tailors in Cartagena likely would have been held in high esteem, as their skills and reputations would have elevated their social profile above the city's many unskilled or marginally skilled black workers. Not only was tailoring considered generally to be a respectable trade irrespective of who was engaged in it, tailors would have had frequent opportunities to interact with their customers, people who would have likely been reasonably well off economically. Not all tailors would have encountered the same degree of success, but it is reasonable to assume that at least some would have derived significant social benefits from their position as skilled tradesmen in an occupation that necessitated frequent interaction with well-to-do clients.

Other popular artisan trades would have held similar benefits, if perhaps less pronounced than tailoring. Such occupations as carpenter, shoemaker, barber, and silversmith all required varying degrees of skill and would have required direct interaction with clients (particularly wealthy ones, in the case of silversmiths). Each of those occupations can be considered among the most popular occupations for skilled men of African descent. Between 1777 and 1780, Cartagena was home to 128 carpenters, 121 shoemakers, 52 barbers, and 46 silversmiths in 1780, nearly all of whom were of African descent, mostly *pardos*.[55] In fact many of these skilled blacks and *pardos* lived in the city's racially mixed, often upper-class neighborhoods. Though many of the city's carpenters and shoemakers—jobs more likely than other skilled trades to be plied by men classified as *negros*—lived in the predominantly black, poorer neighborhood of Getsemaní, many of the artisans of color engaging in skilled occupations would have lived inside the walled city among wealthy white neighbors. Like in Charleston, racial segregation was low in Cartagena, and upper-class free artisans of color would have been widely dispersed throughout the city.

RESIDENTIAL PATTERNS AND SLAVE OWNERSHIP

Engagement with skilled craftwork of various kinds allowed free people of color to establish crucial class distinctions between themselves and the unskilled or semiskilled black lower classes. The service-oriented nature of their work often necessitated the cultivation of social ties with prominent members of the community and allowed free people of color to develop a broader reputation for respectability. More broadly it allowed them to challenge prevailing views that people of African descent could not survive in freedom. The money earned from skilled work and the need to maintain relationships with a predominantly white clientele meant that for many free people of color, establishing residences in racially mixed, desirable neighborhoods was crucial. Living among clients as neighbors helped free people of color establish themselves as part of the community fabric, far more so than their African-descended counterparts living in more racially segregated parts of the city.

In Charleston, while neither free blacks generally nor black artisans in particular ever constituted a sizeable proportion of the city population, their ability to own property in desirable, popular locations within the city likely served as a mark of distinction, affording black artisans frequent opportunities to interact with white neighbors. Because of the ubiquity of their labor, the presence of and interaction with black artisans would have constituted an indelible aspect of daily life in Charleston, even as the presence of unskilled free and enslaved black workers may have been far more common for much of this era. Although the sight of enslaved people and unskilled workers would have surely been common in such a bustling city as Charleston, black artisans residing in the city gained the opportunity to distinguish themselves from that class, carving out reputations for themselves as skilled, hardworking, and respectable.[56]

Mapping the locations of free black artisans listed in the city's 1831 directory reveals that they were indeed spread throughout city, though groups of free black artisans are often clustered around particularly prominent intersections (figure 3.1). This apparent lack of residential restrictions on free blacks made the financial advantages of artisan labor all the more important. As the visualization below illustrates, Charleston's most prominent black artisans lived and worked throughout the city proper, among white neighbors and fellow black artisans that matched their social, economic, and often complexional profiles.

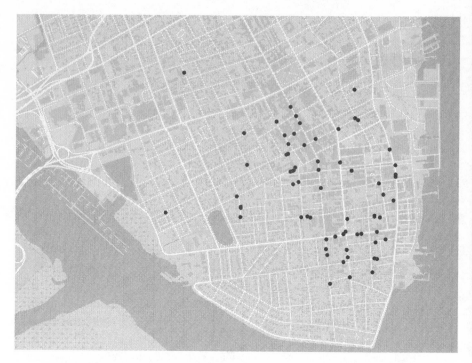

FIGURE 3.1 *Free artisans of color listed in Charleston's 1831 city directory.*

Because so many free artisans of color maintained residences in the city proper (be it through ownership or rental), the presence of and interaction with relatively wealthy free black artisans would have become an unmistakable feature of daily life in Charleston. The wide dispersal of a certain class of free people of color throughout the city would have made it eminently possible for them cultivate relationships with other members of their community, even those who may not have patronized their businesses or services. Much of the scholarship that recognizes the ability of free blacks to avoid some racial proscriptions focuses specifically on their need carefully to maintain prominent white patrons; the ubiquity of black artisans in Charleston likely would have made maintaining individual patrons less crucial than developing a broader reputation for respectability.[57]

During the 1830s, and likely for much of the eighteenth and nineteenth centuries, walking for more than a few blocks almost anywhere in the city's center would have brought an individual into contact with a number of prominent free black artisans. For whites this would have meant that the sight of relatively affluent, skilled free people of color would have been a daily occurrence in the city. Free blacks, particularly those who considered themselves part of the artisan class, would have had the opportunity to cultivate further social ties with individuals matching their occupational and racial profiles.

To return to Jehu Jones, we can imagine the contact he would have had with other prominent free black artisans in his day-to-day life. Just three doors down from Jones's hotel on Broad Street, Edward Lee maintained a barbershop. If Jones headed west from the door of his boardinghouse and turned left at the next block, on Meeting Street, he would have passed the shops or residences of three black artisans. Jane Monies worked there as a mantua maker, Thomas Ingliss as a hairdresser, and John McBeth as a carpenter. Turning right at the next block, Tradd Street, Jones would have passed Eliza Lee, a pastry cook. Heading right once again at the next block to go north on King Street, he would have passed the shops of John Brown, a cabinetmaker; Diana Trezevant, a nurse; and at the corner with Broad, William Irving, another barber. Heading west back to his boarding house, he would have passed yet two more artisans on Broad Street: Gilbert Wall, a tailor, and Camilla Johnson, a pastry cook.[58]

This hypothetical stroll serves to illustrate how free artisans of color established themselves as part of the fabric of their neighborhood. As artisans these individuals maintained businesses and residences in the heart of Charleston, affording them the opportunity to distinguish themselves from both the enslaved and the unskilled laborers that constituted the black lower classes more generally. Additionally many of these individuals were of mixed racial backgrounds and likely of lighter complexions; many were also members of the elite Brown Fellowship Society, revealing the importance of complexional distinctions, as well as economic ones, among free people of color in Charleston. Nevertheless that they kept residences in the heart of the city reflects more broadly both the advantages of artisan labor for some free blacks as well as the wealth of the individuals distinguished enough to be included in the 1831 city directory. The ability to live and work in that area of Charleston was a distinction that likely allowed free artisans of color to cultivate social ties with neighbors, both black and white, and generate a client base that likely included prominent members of the community. As we saw with the case of Jehu Jones, such a social network could be called upon during times of need.

Data from later in the antebellum era, however, suggests that these residential patterns changed rapidly in the years that followed. After 1840 some free and enslaved African Americans began leaving the city. In 1848 the City of Charleston was home to 14,187 whites, 10,772 slaves, and 1,492 free people of color, marking the first time since at least 1790 (and likely much earlier) that whites outnumbered blacks in the city. Between the federal census of 1840 and the city census of 1848, the black population of Charleston declined precipitously, by 24 percent. The editors of the 1848 census attributed the decline to the fact that the "slaves and free colored" in Charleston "have removed to the Neck, beyond the corporate limits of the city, where the class of houses suited to their condition are numerous, and obtainable at moderate rents."[59] The 1850 federal census taken two years later allows for the development of a more complex racial-occupational comparison between the residents of Charleston Neck and those who resided in the city proper, in Wards 1 through 4. Specifically the 1850 census suggests that wealthier, better-skilled workers were able to maintain their place in the city, while less skilled, poorer free blacks moved north to Charleston Neck.

The 1850 census offered a degree of specificity not available in earlier censuses, including occupation, place of birth, education level, and property values. It is this final category that reveals one of the starkest differences between the city and neck suggestive of the economic benefits of skilled labor and the way the relationship between race, labor, and residential patterns shifted after 1840. In 1850 just 10 of the 1,441 free black residents of Charleston Neck (0.69 percent) owned real estate. The average value of real estate owned by free black residents of Charleston Neck was $1,410, while the median value was $1,000. In the city, meanwhile, not only did more free blacks own real estate, the real estate they owned was far more valuable than that owned by their counterparts in the neck. This is unsurprising, as the 1848 city census claims that property values were lower north of the city. But the value of property owned by free blacks in the city also reveals that it was wealthier free people of color, nearly all of whom worked as artisans, who were able to maintain their place in the city rather than moving north to Charleston Neck. In the city at least 26 of 1,998 free black residents owned property (1.3 percent), proportionally nearly twice as many as in Charleston Neck. The average value of real estate owned by free blacks in the city was $4,423—more than three times the average value owned by black property owners in Charleston Neck. The median for free black city residents was $3,000 (table 3.5).

TABLE 3.5 **Value of real estate owned by free people of color in Charleston, 1850**

	Ward 1	Ward 2	Ward 3	Ward 4	City	Charleston Neck
Average Value	$5,166	$2,083	$2,214	$3,714	$4,423	$1,410
Median Value	$3,500	$3,000	$2,000	$3,000	$3,000	$1,000

Not only did free black city residents own more valuable property, but free black property owners were also a more skilled group in the city than they were in the neck. In Charleston Neck, Alexander Noisett and George Jones, the owners of the two most valuable properties, were both farmers, suggesting perhaps that the value of their real estate lay in its size. Among the other property owners were three carpenters, two tailors, two wheel-wrights, and one butcher. In the City of Charleston's fourth ward—the most populous of the city's four wards—the owners of the two most valuable prop-erties among free blacks were Jacob Weston and Samuel Wilson, both tailors, and John Francis, a hairdresser. Other property owners included another tailor, a cotton-gin maker, and two carpenters—one of whom was Richard Holloway Jr., a member of one of the wealthiest and most prominent free black families in Charleston. Free black property owners comprised a simi-larly skilled group in the city's other wards, including one each of a barber, boot maker, butcher, confectioner, cooper, hairdresser, hotel keeper, painter, shoemaker, tailor, and tavern keeper. While these property owners also in-cluded marginally skilled workers such as bricklayers, carters, and draymen, they on the whole constituted a far more skilled group than the property owners of Charleston Neck.

After 1840, while the confluence of deteriorating economic conditions and the perceived threats to the institution of slavery created social pres-sure on Charleston free blacks, wealthier, more skilled free people of color maintained their residences in the city, while poorer, less skilled free blacks tended to move north toward the neck. The percentage of free people of color engaged in the most prominent occupations discussed above—barber, carpenter, tailor, shoemaker, and boot maker—reveal the higher skill level of free black artisans who were able to maintain their residences in the city rather than move out to Charleston Neck (table 3.6). Two hundred thirty-four free blacks were recorded with occupations in Charleston Neck, compared with 354 in the city (161 of whom were in the city's fourth ward). Within that population Charleston Neck was home to just 4 barbers (1.7 percent of the free black males listed with occupations), while the city was home to nearly four times as many with 15 (5.2 percent). Among shoe and boot makers, the neck was home to 11 (4.7 percent) versus more than twice as many,31 (10.7 percent), in the city proper. A similar pattern was evident among tailors, though the difference was not quite as stark as it was for other occupations. The neck was home to 28 tailors, 12.1 percent of the occupied free black men; the city was home to 50, comprising 17.3 percent of the free black men recorded with occupations. The occupation that deviates from this pattern is carpenters, suggesting perhaps the higher necessity for their skills in the neck, as free blacks and enslaved people (along with German and Irish

immigrants) flooded the neighborhood in search of more affordable hous-
ing. While the neck was home to 59 carpenters (25.4 percent), the city was
home to just 41 (14.2 percent). After 1850, amid the exodus of free blacks and
enslaved people from the city to the neck, it seems likely that the ability of
free blacks to maintain residences in the city proper may have taken on a
greater social value when compared with previous decades—as poorer and
less skilled people of African descent left the city, those who remained would
have been all the more distinct.

TABLE 3.6 **Free people of color in skilled occupations in
Charleston and Charleston Neck, 1850**

	City		Charleston Neck	
	Number	Percent of Free People of Color	Number	Percent of Free People of Color
Barber	15	5.2%	4	1.7%
Carpenter	41	14.2%	59	25.4%
Shoe/Boot Maker	31	10.7%	11	4.7%
Tailor	50	17.3%	28	12.1%

SOURCE: Seventh Census of the United States (1850).

Other data from the 1850 federal census reinforces the notion that free
black artisans with greater skill were better able to maintain residences in
the city. For example Charleston Neck was home to many more free blacks
engaged in the transportation trades—carter, drayman, porter—than those
in the city proper. Fully 18 percent of free blacks with occupations were engaged in such trades in Charleston Neck, compared with just under 9 percent
in the city proper. Likewise the city was home to more free blacks engaged
in such entrepreneurial or mercantile trades as shopkeeper, tavern keeper,
and hotel keeper. In the city those trades constituted 4 percent of free black
employment, while they comprised just 2 percent in the neck (nearly all of
whom were wood factors).[60] While eighteen free blacks in the neck were
engaged generally in food service occupations, all but one of those were
butchers, likely because of the greater presence of small farms in the area
north of the city. Thus when other food service occupations—sugar maker,
baker, confectioner, and pastry cook—are considered, we see the much
higher prevalence of these trades inside the city, where they constituted
2.5 percent of free black occupations, compared with less than 0.5 percent
in Charleston Neck.[61] Even outside traditional artisan trades, free people of

color who possessed significant skills constituted a much larger proportion of the free black population in the city than they did in Charleston Neck.

Yet for free artisans of color to maximize the benefits of skilled labor and their presence among wealthy, white neighbors, they needed to demonstrate shared cultural values that extended beyond labor and industriousness. While skilled labor was essential to achieving social respectability in Charleston, free artisans of color who wanted to solidify a place for themselves and their families sought ways to demonstrate not just their economic self-sufficiency and habits of industry but other values as well. Men of similar means founded and joined voluntary associations, many of which were explicitly dedicated to the cultivation of respectable moral habits (see chapter 4). Likewise the complexional distinctions of these organizations and the greater presence of individuals of mixed racial ancestry in the city proper suggest as well that color distinctions within Charleston's free black community played an important role. More clearly, however, as social pressure on free blacks increased in the late antebellum era because slavery became an increasingly contentious issue in national politics, many free black artisans in Charleston turned to slave ownership as a way to demonstrate their engagement with the dominant social values of the city.

Free people of color owned slaves for a variety of reasons throughout the eighteenth and nineteenth centuries, and the nature of evidence of slave ownership often makes it impossible to determine individual motivations precisely. Many free people of color, particularly after 1820, owned enslaved spouses, children, and other relatives. These individuals likely lived as functionally free people, though South Carolina laws made it either difficult or impossible to manumit them (see chapter 1). Other free people of color, particularly those engaged in artisan trades, likely took in enslaved apprentices. Finally some free people of color surely owned enslaved people for less philanthropic reasons, seeking to derive the same kinds of economic and social benefits from slave ownership as whites. Through slave ownership free people of color could distinguish themselves from enslaved and less wealthy free blacks. As historians such as Michael P. Johnson, James L. Roark, and Walter Johnson have argued, free people of color likely derived significant social benefits from owning slaves, as it allowed them to occupy a social space in the city in which they could interact with prominent whites.[62]

To return to Jehu Jones's hypothetical stroll, for example, four free black artisans living within a square block of Jones were listed as heads of families in the 1830 census, and all of them recorded at least two enslaved people within the household. Gilbert Wall, a tailor, lived at 89 Broad Street with three other free people of color: two males under ten years old and a free woman of color, likely his children and spouse. His household was also home to two enslaved people, males between the ages of ten and twenty-three.[63] Nearby, hairdresser Thomas Ingliss had eleven slaves in his household; carpenter John McBeth and cabinetmaker John Brown each had three. Ultimately, though it may not be possible to determine the exact relationship between enslaved people and these men, each of the possible explanations outlined above offers some sense of how artisan work made social and economic mobility possible for Charleston's free people of color. Whether they owned family members, trained enslaved apprentices, or entered into the slaveholding class alongside whites, free artisans of color gained economic advantages that afforded them the opportunity to draw clear class distinctions between themselves and other people of African descent in the city. For some, slave ownership also allowed them to demonstrate their commitment to shared cultural values with whites.

More broadly the 1830 census suggests slave ownership was relatively common among free people of color in Charleston, both in the city proper as well as in the neck. Historian Carter Woodson identified 260 free black slave owners in the 1830 census, distributed between the city's four wards, and an additional 133 free black slave owners in the neck. In the city free blacks slave owners tended to be younger than their counterparts in the neck, though their slaveholdings were smaller. The average free black slave owner in the city in 1830 owned four and a half slaves, while in the neck they owned nearly seven. The median number of slaves owned was three in the city and six in the neck. In the neck, which was more rural at this time, nearly 70 percent of free black slave owners were over the age of thirty-six in 1830, while just 50 percent were over that age inside the city.[64] While the nature of slave owning among free people of color may have differed between the neck and the city, free people of color throughout Charleston owned enslaved people throughout the antebellum era.

Evidence of free black slave ownership in the 1850 census reveals the continued importance of slave ownership for free blacks as well as the changing neighborhood dynamics of the city. In 1850 the prevalence of free black slave ownership in Charleston Neck clearly declined, while it increased in the city proper. In 1850 free blacks in the city owned, on average, more slaves than their counterparts in the neck. While the average size of slaveholdings held steady in the city between 1830 and 1850, it declined by half in Charleston Neck, illustrating at least in part the influx of poorer free blacks and enslaved people from the city in the intervening decades.[65] Further, not only did free blacks in the city in 1850 own more slaves, but the enslaved people they owned also tended to be younger and were more likely to be males than in the neck, characteristics that likely would have made them more expensive as well.[66] Slave owners comprised a larger proportion of the free black population in the city than in the neck, both among free blacks listed with occupations as well as within the free black population more broadly.[67] Finally free blacks comprised nearly double the proportion of all slave owners in 1850 in the city when compared with Charleston Neck.[68] Just as the economic benefits of artisan work allowed many free people of color to maintain their residences within the city proper in the years after 1840, it appears that slave ownership among free people of color took on greater importance there as well.

The racial-occupational portrait that emerges from this examination of census data, city directories, and legislative petitions reveals the fundamental importance of skilled labor to the city's free blacks and the way it, along with other factors, contributed to the ability of free people of color to achieve economic and social distinction in the city. Skilled labor allowed a segment of black Charlestonians to achieve freedom, economic security, and family stability and enabled them to become an indelible part of their local community. Through the higher wages they received and their ability to cultivate social links with both prominent whites and other black artisans, these individuals would have gained opportunities simply unavailable to Charleston's many unskilled or marginally skilled workers. Further, the presence in the city of blacks across the class spectrum would have made even the modestly successful black artisans all the more distinct. Because of the diffuse nature of black residences in Charleston, artisans gained the opportunity to distinguish themselves as a class apart through their occupations, consumption patterns, and relationships.

Yet ultimately engagement with artisan work was never enough to provide the kind of social stability or community permanence many free blacks sought. While artisan and entrepreneurial occupations were some of the highest positions to which free blacks could aspire, these occupations alone could not entirely shield free blacks from the pressure that increasingly mounted against black freedom during the nineteenth century. Because they constituted such a small portion of the population of Charleston (unlike in Cartagena), free black artisans were forced to compete in many occupations with both whites and enslaved people. Thus while skilled work was essential to free black efforts to achieve economic success and social prestige, the fact that artisan occupations stretched across race and class divisions often meant that while it was a necessary precondition of social status, skilled work was not in and of itself sufficient. Such distinctions as complexion took on greater importance, and free artisans of color relied on other means—namely slave ownership and voluntary associations—to demonstrate their engagement with a shared set of cultural values and to signal their acceptability to white neighbors. While skilled labor constituted a central component to the ability of some free blacks in Charleston to achieve economic success and social distinction, industriousness and skill alone could not shield free blacks from the pressure that mounted against black freedom as the antebellum period wore on.

In Cartagena artisans of African descent likewise used their skills and earnings to establish themselves as a class apart from less skilled, lower-class black laborers. Like black Charlestonians living in the city proper, artisans of color in Cartagena used their skills not just to gain economic stability but also to maintain residences in racially mixed, wealthier neighborhoods inside the walled city, where they could more easily cultivate relationships with prominent Spaniard and creole whites. While artisans of color living in the mostly black neighborhood of Getsemaní were often heads of household, people of African descent living within the walled city tended to occupy parts of larger residences owned by whites, usually living on lower floors while the owner or head of the household occupied the higher ones. Some artisans occupied storefronts or offices attached to these larger white-owned homes, though their exact living arrangements are unclear. Living inside the walled city and maintaining workshops there would have been an important distinction for artisans of African descent, facilitating interaction with prominent neighbors and engagement with the social and cultural life of the city. The ability to maintain a residence or workshop in prominent neighborhoods offered free artisans of color in Cartagena the ability to accentuate their class status and social distinction through physical separation. Living in racially mixed neighborhoods separated from the lower classes in Getsemaní, free artisans of color physically distanced themselves and emphasized their status as part of a distinct socioeconomic class.

The house of Spanish merchant Don Bartholomé Javier Marquecho, located in the neighborhood of Santo Toribio, seems typical of the living arrangements of many black and *pardo* artisans in the city. Located on Calle del Dulce Nombre de Maria, Marquecho's house is recorded as "Casa Alta" number 26. Along with Don Marquecho lived his wife, Doña Maria Manuela de Leon, and their children, Don Joseph Javier, three; Don Adrian Joseph, two; and Doña Ana Theresa, aged eight months. Another Spanish man, Don Joseph de Tela, aged thirty, also occupied the house. In addition to these Spaniards (all of whom received honorific titles, even eight-month-old Ana Theresa), Maria Rosario, a twenty-year-old "mulata libre," also lived in the house, though her exact relationship to the rest of the family is unclear.[69] Listed at the bottom of the residence were five enslaved people: Maria Petrona, eleven; Maria Pio, twenty; Maria Francisca, twenty-three; Juan Ygnacio, twenty-three; and Juan Joseph, fourteen. All of these enslaved people were of mixed racial ancestry, recorded as *mulato or mulata*, though their exact relationship to Marquecho is unclear. Finally, the house is listed with an "Asesoría (carpintería)," a carpenter's workshop. In it worked Manuel Ynitola, a *negro* of unknown age and marital status. Though he did not own the house, Ynitola appears to have used his skills as a carpenter to maintain a residence and workspace inside the walled city, an important distinction in colonial Cartagena and likely a point of pride for Ynitola.[70]

Many other skilled craft workers lived in similar arrangements, occupying workshops and residences attached to the houses of prominent whites within the walled city. For example *pardo* shoemaker Manuel de Herrera, along with his two teenage sons, Thoribio and Julian Estevan, occupied a workshop on Calle de Nuestra Señora de los Reyes in the Santo Toribio neighborhood. The head of that house (Casa Alta no. 4) was Don Rafael de Escovar, a royal official, who lived there with his wife, Doña Mariana; their free servant, Baltasar Ysaquierre; Ysaquierre's wife, Theodora Alvarez; and their daughter, Estefana. Seven enslaved people occupied their residence as well, four female and three male, ranging in age from twelve to twenty nine. Casa Alta no. 4 was also home to five other households, all of which were headed by prominent whites, mostly Spaniards, most of which included enslaved people. These households, along with Escovar's, occupied the upper floors of what appears to have been a very large edifice. Listed below these prominent royal officials, military leaders, and slave owners were people including Manuel de Herrera and his family, who occupied the "casa en lo bajo," or the lower portions of the house. This designation likely meant they occupied the first floor of the house, with the house's more prominent residents occupying the upper floors away from the noise, smells, and dirt of Cartagena's busy streets. Herrera, a mulatto shoemaker and militia member, lived there with his wife, Ygnacia Vallestras; his aforementioned sons, Estevan and Thoribio; and three other children: Tomás, Maria Merced, and Pedro Volazco. Seven other households made up this lower portion, including two black *tallistas* (woodcarvers), a *pardo* silversmith, and a black carpenter, each of whom were also militia members.[71]

Similarly *pardo* brothers Manuel, José Concepción, and Mateo Blanquezel, all tailors, kept a workshop attached to a large house elsewhere in the neighborhood—Casa Alta no. 19—located on the Plaza de Santo Thorivio. The 1777 census reveals that the head of this household was Don Juan Marzan, who lived there with his wife, Doña Feliciana Hurtado de Mendoza, and their seven children, each of whom received the same honorific title. In addition to this family, eight other households and a total of thirty-three people occupied this house, though the Blanquezel brothers were not listed among them. Included within that thirty-three are Joseph and Pedro de Vega, a silversmith and tailor, sons of *quarterón* Joseph Antonio; Mauricio Yturre, a *pardo* shoemaker and son of a retired militia sergeant; and Joseph Montaño and Pasqual Hurtado, both tailors. The house's workshop was occupied by Maria Dominga Espinosa, *negra,* and Marcela Josefa de Caña, *parda,* though they are not listed with occupations. It seems possible this is the workshop taken over by the Blanquezel brothers three years later.[72]

These examples help illustrate the residential dynamics of free black artisans in late eighteenth-century Cartagena and reveal some of the social and economic benefits of skilled craftwork for African-descended people in the city. Whether as heads of household or as renters, artisans of African descent gained tangible benefits from the skilled nature of their work as they acquired the resources to maintain residences and workshops within the walled city in Cartagena. By maintaining residences in racially mixed, often upper-class neighborhoods such as Santo Toribio, Santa Catalina, and Las Mercedes, free people of color would have interacted daily with other prominent community members, both white and black, distinguishing themselves from the black lower classes in the city. These artisans of African descent were well-off enough financially that they were able to maintain residences in the heart of the walled city, living among royal officials, military leaders, and other prominent whites. Their proximity to these individuals and other black and *pardo* artisans, coupled with the service-oriented nature of their trades, likely allowed them to craft reputations for themselves as industrious and respectable members of their communities, neighborhoods, and cities.[73] For a shoemaker such as Manuel Herrera, living and working on the first floor of a building occupied by so many wealthy whites and Spaniards would likely have offered him a relationship with prominent members of the community that was unattainable to unskilled and semiskilled blacks working around the city's ports and wharves or in Getsemaní. Through skilled labor free people of color were able to cultivate relationships with prominent whites, establish reputations for industry and respectability, and maintain a physical distance from the black lower classes that mirrored the social distance they established through their engagement with skilled occupations.

CONCLUSION

In port cities across the African Americas, skilled labor and artisan occupations played a central role in the lives of free people of African descent and their efforts to achieve social prestige and economic stability. As tailors, shoemakers, carpenters, and barbers, and in a host of other occupations, free people of color used skills and hard work to provide for the needs of urban populations and to provide themselves with a wide array of opportunities not typically available to their enslaved or unskilled counterparts. As artisans free people of color achieved an uncommon level of economic success, affording them with social stability, economic security, and for some, a strong claim to respectability within their local community. Skilled work crucially supported efforts to achieve social advancement by urban free people of color, who were more secure economically than the many free and enslaved unskilled or marginally skilled people of African descent that lived in American port cities,.

Yet the nature of this advancement in Cartagena and Charleston often differed significantly. While artisans of color in Cartagena used their residence inside the walled city to create physical distance between themselves and the black lower classes that matched the social distance they wished to emphasize, their counterparts in Charleston were not so easily able to maintain such distinctions, though after 1840 skilled work did allow free blacks in Charleston to maintain residences in the heart of the city. Beyond these residential distinctions, the public dynamic of respectability represents a crucial distinction in the worlds of free people of color in Spanish America and in the U.S. South. In Cartagena nearly all artisans of color also joined the city's voluntary militia. Skilled labor directly affected the ability of free people of color to access this crucial public institution, and their status as militiamen afforded them the opportunity to gain concessions of various sorts that supported their efforts to achieve economic and social advancement. In Charleston, where no such public dynamic existed, the city's much smaller population of free artisans of color looked to the support of neighbors and friends to achieve similar ends. Free artisans of color worked to construct and demonstrate publicly their commitment to shared cultural values with the city's white elites by founding voluntary organizations capable of supporting the free colored elite and, crucially, through slave ownership. Because free blacks in Charleston shared artisan work with both whites and slaves, they often turned to slave ownership as a means of furthering their individual wealth and gaining the social prestige that came with entering the slave-owning class.

This social distinction often came at the expense of a broader racial identification. Charleston's free artisans of color actively distanced themselves from enslaved people and the free black poor, and they declined to use their social connections and reputations to push for the broader political reforms attempted by their northern counterparts—the abolition of slavery and black citizenship rights in particular. While the free *pardo* artisans of Cartagena were active in the local militia and the war for independence from Spain, they were fairly measured in their use of their social prominence and demographic advantage to demand racial reforms, actively placing both social and physical distance between themselves and the city's more numerous black popular classes. Yet despite crucial differences in white attitudes toward racial difference in Spanish America and the United States, the social and cultural worlds of free artisans of color reveal broad parallels in the experience of black freedom in the urban Atlantic.

Chapter 4

INSTITUTIONS AND ASSOCIATIONAL LIFE

The community [has lost] an Honest, Upright,
Industrious, intelligent member.

Comments delivered upon the death of
Richard Holloway, Charleston, 1845

This . . . increases the unjust pretensions of
Pardos who aspire to leave the sphere of their birth.

White militia officer commenting on privileges of
pardo militiamen, Panama, 1779

Organizational and institutional affiliations were central to the lives of free people of color as they worked to shield themselves from racial discrimination and improve their lives during the eighteenth and nineteenth centuries. While free people of color gained economic stability and a measure of social prestige through their work as artisans, many within that group sought to bolster further their claims to expanded rights and social privileges through their involvement with a variety of institutions and organizations. In Cartagena, Charleston, and throughout the urban Americas, free people of color utilized their ties to a variety of mutual aid and benevolent societies, voluntary organizations, and military and religious institutions to achieve social advancement and distinction. From elite social clubs to voluntary militia units, associational and institutional affiliations held a central place in the social and cultural worlds of the Atlantic world's free people of color.

In Charleston some free people of color belonged to the city's several African American mutual aid and benevolent societies. These groups supported a select group of free people of color through the distribution of mutual aid to members and their families and offered an opportunity for free people of color in Charleston to associate with others matching their social, economic, and complexional profiles. These voluntary associations discussed ideas about racial uplift and respectability throughout the early national and antebellum eras, and some free people of color used their public affiliations with these organizations to demonstrate their ability to thrive in freedom. By publicly establishing themselves as models of freedom, free Charlestonians of color challenged—if indirectly and for the most part unsuccessfully—whites' view that people of African descent could function only in slavery. By maintaining exclusive, private institutions, some of which existed explicitly to cultivate bourgeois respectability, elite free people of color in Charleston signaled to the broader white community that they shared social and cultural values with whites and deserved a place in the community life of the city, even as they declined to pursue a broader agenda of political reform.

In Cartagena, meanwhile, free people of African descent used their affiliation with very different types of organizations and institutions to achieve some similar ends. First, both free and enslaved people of African descent maintained *cabildos de nación*, organizations with origins as religious brotherhoods that by the late eighteenth century had largely shifted into mutual aid societies linking those who identified with particular West African ethnic groups. Though the groups' explicit links to West Africa and their inclusion of enslaved as well as free people make them distinct from the mutual aid societies in Charleston, they nevertheless served some similar purposes: they provided financial assistance to members, particularly for burials and funerals, and fostered a sense of community among people of African descent with common backgrounds, in this case around ethnic identity. Likewise, though evidence for these organizations in Cartagena is scant, it seems likely that these brotherhoods also fostered a degree of social prestige among their members and leaders. In addition to their involvement with the cabildos, free people of color in Cartagena looked to the city's voluntary militia as an institutional means of gaining social advancement within their community and in the eyes of the Crown. Joining the voluntary militia was only a possibility for men of a certain economic class, and thus the militia was populated largely by African-descended artisans, men who already possessed the various distinctions skilled work could confer. More broadly, however, the membership of free people of color in Cartagena's militia increased their bargaining power and allowed them to gain the distinction of the *fuero militar* and a variety of other concessions from both local and royal officials.

This access to a crucial public institution and the channels of royal authority represented one of the most fundamental differences between Latin America and the United States in the lives of free people of color and their efforts to establish social distinction. In Cartagena free people of color derived a variety of privileges—special legal considerations and concessions from local and royal authorities in particular—from their membership in a public, corporately ordered society. By providing a crucial public service, free people of color used their institutional status to support their claims to expanded rights, an approach that was simply unavailable to free people of color in Charleston. In Charleston free people of color instead focused on cultivating bourgeois respectability grounded in the cultivation of personal relationships and the demonstration of the kinds of moral habits and cultural values privileged by the city's white elite. By establishing and joining mutual aid and voluntary societies, free people of color could publicly demonstrate to the broader community their commitment to these private values, even as they sometimes couched discussions of personal respectability within a broader rhetoric of racial uplift. By modeling their private lives around such concepts as sobriety, piety, and industriousness, prominent free people of color in Charleston distinguished themselves from enslaved people and culti-vated relationships with wealthy whites in ways that supported their broader efforts to achieve social prestige. This distinction between the public, institu-tional nature of respectability in Cartagena and the more personal bourgeois respectability possible in Charleston affected not just the organizational and associational lives of free people of color in these cities but shaped the social lives of free people of color in a wide variety of ways.

MUTUAL AID SOCIETIES AND VOLUNTARY ORGANIZATIONS IN CHARLESTON, SOUTH CAROLINA

Comprised largely of the city's sizeable free artisan class, Charleston's black and colored voluntary organizations provided a way for free people of color to support their collective interests, to gain a measure of social distinction among the city's African-descended population, and to establish themselves as models of both freedom and respectability in eighteenth- and nineteenth-century Charleston. Free people of color founded and maintained at least six different voluntary organizations in Charleston between 1790 and 1850, most of which were organized to serve broadly similar purposes. The Brown Fellowship Society, Friendly Union Society, Friendly Moralist Society, and Society of Free Dark Men and Humane Brotherhood all existed as mutual aid organizations, providing members and their families with financial security and support, particularly when a member fell ill or died. Some of these groups maintained private burial plots in which they provided space for their members and their families, as the churches to which these men belonged often excluded blacks and mulattoes from their burial grounds. Other organizations in the city were dedicated more specifically to moral improvement, education, and racial uplift. The Minor's Moralist Society, for example, founded in 1803, provided education to "indigent" and orphaned free children of color in the city, and the Clionian Debating Society sought to fulfill the intellectual aspirations of Charleston's free people of color, offering a venue in which members of the city's free black elite debated the political and philosophical questions of the day.

Many of these voluntary associations had counterparts in white society, as free people of color in Charleston engaged with the local intellectual world in addition to broader national and international ideas. The Brown Fellowship Society may have taken inspiration from white Masonic lodges in the city, for example. The Friendly Moralist Society developed rules that paralleled those of Charleston's German Friendly Society, founded decades earlier. The Clionian Debating Society took up many of the same questions debated by the Cliosophic Debating Society (founded in 1838) and, later, the Chrestomathic Literary Society (1848), both of which found homes at the College of Charleston. Like white voluntary societies, organizations established by free people of color "bound together" members by their "financial status" and "consumer habits," as well as their belief in "thrift, industry, sobriety, and piety."[1]

To varying extents, as other scholars have shown, the parallels between black and white voluntary societies reveal the desire among a portion of Charleston's free people of color to gain acceptance by the city's white elite.[2] Yet, in addition to white counterparts, these societies have roots as well in West African institutional traditions and held meaning and importance for African Americans that extended far beyond mirroring white social mores. For one thing the focus on burial, funerary, and mourning practices by these societies at least suggests some kind of link with voluntary and secret societies in West Africa. More directly, however, the concern with respectability, social advancement, and moral uplift places the members of these societies well within the mainstream of early nineteenth-century free black thought, as the black voluntary societies in Charleston parallel neatly those found in many other U.S. cities. Thus while historians have typically analyzed groups such as the Brown Fellowship as evidence of the efforts of Charleston's free colored aristocracy to engage with white society, a broader consideration of the role of voluntary organizations among free people of color reveals they also served as a way for a much larger portion of the city's free colored population to maintain social links with individuals matching their racial and economic profile, to bolster social prestige, and to establish themselves as models of freedom in a society that by and large viewed African-descended people as suited only for slavery.[3] By establishing, maintaining, and joining voluntary organizations, free people of color in Charleston countered white notions of black freedom that saw free people of color as dangerous, poor, and susceptible to lives of vice and crime. While the members of these organizations rarely (if ever) pushed for the kinds of racial reforms advocated by their northern counterparts—black citizenship and voting rights or the abolition of slavery, for example—free people of color in Charleston used their affiliation with these organizations to cultivate reputations as respectable in the face of persistent white racism and negative attitudes toward the freedom of African-descended people.

FREE BLACK VOLUNTARY SOCIETIES IN CHARLESTON, 1790–1815

Throughout the early national and antebellum eras, the Brown Fellowship Society was unquestionably the most prominent of Charleston's African American voluntary organizations, and its membership rolls included many of the city's wealthiest free people of color—namely its mixed-race, light-skinned artisan elite. Organized in 1790 by James Mitchell, George Bampfield, William Cattle, George Bedon, and Samuel Saltus, the Brown Fellowship Society functioned as a source of mutual aid and financial relief to members, their families, and, at least in theory, the broader community of free people of color in Charleston. The society's rules and regulations stated that it was formed in order to "relieve . . . in the hour of their distresses, sickness, and death" the "unhappy situation" of members and their families, as well as a select number of "worthy" poor petitioners. When members fell ill or otherwise became incapable of providing for their families, the Brown Fellowship Society used funds regularly collected from members to provide financial assistance. Sick members, in addition to being called upon by their fellow members, received a stipend of $1.50 per week from the organization.[4]

Further, the society regularly helped defray the cost of funerals and burials for deceased members as well. As most of the founders and early members of the Brown Fellowship Society were parishioners of St. Phillip's Episcopal Church—parish home for many of Charleston's aristocratic white families and its mulatto elite—but excluded from the church's burial ground, the Brown Fellowship Society maintained a private burial lot north of the city in which members could be interred.[5] When society members died unable to afford funeral services and burial, the society used their funds to provide financial assistance to their families. Members also mourned the death of members by displaying "a black crape around the left arm."[6]

The society also provided assistance to the children of deceased members as well, educating them and setting them up in apprenticeships. As nearly all members of the Brown Fellowship Society were counted among Charleston's free colored artisan class, opportunities for apprenticeship would have been ample for such children, many of whom likely gained membership in the organization when they came of age. Finally, in keeping with their motto of "Charity and Benevolence," the Brown Fellowship Society also accepted applications for assistance from "any poor colored orphan or adult, being free, whose case requires needful assistance."[7] Although the society's regulations leave unclear the process for deciding who could receive such assistance as well as the extent to which such aid was ever doled out in practice, the organization's willingness to accept petitions from nonmembers suggests at least some concern for the broader community of free people of color in the city, even if, like its membership, it only extended to people of relatively light complexion. In 1833 the society passed a resolution approving the creation of an education committee empowered to hire instructors as necessary to provide for the instruction of the children deemed eligible by the society's constitution. The committee was also assigned the task of assessing the "progress of learning" of each child and reporting those found "inattentive at school."[8]

In addition to its direct functions (and in some ways because of them), the Brown Fellowship Society provided members with a measure of distinction and helped facilitate important social connections in the community. With membership limited to just fifty members and a substantial initiation fee of fifty dollars, as well as the requirement to pay regular dues, the Brown Fellowship Society restricted its membership to very few of Charleston's wealthiest free men of color. Membership, therefore, offered a degree of distinction for certain free people of color in Charleston, cementing their status among the city's elites. The society tried to reinforce their respectable reputation at their meetings: they not only required "that a decent, peaceable, and orderly behavior be observed" at their meetings but imposed a fine of twenty-five cents "for taking God's name in vain."[9] The distinction afforded by the society was likely mutually reinforcing: members were each relatively wealthy and well-known in the community as individuals but gained greater benefit through their association with other free men of color matching their economic, occupational, social, and complexional profiles. Indeed, as historians Michael Johnson and James Roark noted, the membership roll of the Brown Fellowship Society reads like "a social directory of the free mulatto elite."[10] At its most basic level, the Brown Fellowship Society allowed a small number of Charleston's wealthiest residents of mixed racial ancestry to strengthen links of a tightly knit community within the city's broader population of free people of color.[11]

The experience of free colored Charlestonian Richard Holloway—his entry into the society and the connections and reputation it supported—helps reveal how voluntary association could have a real impact on the individual and family circumstances of free people of color in the city. Born in 1776 in Essex County, Maryland, Holloway worked in his youth as a sailor. Of mixed racial ancestry, he stood about "five feet eight inches high" and had "black wooly hair, brown eyes" and a "yellowish complexion"—a characteristic he

FIGURE 4.1
*Portrait of Richard
Holloway, from
Holloway family
scrapbook. Source:
Avery Research
Center.*

shared with many of his Brown Fellowship counterparts. Holloway and his family rose to become some of the best-known and wealthiest free people of color in antebellum Charleston, and many of his social connections among the mulatto elite of Charleston stemmed from his affiliation with the society. Shortly after settling in Charleston, Holloway established a friendship with James Mitchell, one of the society's founders. On January 19, 1803, Holloway married Mitchell's daughter Elizabeth in St. Philip's Church. It was in that same year that he gained admittance to the Brown Fellowship Society. In 1806 Mitchell gifted Holloway a plot of land that Holloway established into a successful carpentry business, one that would provide for the Holloway family for generations.[12]

Holloway achieved uncommon success as an artisan in Charleston, success facilitated at least in part by his entry into the Brown Fellowship Society and the social links it strengthened. In 1826 he agreed to build a shop for tailor Joseph Humphries. Not only was Humphries a member of the Brown Fellowship Society, but he and Holloway were cofounders of the Minor's Moralist Society as well. For sixty-five dollars Holloway agreed to build Humphries a twelve-by-eighteen-foot shop, including all materials except the front door. Humphries's payment would be half in cash, and half "in taloring [*sic*], furnishing whatever artical [*sic*] in the taylors [*sic*] line that the said Holloway may order."[13] This arrangement, in which Holloway exchanged carpentry services for tailoring, was likely facilitated through their comembership in the Brown Fellowship Society.

As successful artisans, both Holloway and Humphries gained membership in the society, cementing their status as members of Charleston's mulatto elite. The two also lived just a few blocks away from one another. The agreement reached between these two men begins to reveal the way voluntary associations linked racial and class distinctions in important ways for free people of color in Charleston. First, both men were clearly within the city's free colored elite. That Humphries could afford the construction of a new tailor's shop suggests a level of wealth only the luckiest and most industrious free people of color in Charleston could obtain. Holloway, for his part, was even wealthier, and his agreement to accept half of his payment in tailoring services suggests he owned the amount and type of clothing to make such a payment worthwhile. Additionally the arrangement to exchange services reveals the way fraternal organizations such as the Brown Fellowship Society could facilitate social and financial links between members. In a city home to hundreds of free black and enslaved carpenters and tailors, it seems significant that as two of very few comembers in an elite voluntary organization, Holloway and Humphries struck such a deal with one another. Perhaps the decision to enlist one another's services not only reflects the way the Brown Fellowship Society facilitated social and financial relationships but also reveals a broader impulse among Charleston's free mulatto elite to support one another, maintaining and strengthening ties within their group.

Holloway was also an active member of the Cumberland Street Methodist Episcopal Church in Charleston. He served there as a class leader, presumably offering religious instruction to other African American parishioners. In November 1821 he traveled from Charleston to Savannah on church business. Traveling outside of one's community was dangerous for free people of color during the antebellum era, all the more so when crossing state lines. As such Holloway was furnished with an explanation of his business from a preacher in Savannah. It explained that he was a "freeman of reputable character" who had come to Savannah "in the capacity of an exhorter in the Methodist Episcopal Church."[14] In 1830 Holloway purchased a subscription to the *Wesleyan Journal,* the first Methodist weekly newspaper in the South and the second published in the United States.[15]

When Holloway died in 1845, members of the Brown Fellowship Society and the Cumberland Street Methodist Episcopal Church delivered exhortations testifying to his unique character and shared them with his wife, Elizabeth. They noted Holloway's outstanding traits, revealing in plain language the contours of Christian respectability for Charleston's free mulatto elite, characteristics both the church and the Brown Fellowship Society endeavored to foster. They mourned that "the church have lost a pious and useful member, a sound and zealous exhorter and a faithful leader. The poor have lost a true friend; Society an ornament. The community an Honest, Upright, Industrious, intelligent member; and We his brother leaders one in whom we could confide with assurance for counsel and advice." They urged one another to "endeavor to be like him—like him in piety: ardent, deep, devoted to his God; In charity: kind, benevolent, liberal, remembering the poor; In friendship: with candor, openness, and hospitality; In courteousness, mild, civil, compliant; In temper: gentle, even, composed; In conduct, living for God and the salvation of dying men." They prayed they might be like Holloway, "useful in our day and generation as he also was eminently useful."[16] In their mourning of Holloway's death, his fellow parishioners and society members made clear the traits they sought to emulate and support within the membership of the society.

Despite its noble intentions, the founding of the Brown Fellowship Society seemed to have unnerved some prominent white Charleston residents. Just a few months after the society's founding, the South Carolina legislature expressed anxiety that blacks in the city were being actively introduced to freemasonry. In February 1791 a legislative committee presented their concern over black Charlestonians both free and enslaved "assembl[ing] privately in great numbers under the pretence [sic] of being initiated in the mysteries of freemasonry." The committee expressed anxiety that under the guise of freemasonry, "some nefarious person may communicate to the slaves of this state a bond of union prejudicial to the peace of the good people" of South Carolina.[17] While the committee did not name the Brown Fellowship Society specifically, the broad connection between the society's stated goals and the tenets of freemasonry, in addition to the timing, certainly suggest they may have been referring to that organization—perhaps one among others.

During the 1790s in Charleston, there appear to have been at least two different white Masonic lodges that may have offered a model for prominent black Charlestonians' organizational aspirations. Further the frequent exchange at the port of Charleston of news and information from both the North and broader Caribbean world would also have provided black Charlestonians information about freemasonry elsewhere in the United States and Atlantic world, including information about African American freemasonry in particular.[18] In their rules and regulations, the founders of the Brown Fellowship Society called attention to the models for their organization in the city, noting that they had observed "the method of many other well disposed persons of this State," who "by entering into particular societies" had dedicated themselves to "relieving the wants and miseries, and promoting the welfare and happiness of one another." In the years immediately following the American Revolution, black Freemasonry spread rapidly in northern cities, particularly places such as Boston and Philadelphia. The founding principles of the Brown Fellowship Society, "Christian love, charity, and benevolence," reveal that free black Charlestonians held commitments similar to those of Masonic brotherhoods. Given Charleston's ties to other American port cities, it seems possible that the city's free black elite may have seen in Freemasonry another opportunity to achieve social distinction, particularly through common organizational membership with whites. It seems probable as well that Freemasonry's commitment to the ideals of fraternity, equality, and charity may have been part of its appeal to Charleston's free people of color. These same ideals, however, were likely at the core of white South Carolinians objections the involvement of "free negroes" in the institution.[19]

Peter Hinks has argued that for many early black Masons in northern cities, part of the appeal of Freemasonry was its potential to "overcome racial otherness and social distance," as well as its ability to provide a "racially informed fraternal identity that was portable in the Atlantic world."[20] The South Carolina legislature's worry about black involvement in Freemasonry —likely fueled by the founding of the Brown Fellowship Society—perhaps suggests that this appeal reached the Atlantic ports of the United States South. Not only did the Brown Fellowship Society allow a small segment of Charleston's free blacks to achieve social distinction and respectability, but these organizations also exhibited at least some parallels with northern African American masonic lodges. Though the links between Brown Fellowship Society members—namely complexion and class—differed significantly from the broader ties of Africanness that bound together members of northern lodges, members used both organizations to demonstrate publicly their commitment to a shared set of values and achieve a degree of social distinction normally not afforded to people of African descent.[21]

While potential Masonic links of the Brown Fellowship Society may have offered free black Charlestonians a source of common identification in the Atlantic world, the society clearly held more immediate advantages within their local community. Through their public affiliation with an exclusive social organization dedicated to charity and benevolence, Brown Fellowship Society members signaled to the broader Charleston community a commitment to values shared among black and white residents alike. As relatively wealthy free people of color dedicated to the assistance of one another as well as the free black or colored poor, Brown Fellowship Society members carved out spaces of respectability for themselves in Charleston, raising their individual and collective social profiles. In a region where enslaved people made up the vast majority of the local population, Brown Fellowship

members used their public affiliation to offer a counterexample of the capabilities of African-descended people, living as models of respectability.

The Brown Fellowship Society's exclusivity was bolstered by the fact that
membership in the organization seems to have been difficult to obtain. Aside
from the high initiation fee, there simply were not many available openings
in the organization. Between its founding in 1790 and the publication of its
rules and regulations in 1844, the organization admitted a total of 132 individuals, including the founding members. While membership was technically
open to all free people of color over twenty-one years old, membership was
often granted on the basis of legacy, as new members were often related to
existing ones. For example, founding member George Bedon's son George H.
gained admittance thirteen years after the group's founding, in 1804. William
Clark gained entry in 1804 as well, and three more Clarks gained entry later:
James R. in 1829, William B. in 1830, and John E. in 1844. William Cooper,
who rose to become one of the society's most prominent leaders, gained admittance in 1807, and his son Thomas became a member in 1829. Many other
examples exist where new members share a surname with older members, at
least suggesting a familial relationship where the exact specifics remain unclear. This process of succession by younger family members was by design,
as the initiation fees for the sons or male heirs of existing members were one
quarter of what they were for new outside members.[22]

In 1817 the society expelled a man named George Logan, calling attention to the need to maintain unassailable reputations within the Charleston
community and, perhaps, to the need to police carefully boundaries between
slavery and freedom. Logan joined the society in October 1800 but was expelled in 1817 when the society discovered that he had attempted to enslave
a free black man named Robinson. Historian Robert Harris points to this case
as evidence of the Brown Fellowship Society's "concern for the rights of all
free Afro-Americans in Charleston and not just the welfare of its ingroup."
That the society labeled his actions "base and notorious" suggests as well that
they could ill afford any of its exclusive membership's being associated with
criminality or vice, lest his individual reputation reflect poorly on the group
as a whole. Finally that the affair began as a result of wrongful enslavement
suggests the concern of free people of color for ensuring that the dividing
lines between slavery and freedom never be blurred.[23]

While the Brown Fellowship Society may have in theory accepted
applications for aid from Charleston's free black poor, free people of color
founded a new organization in 1803, the Minor's Moralist Society, dedicated
exclusively to that end. Six of the city's most prominent free black leaders—
Richard Holloway and Joseph Humphries, as well as Thomas S. Bonneau,

William Clark, William Cooper, and Carlos Huger—founded the organization; they all later gained entry into the Brown Fellowship Society. Some of these men held membership in other black voluntary societies as well, including Bonneau and Huger, who were members of the Friendly Union Society, and Holloway, who was a member in the Friendly Moralist Society. Like other voluntary organizations in Charleston, the Minor's Moralist Society was limited to fifty members, each of whom contributed an initial five-dollar fee and thereafter paid twenty-five cents per month. Unlike the Brown Fellowship Society, whose efforts were primarily focused on supporting members and their families, the Minor's Moralist Society was founded explicitly to provide education to the city's orphaned and "indigent" free children of color—though they left unclear whether this was open only to individuals of relatively light complexion, like the founders, or if it was also open to darker-skinned free people of color as well.

The Minor's Moralist Society likely conferred many of the same social benefits as membership in the Brown Fellowship Society. The group's exclusivity meant that affiliation with this organization conferred a degree of social prestige within Charleston. The founders and members of the organization took on a position of leadership within the city's free colored community, offering education to those who possessed freedom but few other opportunities for social mobility. Those affiliated with this society gained the opportunity not just to distinguish themselves as leaders but also to signal to the broader community their commitment to a shared set of values, including education and moral improvement. Rather than functioning as a social club for individuals matching a particular complexional and economic profile, the Minor's Moralist Society reveals a significant commitment among relatively wealthy free people of color in Charleston to pursuing a broader agenda of individual improvement and racial uplift through education, even if it remained within the sphere of free people of mixed racial ancestry.

While the activities and structure of the Brown Fellowship Society suggest a desire among prominent free blacks to align their comportment with that of prominent whites, the concern of at least some Brown Fellowship Society members with the welfare of free people of color more broadly suggests at least a slightly broader worldview. Some evidence suggests these education efforts were at least relatively successful as well. For example one beneficiary of the Minor's Moralists' efforts, Daniel Alexander Payne, later opened his own school for free children of color in Charleston and went on to become one of the leaders of the African Methodist Episcopal Church and black educational efforts during Reconstruction. At one time Payne taught more than sixty pupils in his Charleston school, but South Carolina's legislature forced him to cease his efforts in 1835. Facing growing pressure from the state, the Minor's Moralist Society ended its education efforts twelve years later, in 1847.[24]

Free Charlestonians of color who desired the benefits of associational membership but were unable to gain entry to the Brown Fellowship Society often joined one of a number of other voluntary organizations—some of which not only paralleled the goals and structure of the Brown Fellowship Society but were also used as stepping-stones to gaining membership in that organization. One such organization was the Friendly Union Society, organized in May 1813. Like the Brown Fellowship Society, the Friendly Union was established as "a Society for mutual aid in the time of distress," providing aid and funeral assistance for its members. Along with the Friendly Moralist Society, the Friendly Union Society seems to have borrowed its naming conventions from the German Friendly Society, a white organization founded in the city in 1766. Its purpose and mission, however, were modeled after the Brown Fellowship. Like the Brown Fellowship, the society's membership was limited to fifty individuals, specifying they were required to be "men of respectable character." The Friendly Union Society likewise provided assistance to members and their families in times of need and distress, particularly following death. Likely not as wealthy as their counterparts in the Brown Fellowship Society, the Friendly Union Society seemed to have functioned as a parallel organization. Nevertheless their membership rolls often intersected, as Friendly Unionists occasionally broke into the ranks of the Brown Fellowship.[25]

In total 28 of 111 members of the Friendly Union Society between 1813 and 1844 also gained membership in the Brown Fellowship Society. Among these fully half of the 8 founders of the Friendly Union Society later became Brown Fellowship members. In April 1817 John Mishaw joined the Brown Fellowship Society, followed the next month by John Lee. William W. Seymour joined three years later in 1820. Peter H. Marchant followed in 1828. Of these 4 founding members of the Friendly Union Society, none are listed in the organization's published rules and membership lists as having resigned or been excluded, suggesting they may have maintained simultaneous membership in both organizations. Both Lee and Marchant became not just Brown Fellowship members but also leaders in that organization.

Others first joined the Friendly Union Society even though they had fathers or other relatives who were Brown Fellowship Society members. Benjamin T. Huger, a tailor, gained membership in the Friendly Union in 1814 and in the Brown Fellowship three years later in 1817. James Huger joined the Friendly Union in 1829 and the Brown Fellowship in 1830. Though the exact relationship is unclear, they are almost certainly related to Carlos Huger, a leader in Charleston's free black community who gained membership in the

Brown Fellowship Society in 1801 and who later served as one of the founders of the Minor's Moralist Society. Others—Peter Campbell, Robert Hopton,
John Brown Mushington—all became members of the Friendly Union Society
before later gaining a legacy admission to the Brown Fellowship Society,
suggesting perhaps that some prominent free blacks joined the Friendly
Union Society while they waited for membership space to open in the Brown
Fellowship. Another member, Richmond Kinloch, became a Friendly Union
member in 1816 and later gained entry into the Brown Fellowship Society
in 1828. Richmond's son Robert followed the opposite path. Robert Kinloch
became a member of the Brown Fellowship Society in 1843 and the following year became a member of the Friendly Unionist Society, one of the few
members to move in that direction.

That so many free men of color affiliated themselves with both the Brown
Fellowship and Friendly Union societies reveals a strong link between the
two organizations and suggests that both would have offered similar social
benefits for their members. Further the path to membership for many Brown
Fellowship members suggests the society functioned as a gateway to something of a free colored aristocracy in early nineteenth-century Charleston.
One could be born into membership, while limited space existed for other
individuals to move into it over time. Despite the greater exclusivity and social prominence of the Brown Fellowship Society, however, both the Friendly
Union Society and Brown Fellowship Society provided social space for select
free men of color in Charleston to demonstrate publicly their status as industrious, pious, sober, and respectable members of the local community.

FREE BLACK VOLUNTARY SOCIETIES IN CHARLESTON, 1815–50

A shift occurred within the black voluntary societies in Charleston after the
early national period, as a new generation of free people of color, many of
whom never experienced slavery, became concerned not just with maintaining their individual freedom and supporting the members of an elite cohort
but also with the cultivation of social respectability that might demonstrate
the fitness of free people of color for inclusion in community life. Although
complexional distinctions remained salient in the city throughout the antebellum era, the rhetoric of these later voluntary associations engaged a
broader national discourse about racial uplift. One such organization, the
Friendly Moralist Society, was founded in 1838, much later than either the
Brown Fellowship or Friendly Union Society. While the operative referent
for the Brown Fellowship Society seems to have been Freemasonry, the
Friendly Moralist Society was more likely influenced by the growing reform
movements of the mid-nineteenth century. The Friendly Moralist Society
was focused far more directly on moral improvement and the cultivation of

virtuous citizens, as the Friendly Moralists (along with other black organizations founded in the 1830s and 1840s) seem to have been in more direct conversation with free black communities in the North and elsewhere about the value of moral uplift, education, and the politics of respectability. While the Brown Fellowship and Friendly Union societies focused the bulk of their efforts on supporting one another, societies founded in the next generation placed greater emphasis on concepts such as moral reform and racial uplift.[26] The Friendly Moralist Society's regulations and the activities of its members seem to suggest that the society sought to demonstrate the integrity and moral standing of its members as an opportunity to cultivate a public identity centered around respectability and to serve as a model of freedom among African-descended people in the Charleston community.

Membership in the Friendly Moralist Society was open only to "Free Brown Men . . . of respectable character." Continuing to build on the model provided by the Brown Fellowship Society, Friendly Moralist membership was capped at fifty, and the organization provided assistance to members and their families, including funeral expenses and burial.[27] Applicants had to be recommended by two current members (a rule adopted by the Brown Fellowship Society as well). These members had to certify that the applicant was not only "a bona fide free brown man" but also that he was "of moral character, and of good standing in the community."[28] Such concern with reputation and morality, in addition to complexion, suggests that the society functioned as far more than a safety net and source of financial assistance. Rather membership in an exclusive social organization such as this seems to have served as way for a portion of the city's free colored population to gain a level of social recognition within the local community, to cultivate and maintain reputations for respectability, and to defy negative stereotypes of black freedom.

At least some members of the Friendly Moralist Society were also members at one time or another of the Brown Fellowship, revealing that even while this new generation of organizations may have had slightly different goals, older organizations continued to serve as important social institutions for Charleston's free people of color and that the Brown Fellowship Society in many ways continued to serve as a model. For example William Mitchell and Philip Saltus, sons of two of the founding members of the Brown Fellowship Society, also held membership in the Friendly Moralist Society. Perhaps coincidentally, both Mitchell and Saltus gained admission to the Brown Fellowship Society in 1838, the same year the Friendly Moralist Society was founded. Other Brown Fellowship members—Francis David, John Gordon, Charles Holloway, and Robert Mishaw—also became members of the Friendly Moralists. That these individuals, each of whom was born into one of Charleston's free black artisan families, joined the Friendly Moralists either in addition to or instead of the Brown Fellowship Society reveals the way institutional life for free people of color transformed during the middle of the nineteenth century. Not simply content to associate with and offer financial support to others matching their class and complexional profile, Friendly Moralists emphasized active moral and intellectual improvement as a means of bolstering their claims to respectability and providing a model of black freedom that ran counter to prevailing white racial ideologies.

Objections periodically emerged about the institutional affiliations of potential members. In 1844 one Friendly Moralist, Robert Mishaw, objected to the membership application of Richard Gregory, on the grounds that he did not meet the complexional qualification that called for the admission of only "free brown men." Mishaw called for a dismissal of the application, arguing that Gregory, having already associated himself with Charleston's Humane Brotherhood—an organization (discussed below) that admitted only "free dark men"—was disqualified from membership in the Friendly Moralist Society. President Job Bass disagreed. Bass argued that even if Gregory "were to be exposed to the scorching rays of the sun on the shores of Africa, he would still be a Brown Man. The fact of him being associated with Black men could never make him a Black man."[29]

Mishaw, himself associated with another of Charleston's African American voluntary associations, called attention through his objection to the crucial importance of maintaining the society's complexional distinctions and perhaps of policing the boundaries of respectability to ensure they extended only to the mixed-race artisans. Bass's response, while perhaps suggesting the ways the Friendly Moralist Society included a broader segment of Charleston's free population of color, more likely reveals the way visible complexion was at least as important among free people of color in Charleston as performative characteristics were. For Bass the fact that Gregory appeared of light complexion was more important than his association with dark-skinned free blacks. Further that Gregory could associate with both of these organizations suggests that free people of color of darker complexion were more likely to accept their lighter skinned, more elite counterparts, while "brown" organizations expressed at least some hesitance toward accepting individuals who had associated with blacks.

This need to maintain social boundaries and the centrality of moral improvement and education to the efforts of Charleston's mixed-race free people of color to distance themselves from their dark-skinned counterparts was made clear by Friendly Moralist Michael Eggart, in his address to the society at their anniversary meeting in 1848. Eggart proclaimed that as members of the city's mulatto elite, Friendly Moralists occupied a "middle ground" in Charleston society between the "prejudice of the white man" and the "hate of our more sable brethren."[30] Responding to perceived prejudice about the "amalgamation of the races" that had produced the mixed-race members of the society, Eggart argued that their "capacities mental and physical are as good as either of the races," clearly positioning the society's mixed-race elites between white and black. Likewise he revealed the way the image of Haiti still held an important place in the minds of Charleston's free people of color, as he called attention to the conflict that persisted between blacks and mulattoes there, which he designated as the "inevitable result of a union of the black and colored races." In order to provide for the survival and success of "colored" men in Charleston, Eggart called on the Society to more explicitly adopt principles of "benevolence or Christian philanthropy" into its constitution, offering greater assistance to other mixed-race individuals who found themselves outside the membership rolls of the organization.[31]

Eggart also emphasized in his address the ways in which free people of color could prove themselves worthy of freedom and social inclusion and how the relatively wealthy members of voluntary organizations could offer examples of respectability that would challenge whites' negative attitudes toward free people of color. He argued vehemently for the need for the Friendly Moralist Society to work with other organizations in the city, even proposing the foundation of a "society of societies" to better carry out a broad plan to provide "education . . . our life[,] our sun shield" to Charleston's free people of color. Eggart's equating of education with a "sun shield" suggests that he viewed intellectual improvement as an opportunity to draw clearer distinction between light-skinned and dark-skinned free people of color.[32]

Eggart argued that "the Amelioration of our race can never be Effected" —leaving unclear whether he meant people of mixed racial ancestry or free African-descended people more broadly—until free people of color in Charleston began to offer greater assistance outside the narrow membership of their societies. He called on the members of these voluntary organizations to look "beyond ourselves and those immediately connected with us, to the welfare of our people generally." Like the Minor's Moralist Society earlier, Eggart stressed the need for the relatively affluent free people of color who populated these organizations to help lift up all free people of color, not just those fortunate enough to have obtained organizational membership. Through educating free people of color, he argued, "we add bone and sinew to our strength as a people." "What but Education," he asked, "raises us Above the level of the slaves[?] [I]n this land the ignorant and degraded are taken as the Representatives of our people." He continued, noting "how much brighter . . . the line of seperation [sic] . . . between us and the slaves" would be if the city's free people of color, particularly members of its prominent voluntary organizations, placed greater emphasis on intellectual improvement. "It would bee so bright," he argued, "that it would Eventually trump over the prejudice of the white man." Eggart called upon "our several societies to take their part in this great moral Reformation, Each body educateing [sic] besides its own Incumbents as many children as the strength of its fund will admit."[33]

By referencing "our race," "our people," and "our strength," Eggart may have been making an argument about free people of color in Charleston writ large, though his earlier comments about the incompatibility of mixed-race people and free blacks suggests he may have only been referring to the city's mixed-race free people of color. But even if Eggart only intended to for Charleston's voluntary societies to support light-skinned people of mixed racial ancestry, his call for action beyond the membership of these organizations dedicated to education and racial uplift reveals the centrality of demonstrating commitment to moral and personal values for free people of color in the city. The sentiment that moral and intellectual improvement and a demonstration of commitment to education could triumph over white racism places the Friendly Moralists in direct conversation with northern free black communities during this era. Indeed throughout the United States, free blacks during the antebellum era emphasized that through appeals to shared cultural values and the cocreation of respectability, free people of color could elevate all African Americans. While northern free blacks used these arguments in their efforts to gain citizenship and voting rights, however, free people of color in Charleston seem to have been more conservative and more locally focused in their aims.

Eggart called upon the city's free people of color to cooperate to "drive depravity and ignorance from amongst us and raise up in their stead Intellectual and Moral worth." This, as far as Eggart could tell, was the only way for Charleston's free people of color to "dispel the heavy cloud that hangs upon our political horizon."[34] Eggart's call for education came the year after the educational efforts of the Minor's Moralist Society had ceased, suggesting that while the content of his speech entered a much broader conversation about moral and intellectual improvement among free people of color, he may have been speaking directly to local concerns.[35] Eggart argued that by proving their intellectual capacity and moral worth—all of which contributed to nineteenth-century ideas about respectability—Charleston's free people of color could prove themselves worthy of freedom and social inclusion in antebellum Charleston. Education and moral improvement, coupled with the distinction of membership in elite fraternal organizations dedicated to charity and Christian benevolence, served as a way not just of drawing dividing lines between mulattoes and blacks but also of drawing an additional level of distinction between slavery and freedom. By actively cultivating respectable identities, mixed-race free people of color attempted to prove themselves as exceptions to white ideas about African-descended people, even as they declined to refute the applicability of such ideas to their dark-skinned counterparts elsewhere in the city.[36]

The Brown Fellowship Society served as a model for the city's other African American voluntary associations, particularly in its emphasis on complexional distinctions and preference toward light-skinned free people of color; similarities extended as well to policies such as membership and dues. Yet Charleston's mixed-race artisans were not the only free people of color in the city engaging with ideas about respectability and reform in the late antebellum era. Charleston's Society of Free Dark Men and Humane Brotherhood scoffed at the pretensions and exclusion of groups such as the Friendly Moralist Society. Organized in 1843, the Humane Brotherhood declared their organization open only to "respectable Free Dark Men," challenging the mulatto elite's monopoly on respectability in Charleston. The Humane Brotherhood, like its predecessors, declared its purpose to be the mutual aid of its members in times of sickness or distress. While groups such as the Brown Fellowship or Friendly Moralist Society either implicitly or explicitly restricted their membership to individuals of mixed racial ancestry, the Humane Brotherhood stipulated in its constitution that the "Society shall be exclusively supported by any number of free, dark men."[37] Nevertheless, as historian Robert Harris points out, of the seven founders whose race can be gleaned from the 1850 census returns, three were listed as mulattoes. While this may point to the ability of men of mixed racial ancestry to enter into societies open only to dark-skinned free people of color, it is equally possible that, though considered by whites to be mulattoes, their visible complexion was still too dark to gain acceptance into the Brown Fellowship Society or other "brown" organizations. It seems likely as well that census administrators were more likely to list relatively wealthy people of African descent as mulattos and free people of color who were less well-off as blacks, regardless of physical appearance.

That the Humane Brotherhood explicitly defined itself as an organization of "free, dark men" reveals a desire to distinguish itself from other voluntary organizations in the city and to extend the benefits of fraternal organizations to a broader swath of free people of color in Charleston than groups such as the Brown Fellowship and Friendly Moralists allowed. The founding of the Humane Brotherhood reveals as well the way conversations about respectability were not confined to the organizations of the mulatto elite but were engaged by darker free people of color in the city as well. Not only did the Humane Brotherhood's bylaws stipulate that only "respectable" men would be admitted, but they also included various restrictions aimed at moral reform among its members. They would dismiss members from meetings and levy fines, for example, to any members who disrupted meetings by smoking or whispering and to members who were "under the intoxicating influence of liquor."[38]

The Humane Brotherhood parallels the city's other African American voluntary societies in a number of important ways but seems clearly to have been open to black Charlestonians who found themselves outside of the mulatto aristocracy that populated those organizations. Unlike other organizations, very few members of the Humane Brotherhood gained membership in any of the other voluntary societies in the city. John Mishaw, an originator of the Friendly Union Society and Brown Fellowship member beginning in 1817 was counted among the Humane Brotherhood's members. Brown Fellowship member William Mitchell was as well. Just one other member, Friendly Moralist and barber Paul Poinsett, was counted as a member of another group. Humane Brotherhood members, then, seem to have been excluded from (or rejected membership in) the many organizations in the city that were founded by and catered to mixed-race artisans, yet they were equally engaged in a national conversation among African Americans about public virtue and sought the social benefits of respectable public affiliations just the same.

Other evidence seems to reveal the way considerations of class and complexion overlapped in antebellum Charleston. Members of the Humane Brotherhood, for example, owned real estate and enslaved people of much less value than their counterparts in the Brown Fellowship Society. Robert Harris has calculated that while the average value of real estate owned by Brown Fellowship members was almost $9,000, that of members of the Humane Brotherhood averaged only $1,832. Similarly Brown Fellowship members were more likely to own enslaved people and owned them in larger numbers.[39] Class distinctions between the Brown Fellowship and Humane Brotherhood extended to occupational patterns as well. Brown Fellowship members typically occupied jobs, such as tailor, requiring greater skill and capital and often owned their own storefronts or workshops. Humane Brotherhood members, meanwhile, most often found employment in trades such as carpentry, typically working in the employ of another. While these organizations were all populated by artisans of color, class distinctions reinforced complexional ones in determining eligibility and admission.[40]

Other free people of color in Charleston turned to another of the city's free black voluntary societies as a means of demonstrating not moral worth but their intellectual capacities, another marker of respectability. While the Brown Fellowship Society's constitution declared, for example, that "debates on controverted points of divinity or matters of nation, governments, states, or churches, shall be excluded from the conversation in this society," such debates found home in Charleston's Clionian Debating Society.[41] Organized in 1847, the debating society's "sole object" was the pursuit among free people of color of "learning and mental improvement." The Clionian Debating Society had counterparts among whites in Charleston, including the Cliosophic Debating Society, founded in 1838 and after which the Clionian Society was likely modeled, and the Chrestomathic Literary Society, founded in 1848. The parallels between the groups extended far beyond naming, as the three groups took up many of the same moral and philosophical questions, and members of white debating societies occasionally attended Clionian meetings.[42] The debating society presented an opportunity for Charlestonians of African descent to demonstrate to the broader community that they had the moral and civic intelligence to make them fit for freedom. Through education and intellectual exercises, Clionian Debating Society members continued their engagement with a broader national conversation about black respectability, attempting to solidify their place in the Charleston community even as they declined to pursue a broader agenda of political reform.

The Clionian Debating Society engaged with a number of questions of political and religious importance. During the Mexican-American War, for example, the society's members debated whether the conflict would "be of any advantage to the United States of America," finding that it would not. They debated whether the United States "was right in declaring her Independence" and even "Was Caesar right in crossing the Rubicon?" They took up questions regarding the schism of the Catholic Church, the merits of various literary and artistic pursuits, and a wide variety of philosophical questions, demonstrating an impressive breadth of interests. The society also debated questions more directly pertinent to black freedom in the United States and Atlantic world. They discussed, for example, "which country presents the brightest prospects for future happiness and permanency, the U.S. or Great Britain," deciding for the former. At a time when free blacks throughout the United States debated a wide variety of emigration schemes, with at least one prominent Charleston free black (then living in New York) of the mind that Jamaica represented more attractive possibilities for freedom, the debating society's declaration that the United States still represented the greatest prospects for freedom speaks to the optimism—or perhaps the fear—of the society's membership.[43] Perhaps explicitly because of their affiliation with the society, members of the Clionian Debating Society believed even in the late 1840s that by demonstrating their intelligence, civic engagement, and public respectability, black freedom remained viable and desirable within the United States.

More broadly that the Clionian Debating Society took up questions engaged by white debating and literary societies reveals that part of their efforts toward intellectual improvement were aimed at developing a local reputation for intelligence and civic engagement. As in northern free black communities, the organizations' members believed that by demonstrating their intellect and ability to engage political questions, they could prove themselves as virtuous residents of the city who deserved inclusion in the civic community. Yet unlike in northern cities, free blacks in Charleston did not use their claims to respectability as a means of pursuing activism and political reform. Even as free people of color in Charleston engaged a national (and as I will argue, transnational) discourse about respectability, the concept of community seems to have been far more central to the world of free black and free colored Charlestonians than it was to their northern counterparts. Likely seeing futility in agitating for the rights of citizenship or advocating antislavery principles (if indeed, they held them; certainly the frequency of slave ownership among the most prominent free people of color suggests that was not the case for many), free people of color in Charleston used their involvement with prominent organizations to gain greater acceptance in their local community. Through moral and intellectual improvement, Charleston's free people of color sought to offer a model of freedom and respectability that countered white racial ideologies that equated African ancestry with slavery. Through appeals to shared cultural values and claims to respectability, free blacks in Charleston gained social prestige and a place in the social and cultural world of their community.

Charleston's various voluntary societies reveal the importance of voluntary organizations for the city's free people of color. Through their public association with other free people of color matching their social, economic, and complexional profile, a portion the city's free people of color solidified their reputations as virtuous and respectable members of the community. All of this seems to cut against prevailing notions of the viability of freedom among people of African descent in early national and antebellum Charleston. The members of these organizations did not occupy "a world in shadow," to use historian Marina Wikramanayake's term, though many such members would have altogether rejected being classified as "negroes." Neither was involvement in voluntary societies only the concern of the city's wealthiest free people of color. In 1840 Charleston was home to 794 free men of color between ages ten and ninety-nine. In 1850 it was home to 696 free men of color older than twenty years old. With six different voluntary organizations operating within the city at any one time, many of which included up to fifty members, it seems likely that affiliation with one of these organizations could have extended to nearly 300 free men of color by the 1840s. Though the exact proportion of the city's free people of color who counted themselves as members of these organizations at any one time is perhaps unknowable, it seems clear enough that public affiliation with prominent organizations served important functions in the lives of a far larger number of free people of color in Charleston than just the artisan elites of the Brown Fellowship Society.

Through their membership in organizations defined in explicitly racial terms and the engagement among members with a national discourse about respectability, these men demonstrated that they were not individuals who simply "imbibed the norms of the predominant white society," and that Charleston's free colored community did not "identify itself, almost completely, with the white man."[44] At the most basic level, that free blacks gave their social organizations such names as Brown Fellowship and Society of Dark Men suggests a certain willingness to accept various racial identifications. Yet the emphasis these groups placed on complexional and color distinctions also undermines the notion that free people of color in Charleston had entirely "imbibed" white understandings of racial difference, as they constructed and policed more complex, more nuanced boundaries. These complex distinctions within Charleston's community of free people of color make clear that fissures among that population were more than a reproduction "at all levels" of the class distinctions "established in white society."[45] Rather the participation of free people of color in the Charleston's public, social worlds through the establishment of and membership in these societies and their attempts to establish themselves as respectable members of the community meant that at least some black Charlestonians participated in what Patrick Rael has termed the "cofabrication" of notions of respectability and of middle-class values in antebellum Charleston.[46]

While free blacks in Philadelphia, New York, Boston, and other northern cities cultivated black respectability as a means of gaining greater political inclusion, agitating against slavery and broadly attempting to change white minds about issues of race, no such radicalism or activism is apparent in Charleston. Free black Charlestonians seem more concerned with achieving far more limited ends focused closer to home: proving African-descended people could thrive in freedom and demonstrating commitment to shared moral values as a means of improving their individual or family circumstances. While free people of color in Charleston discussed issues of race, engaged a national and transnational discourse about respectability, and expressed concern for the welfare of free people of color more generally, these efforts seem to have been focused on providing a counterexample to the link, viewed by whites as inextricable, between slavery and African ancestry. By emphasizing education, moral improvement, and sometimes complexional distinction, free people of color in Charleston demonstrated their commitment to a set of shared cultural values with whites in their community and participated in a continuing redefinition of what those values—sobriety, piety, industry, respectability—could look like. In a city and region in which whites believed slavery to be the proper condition for African-descended people, free people of color engaged these social and cultural conversations as a means of refuting such arguments and demonstrating their fitness for freedom. Perhaps recognizing the impossibility of a push for broader political reforms, free people of color in Charleston gained social and economic mobility by adapting a broader conversation about respectability to their more immediate circumstances.

CABILDOS DE NACIÓN, THE VOLUNTARY MILITIA, AND PUBLIC ASSOCIATION IN CARTAGENA

As in Charleston, free people of color in Cartagena used their public affiliation with institutions organized by racial designation as a means of achieving social distinction, establishing lives and reputations that could serve as a counterexample to white creoles' and Spaniards' negative view of the capacities of African-descended people. Throughout Spanish America people of African descent—particularly free men of color—used affiliation with various religious, secular, and military institutions to gain social prestige within their local communities and improve their standing in the eyes of the Spanish Crown. Organizations such as *cabildos de nación* brought together free and enslaved people who identified with specific West African ethnicities, supporting funerals, burials, and mourning much in the same way U.S. mutual aid societies did, though their North American counterparts rarely included both free and enslaved people. Affiliation with and the acceptance of leadership roles within these cabildos likely afforded some free people of color in Cartagena a path to community leadership and social advancement. Through the special privileges and distinctions afforded to militia members, meanwhile, free men of color gained a route to social prominence facilitated directly by the Crown. Like free people of color in Charleston, free people of color in Cartagena rarely used their privileged positions and social prestige to challenge or resist state power directly—and indeed often directly supported it—in large part because, unlike in Charleston, the state conferred many of the social privileges free people of color sought to achieve. Yet even as free people of color rarely confronted white authority directly, their efforts to improve their circumstances through institutional affiliations called into question white racial ideologies and the logic of racial hierarchies.

The role of public institutions in the lives of free people of color in Cartagena marks a major difference from experiences of free black Charlestonians.

While free people of color in Charleston were for the most part forced to found independently and maintain the institutions they used for social advancement, the role of the church and Crown in Spanish American society provided institutional outlets that free people of color could bend to their needs. Through their involvement in the voluntary militia, for example, free people of color gained the opportunity to appeal directly to the Crown to express their displeasure with local circumstances as well as the right to be tried in separate military tribunals, where they would likely receive more preferable treatment, an engagement with the state rarely available or pursued by free people of color in Charleston. Yet despite this greater involvement, free people of color in Cartagena transformed these institutions to serve their specific social and cultural needs, as neither the militia nor *cabildos de nación* were designed to provide social advancement to African-descended people. Rather, like in Charleston, a segment of the free colored population in Cartagena used the institutional and organizational opportunities available to them to establish respectable reputations for themselves, achieve a measure of social prestige within their local communities, and challenge the racial discrimination they faced at the local level.

CABILDOS DE NACIÓN IN LATIN AMERICA

Cabildos de nación emerged throughout colonial Iberian America as early as the sixteenth century, providing a religious, social, and cultural home to the thousands of Africans forcibly brought to South America and the Spanish Caribbean during that era. Between the sixteenth and nineteenth centuries, these organizations transformed from lay religious brotherhoods into collective voluntary associations dedicated to mutual aid, particularly the support of funerals, burials, and mourning. In addition to this material assistance, cabildos provided opportunities for building and strengthening social connections among fellow people of African descent and white church officials as well as for preserving, nurturing, and at times re-creating elements of West African culture in the Americas. With naming conventions connecting the institutions to particular African identities, cabildos established a space in which Africans and their descendants could convene with others holding similar ethnic ancestry.

These *cofradías,* or lay brotherhoods, emerged during the sixteenth and seventeenth centuries in the cities of Spain and its growing empire in the New World, "helping settlers integrate into the urban milieu."[47] As Spanish American societies grew during the seventeenth century, the nature of these organizations transformed as Africans in Spanish America founded new brotherhoods to serve both body and spirit in cities throughout the empire. As historian Nicole von Germeten has shown, *cofradías* founded by and serving African-descended people in colonial Mexico during the seventeenth century provided both religious community and crucial health care functions, reflecting the institutions' Hispanic origins as well as Central Africans' familiarity with "communal societies addressing health and mortality."[48] With more than a dozen distinct organizations, confraternities in Mexico City "helped seventeenth-century Africans and descendants of Africans survive through fostering community and providing health care and burials, and later encouraged a degree of upward social mobility."[49]

Such confraternal organizations emerged in nearly every city of Spain's American empire. In Havana, Cuba, one of the Spanish American cities with the strongest and longest ties to the transatlantic slave trade, lay brotherhoods and mutual aid societies began developing during the sixteenth century and remained crucial sites of community building, spiritual and cultural life, and social mobility for Afro-Cubans well into the nineteenth century. As Matt D. Childs has shown, during the eighteenth and nineteenth centuries, these *cabildos de nación* grouped Africans by shared ethnic identities corresponding to "the numerous African 'nations' forcibly imported to Cuba."[50] The naming of these institutions reveals how "people of African descent emphasized their place of origin in terms of where they were born, and also how they remembered, reconnected, and recreated Africa in the New World."[51] Many of these organizations owned houses, providing a physical space for their cultural, social, and political activities. Cabildo houses served crucial communal functions: they "provided rooms to rent for urban members who often were the elected leaders of the society" and also functioned as "a place for holding weekly meetings and special festivities," "an informal bank," "a theater for dances," and "funeral parlors for their members."[52]

Cabildos existed in Cartagena as well, providing unique insight into worlds of the city's African and African-descended residents during the seventeenth and eighteenth centuries. Historians such as Pablo Gómez, Jane G. Landers, Luz Adriana Maya Restrepo, and David Wheat have all emphasized the multiethnic Africanness of seventeenth-century Cartagena.[53] The city was one of the most important sites of slave importation to Spanish America during that era. Because of the many different African ethnicities represented in Cartagena and its hinterlands during the seventeenth century, the city "quickly took on the aspect of an African landscape."[54] In an effort to provide for their own spiritual, medical, and cultural needs, free and enslaved Africans in Cartagena developed confraternities in a manner similar to their counterparts in Brazil, Cuba, Mexico, and elsewhere.

While a dearth of notarial and legal records in Cartagena makes direct comparison with these other cities impossible, the centrality of Cartagena for the early Spanish American slave trade and the presence of these cabildos in the 1777 census suggests the *cabildos de nación* functioned in a similar manner as elsewhere in Iberian America. In the late eighteenth century, Cartagena's cabildo houses were located in the neighborhood of Santo Toribio, the largest and most racially mixed neighborhood inside the walled city.[55] Though little additional evidence regarding the cabildos' activities seems to exist beyond references in the city's 1777 general census, by complementing these census returns with what we know about these voluntary organizations in such places as Havana, Mexico City, and Rio de Janeiro and Salvador, Bahia, Brazil, we can begin to get a sense both of the ways that voluntary organizations helped establish and maintain bonds of ethnic community in Cartagena and the extent to which various forms of West African ethnic identification continued to hold meaning for Africans and their descendants in late eighteenth-century Cartagena.

Each of the cabildos in Cartagena corresponded to broadly defined African ethnic groups. Eight cabildos existed for seven different ethnic groups in Cartagena: Ararás, referring to Africans from Ardra or Allada; Caravalí, for which there were two separate cabildo houses, referring to Africans from Calabar; Luangos, likely referring broadly to people brought to Cartagena from or around the port of Luanda in Angola; Lucumí, referring broadly to Yoruba people; Mina, referring to people from Upper Guinea; Jojóes, likely corresponding to the Jeje people; and the Chaláes, whose more identifiable ethnic background I have been unable to discern. Each of these cabildos owned property, likely collectively, in Santo Toribio. The 1777 census refers to most of these cabildo houses as *solares*, which typically indicated some kind of informally organized lot. Others are classified more traditionally as casas. But despite the somewhat murky nature of the physical characteristics of the cabildo houses, we can assume that the cabildos exerted either a formal or informal collective ownership of space in one of the walled city's most prominent neighborhoods.[56]

The "cavildo de los Negros Luangos" was located on Calle de Nuestra Señora de Valencia in Solar number eight. Within it resided Josepha Miranda, a *negra libre*, a free black woman, aged forty-seven. The cabildo house also served as the *habitación* for four unnamed enslaved people, two men and two women, likely married. Other cabildo houses reveal similar arrangements. In the "cavildo de los Negros Jojoes," *casa baja* number 6 on Calle de Nuestra Señora de la Aurora, lived two enslaved men and three enslaved women, whose names were not recorded. In houses on either side of the cabildo house resided other unnamed enslaved people: three (one man, two women) in *casa baja* number 7, and eight (three men, five women) in *casa baja* number 4. Also in house number 4 lived two free women of color, Juana Thomasa Rodriguez, age forty-four, and Maria Ba, age sixty, both of whom were widows recorded as *mulata*. While the exact link between Rodriguez and Ba to the cabildo remains unclear, only in or near cabildo houses were enslaved people recorded without names, so the fact that the two women lived in such a house suggests a link with the cabildo.[57]

Two free women of color lived in the "cavildo de los Negros Minas" as well: Candelaria Zepulveda, sixty, and Bonifacia de la Cruz, forty-four, both listed as *negra libre*. Along with them lived two enslaved men. In the one of the two cabildo houses for "los Negros Caravalies," on Calle de Nuestra Señora del Cavo, lived Juan Phelipe Rondon, a free mulatto man, age forty-five; his wife, Ana Pedrosa, a *mulata*, age twenty-eight; and their daughter, Maria Dionicia, age three. In addition two enslaved men also resided in the house. In the "otro cavildo de los Negros Caravalies," located on Calle de Nuestra Señora del Pino, lived four enslaved men, unnamed. In the Lucumí cabildo, located on Calle de Nuestra Señora de Egipto, lived Cipriana Herrera, a *negra libre*, age fifty-four; Rafaela Esquina, a *negra libre*, age eighty; and an enslaved married couple. The "cavildo de los Negros Chalaes," just a few doors down from the Lucumíes, served as home for four enslaved people, two men and two women.[58]

The "cavildo de los Negros Araraes" was distinct among the cabildo houses in Santo Toribio, as it appeared to serve as home to more than sixteen free people of color in at least four separate families. Miguel Gomez, a *negro libre*, age fifty-nine, lived there with his wife, Maria del Carmen Miranda, a *negra libre*, age fifty-four. Juana Velazco, likewise a *negra libre*, also lived there. Three women lived in the house who were married but whose spouses were for one reason or another absent: Cipriana de Ayala, a married, thirty-nine-year-old *mulata* who lived there with her two children, Barthola, age twelve, and Manuel, age ten; Maria Blasima de la Candelaria, a *negra*, age twenty-seven; and Juana Rosa Carrillo, a forty-four-year-old *negra* who lived there with her four-year-old *negro libre* son, Rafael. Finally Maria Santo Landente, a *mestiza* widow, the only person listed among the cabildos who had Indian ancestry, lived there with her six young children.[59]

While the cabildos in Havana may have provided residence to elected officers, that seems not to be the case in Cartagena. Rather the high prevalence of widows or married women whose husbands were absent suggests that the Cartagena cabildo houses provided aid in the form of residences to African or African-descended women incapable of supporting themselves independently. One of the few adult men who resided in a cabildo house, Caravalí Juan Phelipe Rondon, is listed as an "invalid," further suggesting that residence in cabildo houses functioned as a kind of charitable aid. Such a role would fit neatly with their cabildos' broader purpose of providing mutual aid and bringing together individuals of common ethnic ancestry.

Further the *cabildos de nación* in Cartagena seem to have served people of African descent born in the Americas, not just the African-born, raising questions about their link to the ethnicities reflected in the cabildos' names. Because so many of those listed with a connection to cabildo houses were identified as *negros,* it seems plausible that these individuals were of the second or third generation born in the Americas and had a more recent link to West Africa. More broadly, however, the persistence of these African ethnic identifiers in Cartagena is distinct from similar trends elsewhere in Iberian America in that their use continued long after the slave trade to the region had waned. While in both Cuba and Brazil the African slave trade disembarked the highest number of slaves during the eighteenth and nineteenth centuries, in Colombia the trade peaked in the mid-seventeenth century.

The slave trade to ports in Caribbean New Granada long predated the highest years of African slave trading in Cuba and Brazil—though even the highest years of slave trading to Cartagena were dwarfed, in terms of total numbers, by the trade to those countries.[60] Yet for African-descended people in Cartagena, various African ethnic identities remained salient long after the regular arrival of Africans had declined, with *cabildos de nación* remaining active at least until the end of the eighteenth century. While historians have documented the extent to which African identities and culture shaped the history of Cartagena in the seventeenth century, far less work has been completed examining how these identities persisted into the late eighteenth century.[61] Aline Helg notes that these organizations persisted despite the waning slave trade but maintains they continued to serve the African born.[62] The presence of mulattoes and of free people of color within the cabildo houses and the continued existence of cabildos with seven different ethnic identifiers, coupled with the near termination of the international slave trade to Cartagena, however, reveal that these ethnic identifiers continued to hold meaning for both free and enslaved people of African descent born not in Africa but in the Americas.[63]

More broadly considered, evidence for *cabildos de nación* in late eighteenth-century Cartagena reveals that they brought together free and enslaved people of African descent in mutual association in ways mostly unimaginable to Charleston's free people of color. Links to particular West African ethnic groups brought together African-descended people of a wide range of racial, complexional, and class backgrounds to offer mutual aid and likely the promotion of West African cultural practices. While free people of color may have served as leaders for these loosely defined organizations, the inclusion of both free and enslaved people represents a sharp distinction with their North American counterparts. Yet for free people of color throughout the Atlantic world, founding and participating in mutual aid societies functioned as a distinct and crucial way to forge social links with their counterparts from across the city and offered an important avenue to social advancement. While local particularities may have distinguished these organizations from one another, engagement with mutual aid societies represents a distinct feature of black freedom throughout the urban Americas.

THE VOLUNTARY MILITIA IN COLONIAL CARTAGENA

A different type of organization, the voluntary militia, had an impact on the lives of a far greater number of free people of color in Cartagena and, though in many ways different, offers another point of comparison with Charleston's black voluntary associations. Comprised almost exclusively of men counted among Cartagena's free black and mulatto artisan class, the voluntary militia in Cartagena offered a certain segment of the city's free people of color a variety of economic and legal distinctions and provided them tangible advantages over other people of African descent. The voluntary militia offered free people of color in Cartagena the opportunity to claim privileges directly from the Crown by virtue of their membership in a corporately ordered society, a major difference from Charleston, where such a public-institutional dynamic never existed for African-descended people. In Charleston free people of color focused their efforts on the cultivation of private moral habits and bonds of personalism, claiming a bourgeois respectability very much unlike that in Cartagena. Yet in the broadest of terms, free people of color in both cities used their affiliations with elite organizations as a means of achieving social prestige, even as the source of that prestige often differed. Additionally militiamen of African descent, like the members of Charleston's voluntary societies, declined to use these positions of relative prominence to push for broader racial reforms. Free colored militia members focused their efforts on improving the lives of themselves and their families rather than using their demographic advantages and military capacity to challenge institutional power more forcefully, in large part because they depended on the state so directly for these sources of privilege. Even as the free militiamen of color in Cartagena never directly challenged the state, however, the privileges, concessions, and rights they won represented a challenge to the logic of racial hierarchies. As free people of color attempted to improve their individual circumstances, their actions called into question the very nature of white authority.

Like elsewhere in Spanish America and the greater Caribbean, free people of color in Cartagena used their affiliation with local militias to exploit rifts between military and civilian authority to their advantage, to stake their claims to social distinction and respectability, and to cultivate broader social networks capable of supporting them in times of need.[64] As historian Ben

Vinson III has noted in his study of the free colored militia in colonial Mexico, in Spanish America "few institutions offered the same amount of legal and political strength as did the militia," as the militia's strategic importance provided men of African descent with significant bargaining power with local and Crown officials.[65] Likewise Aline Helg, Marixa Lasso, Allan Kuethe, and Sergio Paolo Solano D. and Roicer Flórez Bolívar have all emphasized the centrality of the voluntary militia in the efforts of Cartagena's free people of color to achieve social distinction. Solano D. and Flórez Bolívar have argued that through military service, free people of color took advantage of fissures between civil and military authorities, affording them the opportunity to improve their social position. Helg specifically notes that the militia presented a clear avenue toward social prestige for free people of color during the late colonial period.[66]

In 1773 Spain's royal government initiated a reorganization of the military in New Granada, strengthening the regular army in the crucial Caribbean port of Cartagena and creating a new provincial militia there. Amid increasing interimperial tensions in the late eighteenth-century Caribbean, Spain sought to provide greater security to important port cities through the creation of these regional "disciplined" militias, who would receive training from officers and provide support to the regular army in times of crisis. Despite white views of Africanness as a "defect," their doubts about the capacities of men of African descent, and a variety of discriminatory policies, free people of color constituted a majority of both the militia and the general population of Caribbean Colombia. In fact they were disproportionately represented in the disciplined militias, as the city's minority Spaniard and white creole populations typically took advantage of a variety of exemptions. The Spanish imported men of African descent to Caribbean Colombia to construct Cartagena's fortifications in the sixteenth and seventeenth centuries, and at the end of the eighteenth century and through the wars of independence, Spanish colonial authorities relied heavily upon these slaves' free ancestors to man them.[67]

Free people of color were technically split into two different militias—that of *morenos,* for men born to free parents of entirely African descent, and that of *pardos,* which included free men of various racial complexions—but colonial authorities generally referred to all of these militiamen and their units as *pardos.* Though separated into racially classified units and never viewed as equal with whites within the military, free people of color in Cartagena used membership in the militia as an avenue to social distinction within the city and as a means of differentiating themselves from Cartagena's black lower classes. This differentiation between men of various complexions and racial backgrounds suggests an interesting parallel with Charleston's voluntary associations: though men of African descent of all complexions utilized the militia to gain social advancement, that route was more difficult for men of darker complexions or entirely of African ancestry.

The economic status required to join the militia made it an avenue to social prestige as well. Only men capable of independently supporting themselves were eligible to serve in the disciplined militias, marking the free men of color who enlisted in the militia as men of means. Because of these economic barriers to entry into the colonial militia, nearly all the militiamen of African descent in Cartagena were counted among the city's artisan class. Though the government of colonial New Granada prohibited men of African descent from entering a number of professional occupations and positions, the exclusive nature of the militia meant that it "offered one of the few avenues of social advancement" available to free people of color in the city.[68] While they also barred men of African descent from ascending to officer positions higher than captain, some managed to rise through the ranks, while others eventually became eligible to receive a pension.[69] Free men of color in late eighteenth- and early nineteenth-century Cartagena used membership in this exclusive body as a means of claiming expanded rights and bolstering their local reputations, differentiating themselves within the community from the black popular classes.[70]

One of the most pressing questions for men of African descent serving in the colonial militia was whether they would receive the privilege of the *fuero militar* that white soldiers enjoyed. The *fuero militar* placed those serving in the military under the jurisdiction of special military tribunals rather than of the ordinary or royal court system and limited the power of civilian authorities in a number of ways. Because of the security needs of such a crucial port city, free militiamen of color in Cartagena expected to receive more equitable treatment from a military tribunal than from civilian courts. The privilege of the *fuero militar* provided its recipients with a certain degree of social distinction in colonial Spanish society, and it was one free people of color throughout Spanish America fought hard to obtain and keep.

Following the 1773 reorganization of the Spanish militias, a flurry of legal challenges by free men of color ensued, as they demanded the right to the military *fuero* open to white soldiers, both for themselves and for their families. In the summer of that year, for example, civilian authorities attempted to arrest Florencio Sanmartín, a *pardo* militiaman and silversmith in Cartagena, for the failure to pay a debt. Though *pardo* militias in Cuba and Puerto Rico had already gained the privilege of the military *fuero,* those of Cartagena had yet to determine if this would be the case for them, a situation Sanmartín sought to rectify. After being arrested Sanmartín asked permission from the civil authorities to be brought to the house of Casimiro Jinete, an officer in the *pardo* militia, under the pretense that he needed money from Jinete to satisfy the debt. In reality the two sought to appeal to the military higher-ups to determine whether or not civil authorities had power over them.

Jinete contacted militia *comandante* Domingo Esquiaqui and explained Sanmartín's situation. Though Esquiaqui informed the local alcalde who ordered the arrest that Sanmartín was a member of the local militia, the alcalde argued that the *fuero militar* did not apply to militiamen of African descent in Cartagena. Ultimately Esquiaqui and the provincial governor, well aware of the need to satisfy the militiamen of color on whom they depended so heavily for security, appealed to the viceroy to affirm that men of African descent serving in the disciplined militias would have full enjoyment of the *fuero*. The viceroy acceded to their request.[71]

This incident illustrates well the importance of organizational membership among free men of color in late colonial Cartagena. First Sanmartín and Jinete's presence of mind to bring the case to Esquiaqui and demand the benefit of the *fuero militar* suggests a level of engagement with the intellectual and cultural currents of the Spanish Caribbean and Atlantic world. Sanmartín and Jinete approached their commanding officers armed with the knowledge that free colored militias elsewhere in urban Spanish America had been granted the military *fuero* and understood the benefits the *fuero* conferred. Finally that free militiamen of color were able to gain support for their petitions to the viceroy of Nueva Granada emphasizes the types of crucial social connections membership in the militia made available to Cartagena's free people of color. Not only did militia membership offer an opportunity to gain legal distinctions not open to other free people of color, but it also gave free militiamen of color access to both local and royal officials that they could use to improve their lives and those of their families. While many people of African descent may have petitioned the Spanish Crown seeking privileges and concessions, militiamen of color seem to have been more likely to succeed, particularly given the importance of their public service and their connections with prominent local and royal officials. For free militiamen of African descent in Cartagena, participation in the local militia, and the concomitant enjoyment of the military *fuero*, offered not just social distinction within the local community but enhanced bargaining power and concrete opportunities to improve their individual circumstances.

Cartagena's militiamen of African descent worked to secure the military *fuero* not only for themselves but for their families as well. In 1804 Tómas Morales, a carpenter and sublieutenant in the *pardo* militia, argued that his wife should fall under the jurisdiction of the military *fuero* as well. Morales filed a complaint against local merchant Don Francisco Pacheco, who Morales accused of causing a public scandal. According to the claim,

Morales's wife declined to inform Pacheco whether or not her husband was present at their home, an offense for which she was ordered arrested by the alcalde. Morales argued that not only should she not have been arrested for such a transgression, but also that because he was a member of the militia, civilian authorities had no jurisdiction over his wife. Though his claim was initially denied by the alcalde, upon sending the case to the provincial governor and ultimately the viceroy, the alcalde was forced to concede that the families of militiamen of color were indeed protected by the military *fuero*.[72]

In addition to the military fuero, free militiamen of color in Caribbean New Granada used their uniforms to distinguish themselves as a class apart. In 1794, when the colonial government in Madrid suspended the right of *pardo* officers to wear the same insignia as their white counterparts, they provided an exception for those in Cartagena, a decision that speaks to the outsize importance of militiamen of African descent there and the potential value of militia service for free people of color.[73] In Portobelo, Panama, another important Caribbean port in Nueva Granada, other cases arose to suggest the importance of visual as well as judicial distinctions for free militiamen of color and their families, trends that suggest this was likely the case in Cartagena as well. In 1779, for instance, Felix Martinez Malo expressed the dissatisfaction of white military officials to colonial authorities, complaining of insubordination among black militiamen and officers. He complained that *pardo* militia members failed to show the necessary deference to whites by removing their hats when in their presence in public. Martinez Malo argued that it was a necessity for the peace and good order of the city that black *milicianos* be required to show "respect, attention, and courtesy" to all whites, whether or not those whites were in the military. By not removing their caps for whites, Martinez Malo claimed, militiamen of color demonstrated a dangerous desire to "leave the sphere of their birth," one to which they should remain subject. In response to *pardo* protests, and as part of his effort to maintain the much-needed support of *pardo* militiamen, Panama's governor agreed to not require them to remove their hats except to white officers, and only when conducting military duty. In Cartagena, where both the size of the militia and the black population as a whole was much larger, the necessity of visual distinction from the black lower classes likely would have seemed equally important for free militiamen of color. For black militiamen maintaining a visual, public air of distinction was crucial; the privileges of uniform, like the ability to keep one's hat on when in the public presence of whites, clearly signified a level of distinction and respectability not open to the black popular classes.[74]

Free *pardo* militia officers also requested the right to mourn the death of King Carlos III in the same manner as their white counterparts. In 1789 *pardo* officers in Caracas and Portobelo successfully petitioned colonial authorities for the right to mourn the death of Carlos III by displaying a black band on their hat's cockade, in the same manner as white officers. Here, too, militia membership conferred important benefits on free people of color. Through their uniforms, and in particular their right to don the same insignias as white military men, free people of color obtained the ability to distinguish themselves from the black lower classes. Militia service, through this ability to achieve visual, public distinctions, supported their claims to respectability and provided an avenue to social advancement.[75]

Like with the military *fuero*, free militiamen of color also tried to acquire these important visual distinctions for their wives and partners, likely conferring status on both members of the couple. In 1779 free militiamen of color petitioned colonial authorities, requesting that their wives be given permission to wear velvet skirts and clothing adorned with precious stones in public. The honor of wearing such clothing, they argued, should not be exclusive to the wives of white militia members but should be open to *pardo* wives as well, befitting their station. For these militiamen the denial of the right of their wives to wear this type of clothing represented an affront to their public reputations. Like their right to keep their hats on and the right to mourn the same as white officers, free men of color used their social distinction as members of the militia to gain greater concessions from colonial authorities for their families, offering them a way to gain prestige and social advancement. The ability to wear their uniform hats in the presence of whites, to be seen mourning the death of the king the same way as their white counterparts, and for their wives to be seen dressed in a manner similar to those of white officers, crucially supported the efforts of free people of color to distinguish themselves from the black popular classes in Caribbean New Granada. Through their efforts to achieve these concessions from both local and royal officials, militia membership increased the ability of free people of color to negotiate with colonial authorities and offered a measure of social advancement for African-descended people.[76]

Throughout Caribbean Colombia institutional affiliations proved central to improving the lives of free people of color. African-descended people both free and enslaved founded and affiliated themselves with *cabildos de nación,* mutual aid societies that offered assistance and social connection to individuals of similar ethnic roots while crossing status and complexional boundaries. It seems possible that free people of color took on leadership positions within the cabildos, offering them a degree of social prestige within their specific ethnic community as well as within the broader community of free people of color in the city. Further free people of color took advantage of military necessity to further their social advancement and to win concessions from colonial authorities that distinguished them from the city's black lower classes. Through the legal distinction of the *fuero militar*, the visual distinction of military dress, and the social connections militia membership allowed them to cultivate, free men of color in Cartagena grasped an avenue to social advancement and respectability. Through their public affiliation with organizations and institutions, free people of color in Cartagena seized upon opportunities to improve their individual circumstances and challenge racial discrimination at the local level through appeals to the Crown.[77]

CONCLUSION

By examining the importance of membership in a variety of voluntary organizations for free people of color, we can begin to see how the contours of social status shared distinct parallels throughout the African Americas. In Charleston, Cartagena, and throughout the urban Atlantic, free people of color used membership and participation in exclusive groups or organizations to craft identities as respectable members of their local communities, countering a white racial ideology that viewed African descent as a defect and generally doubted the capacities of free people of color. Though in both Charleston and Cartagena, free people of color declined to pursue broader agendas of political reform or more forceful challenges to white rule—and in fact often relied on privileges acquired through their proximity or connections to white authorities—they used their engagement with an Atlantic discourse about race and respectability to improve their individual and family circumstances. Through their efforts to improve their individual lives, free people of color offered an implicit challenge to the very nature of American racial hierarchies, subtly calling into question the basis of white authority.

In Charleston free men of color used membership in mutual aid and voluntary societies to achieve social prestige and to offer a model of freedom and respectability than ran counter to whites' broader attitudes about the character and capabilities of African-descended people. Although whites in South Carolina continued to view people of African descent as fit only for slavery and incapable of surviving in freedom, free people of color in Charleston—particularly artisans of mixed racial backgrounds and light complexions—used their affiliation with prominent voluntary societies to cultivate reputations for social respectability that allowed them to achieve a degree of social prestige. These private societies fostered a bourgeois respectability among free people of color in Charleston, allowing them to demonstrate their commitment to shared cultural values with prominent whites by actively cultivating such characteristics as industriousness, thrift, sobriety, and piety. By demonstrating their personal adoption of the tenets of moral reform and racial uplift, free people of color in Charleston were able to cultivate respectable reputations and boost their social status.

In Cartagena, meanwhile, affiliation with *cabildos de nación* and the colonial disciplined militia similarly supported free people of color's claims to social status. Yet the basis of these institutions and the nature of respectability in Cartagena were often very different from that in Charleston, particularly in the role of the state in conferring privilege and respectability. While free people of color in Charleston founded private organizations to support their social striving, their counterparts in Cartagena relied on public, corporately ordered societies to achieve broadly similar ends. Service in the voluntary militia afforded a segment of Cartagena's free people of color the legal distinction of the military *fuero,* the visual distinction of their uniforms, and access to the ears of local and royal officials. Along with the social connections militia membership allowed them to cultivate, militia membership provided free people of color in Cartagena a means of distinguishing themselves from the city's black lower classes and of crafting a respectable identity. For free people of color in Cartagena, engagement with a vital public institution and appeals to the Crown allowed them to gain social privileges not afforded to the city's African-descended popular classes.

By achieving social distinction and gaining privileges not normally afforded to African-descended people, the free colored members of these institutions and organizations offered an implicit challenge to the logic of racial discrimination in the urban Americas. Even as these groups declined to demand racial reforms or to challenge state authority directly, the status and privilege free people of color achieved implicitly called into question the logic behind the racial hierarchies that structured American societies during the eighteenth and nineteenth centuries.

Chapter 5

BAPTISM, GODPARENTS, AND SOCIAL NETWORKS

Situated upon the south side of the main square of Cartagena's Getsemaní neighborhood, the Iglesia de la Santísima Trinidad (Church of the Holy Trinity) held a place of central importance for the neighborhood's free and enslaved residents of African descent during the eighteenth and nineteenth centuries. The church and its attendant rites and rituals served not only the spiritual lives of the neighborhood's residents but their social lives as well. In Charleston, though denominational diversity made church affiliation more diffuse, religious life likewise featured centrally in the efforts of free people of color to establish social connections and bolster personal reputations. Indeed throughout the urban Atlantic world, the religious lives and social lives of people of African descent were inextricably linked.

Throughout the Americas the church functioned as a crucial site of social interaction, often bringing together people from different races, legal statuses, and levels of wealth depending on particular local circumstances. For people of African descent, the church presented a unique opportunity to gain recognition of their stature in the local community through their participation in religious rites such as baptism. Through baptism parents selected godparents or baptismal sponsors, entrusting others in the community to assist them in providing spiritual guidance to their children. Beyond this narrow religious function, however, free and enslaved people of African descent recognized that the selection of baptismal sponsors could offer additional advantages to their children as well, through the ability of godparentage to formalize connections to other members of their community. For the free people of color selected as sponsors or godparents by their free and enslaved neighbors, friends, and co-parishioners, their willingness to serve in such a role helped them to develop and to reinforce their reputations as well-respected individuals in the church. The relationships established and strengthened through the process of serving as or selecting baptismal sponsors offered African-descended people in both Cartagena and in Charleston an opportunity to formalize social networks and strengthen bonds of racial community. Networks of baptismal sponsorship built and strengthened mutually beneficial ties of fictive kinship that connected church members of African descent across lines of class and legal status. Those who served as baptismal sponsors more than once situated themselves at the center of a broad network of social connections from whom they could marshal, or for whom they could offer, support as necessary. Baptismal sponsorship in both Cartagena and Charleston helped create and consolidate tightly knit communities of African-descended people. These networks often crossed lines of social class, racial background or complexion, and legal status in ways that rarely occurred in other aspects of daily life.[1]

African-descended people's adaptation of European religious traditions to satisfy local needs was evident throughout the Atlantic world. From the earliest days of interaction with Europeans, Africans and their descendants transformed, accommodated, and resisted various European religious practices to suit better their circumstances. Africans in the Americas adopted and transformed European religious practice, interpreting it within a broader African spiritual worldview and using its rites and rituals to serve their needs. Through candomblé in Brazil and Santeria in Cuba, through vodou in Saint Domingue and obeah in Jamaica, African-descended people transformed religion in the diaspora through their own cultural practices and traditions.[2] While white authorities throughout the Iberian Americas and Caribbean encouraged African-descended people to adopt Catholic religious practice in an effort to assert control, these very practices provided opportunities and structures from which resistance, social mobility, and opportunity of many kinds emerged.[3] James H. Sweet has argued, for example, that for enslaved Africans in Brazil, "religion and spirituality" constituted one of "the most potent weapons at their disposal."[4] In Cartagena, as elsewhere, Africans' ideas about spirituality, health and the body, and life and death often came into conflict with those of Catholic church officials. Beginning in the sixteenth century, enslaved Africans forcibly transported to Cartagena and their free and enslaved descendants interpreted Catholicism through a uniquely West African cosmological frame.[5]

Scholars have likewise examined the role of Africans and their descendants in transforming religion in North America and the United States, where African-descended people transformed European religious traditions not just for themselves but for whites as well.[6] Mechal Sobel, for example, has demonstrated how the spiritual and religious views of Africans and African-descended people in eighteenth-century Virginia transformed the state's—and the nation's—religious culture.[7] Like it did in Latin America, tension existed throughout the era of slavery in the United States between the efforts of white authorities to encourage Christianity to subdue and control enslaved populations and to justify the institution of slavery and the competing efforts of enslaved and free people of African descent to harness Christianity's emancipatory potential. For African-descended people in the lowcountry of South Carolina and Georgia in particular, historian Jason R. Young has argued, "religion operated as a central form of resistance, not only against the system of slavery but also against the very ideological underpinnings that supported slavery in the first place."[8] In the lowcountry Kongolese religious traditions shaped the practice of religion among Africans and their descendants, and this syncretic religion fueled resistance to slavery.

While Africans in the seventeenth and eighteenth centuries transformed European religions in order to mold them to various West African spiritual worldviews, their descendants in the nineteenth century continued to bend various religious practices to suit better their specific social needs. In particular free and enslaved people of African descent used traditional Christian rites such as marriage and baptism to cultivate and strengthen social connections and foster a sense of community among their co-parishioners. Within the specific racial climates of Cartagena and Charleston, free people of color played central roles in these religious rites. Baptism, and the selection of baptismal sponsors or godparents, facilitated the cultivation of social ties, the establishment of broad networks of fictive kinship, and the development of community.

CARTAGENA: CHURCH OF THE SANTISIMA TRINIDAD

On December 18, 1812, an enslaved woman named Cecilia Ortega gave birth to a child named Maria de la O. Felix de Castro baptized Maria at the Church of the Holy Trinity three days later. A white woman named Mauricia Galindo— referred to as *ciudadana* or "citizen" in the baptismal record—owned both Ortega and her daughter. Ortega chose Rafaela Perez as her daughter's sole godparent but declined to select a godfather for the newly baptized Maria. Like elsewhere in the Spanish Americas, Maria's owner did not serve as godmother, nor did members of the owner's family or social circle; rather her godmother was a free woman of African descent.[9]

In a city where African-descended people constituted a majority but the enslaved population comprised only about 8 percent, it was likely advantageous—economically and socially—for enslaved people to maintain these types of "vertical" links with individuals of higher status, in this case free people of color. Perez was surely more secure economically than Cecilia Ortega and her child, and their relationship through baptism may have made Perez more likely to offer any manner of support or assistance in times of need. Perez, for her part, likely gained a degree of social distinction through her formal role with the church, her selection as godmother helping demonstrate that she was a trustworthy and reliable member of the church community to whom others looked for support.[10]

Over the next four years, Perez served as a godmother three more times, one of the few women to hold that distinction in this era. She was the godmother for two other newborn enslaved girls: Maria de las Nieves and Maria Calletana, both born in August 1814. Like Maria de la O, the fathers of both Maria de las Nieves and Maria Calletana were not listed in the baptismal sponsor book, and thus the children are listed as *hijos naturales,* or natural children, a classification used to distinguish them from *hijos legitimos,* legitimate ones. Owned by Mateo Zea y Molina and Mariano Cabilla, respectively, Maria de las Nieves and Maria Calletana are linked, both with each other and with Maria de la O, through their common godmother, Rafaela Perez. Interestingly Maria de las Nieves had a godfather as well: Don Ubaldo Arraje, one of the few *padrinos* to receive the honorific *Don* in the baptismal book for African-descended children, which like elsewhere in Latin America, were recorded separately from white baptisms. Don Arraje was certainly a well-known, respectable member of the community to receive such a title, though his exact racial background remains unknown. Nevertheless his inclusion as a godfather would have benefitted not just the recently baptized Maria de las Nieves but her mother and godmother as well, as each of them would have formalized and cemented a durable social link to a man of means and distinction in the community, an additional example of the kinds of vertical ties *compadrazgo* could facilitate.[11]

In April 1814 Perez once again served as godmother, this time for a boy named Toribio José. Toribio stands out among the godchildren under Perez's charge in a number of ways. First he is the only male child for which she served as godmother. He was also free and had both parents—Agapito de Mesa and Juana Herrera, both also free—recorded in the parish's baptismal book. Toribio José is also recorded with a godfather, Benencia de Mesa, almost surely a relative of Toribio's father, Agapito. Not just the godmother of choice for the mothers of female enslaved children, Perez had ties to free families strong enough that they also chose her for the distinction of godmother.[12]

Ultimately the case of Rafaela Perez allows us to tease out how the Catholic Church and women's roles within it facilitated the development of fictive kinship ties and social prominence for African-descended people in nineteenth-century Cartagena. That so many of Perez's free and enslaved neighbors of African descent thought highly enough of her to request her service as godparent suggests she was regarded as a reliable and respectable member of the church community. Perez's willingness to serve as a godmother for four different children likely cemented her status as a woman of distinction in Getsemaní. Further her role as a godmother linked together more than a dozen individuals in the city, and the mothers of these children likely understood the types of social ties that came with choosing Perez as godmother. The four children became linked to one another, and the four, their four mothers, and the one father involved all gained a social link not just to Perez but also to Don Ubaldo Arraje, Mauricia Galindo, Mateo Zea y Molina, and Mariano Cabilla, wealthy and prominent whites in the city. The "weak" social ties—as sociologist Mark S. Granovetter famously called them—that came with godparentage likely provided a loose system of social support and (perhaps more important) linked together a community of African descent in the city.[13]

The godparentage patterns revealed by Perez's experience parallel those found throughout Latin America, where, at least during the eighteenth and nineteenth centuries, baptism served important social functions for free and enslaved people of African descent. Work by historians of Brazil, Puerto Rico, and elsewhere has revealed that African-descended people frequently selected (and served as) baptismal sponsors in order to formalize and strengthen kinship bonds within their local community. Typically these ties of fictive kinship functioned in one of two ways: *horizontal* ties formalizing the connection between the baptized (and his or her parents) with individuals matching their social, economic, racial, or legal status; or *vertical* ties that established or strengthened connections with community members more prominent than the baptized, whether measured by complexion, legal status, wealth, or other markers.[14] The ties formalized by Perez's role as godmother included both horizontal and vertical, as she sponsored baptisms for both free and enslaved children and served as godparent alongside people of different statuses and backgrounds. As David M. Stark notes in his study of baptism and godparentage in eighteenth-century Arecibo, Puerto Rico, by formalizing relationships through baptismal sponsorship, this process "acted as a cohesive and integrative force within the community," one important for "forging neighbourhood connections" through the development of social networks centered around the church.[15] He further argues that godparenthood not only "strengthened existing kin networks" but also "transformed acquaintances and friends into members of the immediate spiritual family."[16]

The experience of Perez and other free women of color also illustrates the unique role of godmothers in nineteenth-century Cartagena. Like Perez a free woman of color named Trinidad Lambi served as a godmother several times over the course of three years. She served as godmother and sole godparent to three *hijos legitimos:* Antonio Maria Zeferino, born 1814, and Anastacio Antonio and Maria Dolores, both baptized on the same day in August 1815.[17] It is likely that for Lambi serving as godmother for these *legitimos* further distinguished her as a respectable member of the parish community. The critical importance of godmothers is borne out in a broader analysis of baptismal data for Getsemaní: more children baptized between 1811 and 1816 had godmothers than godfathers; women served as godparents multiple times far more frequently than men; and if a child had only one godparent, it was twice as likely to be a godmother than a godfather.[18]

A sampling of the baptisms from Santísima Trinidad reveals that just over half of the children baptized between 1811 and 1816 (54.5 percent) had both a godfather and a godmother present. Fourteen percent of children had only a godfather, while the remaining 31.5 percent had only a godmother (table 5.1).[19] In total, while about 85 percent of infants in this sample had a godmother (either as sole godparent or as one of two godparents), only about 65 percent of baptized infants had a godfather. The greater frequency with which women served as the sole godparent suggests both that the imperative for selecting a godmother seems to have been stronger than for a godfather and that the opportunity to serve as godparent may have been more valuable for women than it was for men in early nineteenth-century Cartagena. It is possible as well that, because the baptisms analyzed here occurred during the wars for independence from Spain and because so many men of African descent participated in the voluntary militia, godfathers were less available during this era than they might have been otherwise.[20]

TABLE 5.1 **Godparents for African-descended children baptized between 1811 and 1816**

Godfather only	Godmother only	Both
14%	31.5%	54.5%

SOURCE: "Libro de Bautismos de Pardos y Morenos, 1812."

These general patterns held true for children baptized at Santísima Trinidad regardless of their birth or legal status. A child's legitimacy status, for example, did not diminish the importance of godmothers. Perez, as we saw, served as godmother for two illegitimate children, only one of whom also had a godfather. People in Spanish America, as Ann Twinam has shown, "employed a precise vocabulary when they differentiated between the layers that composed the birth status."[21] This extended, of course, to the formal recording of status in parish baptismal records. Though the status recorded in baptismal books was not immutable—as Twinam has so masterfully demonstrated—it does reveal the status of a child's parents at the time of baptism.

Children recorded as *hijos legitimos* had parents who were married at the time of the child's birth and who expressed their intentions to raise the child as their own. Children could be considered "illegitimate" for a number of different reasons. The most common of these (and the "least onerous" according to Twinam) was the *hijo natural,* a status for children born to unwed parents. Other, more complicated forms of illegitimacy included *spurii,* or "bastards," *incestuosos, adulterinos,* and *sacrilegos,* each of which involved children being born to parents not only unwed but also for one reason or another unable to marry in the eyes of the church.

Yet despite these differences between *hijos legitimos* and *hijos naturales,* virtually no differences existed in godparenting patterns when children of these statuses are compared. A sample of 221 baptisms from Santísima Trinidad included 103 *hijos legitimos*—slightly more than 45 percent of all baptisms. Of those 15 (14.5 percent) were listed with only a godfather, while 31 (30 percent) were listed with a godmother as the sole godparent. Fifty-seven (55 percent) are listed with two godparents. These proportions are nearly identical to those for *hijos naturales* (and thus to the broader sample). For the 107 *hijos naturales* in the sample, 13 (12 percent) have only a godfather, 35 (33 percent) have only a godmother, and 57 (53 percent) are listed with both.[22] (See table 5.2.) Ultimately the general pattern of privileging godmothers over godfathers in instances where only one godparent was chosen held true regardless of the child's legitimacy status at birth, as there was virtually no difference in godparent practices between legitimate and illegitimate children in early nineteenth-century Cartagena.

TABLE 5.2 **Number and percentage of children baptized at Santísima Trinidad with godfathers, godmothers, and both, 1812**

	Godfather Only		Godmother Only		Both	
	Number	Percent	Number	Percent	Number	Percent
Hijos Legitimos	15	14.5%	31	30%	57	55%
Hijos Naturales	13	12%	35	33%	57	53%

SOURCE: "Libro de Bautismos de Pardos y Morenos, 1812."

Baptisms of enslaved children also seem to have privileged godmothers over godfathers, although relatively few of them occurred during this era compared to the baptisms of free children of African descent. Among the fourteen such baptisms included in my sample, ten (71 percent) are listed with godmothers as the sole godparent, while none are listed solely with godfathers. Four (28.5 percent) were baptized with two godparents. All but one of the godparents listed for these enslaved people were of African descent, and none seem to bear a familial relationship to slave owners.[23] This lack of relationship between slave owners and the godparents of enslaved children seems typical of baptism patterns elsewhere in Latin America.[24] Though the sample size is too small to draw firmer conclusions, particularly in regard to the total absence of godfathers serving as sole godparent, the extant data suggests that for enslaved children and enslaved mothers, the imperative for selecting a godmother was greater than that for selecting a godfather. Perhaps godmotherhood entailed a more direct involvement in the lives of their godchildren, and thus enslaved mothers found that role particularly important. Likewise it is possible that enslaved children required greater assistance from their godparents, perhaps meaning that by serving as a godmother to an enslaved child, free women of color gained additional social prestige beyond that which they could gain by serving as godmother for a free child. Either way the baptismal records of Santísima Trinidad certainly suggest that the link between godmotherhood and enslaved children was even stronger than it was for the free population.

Finally, when we analyze the sample based on the baptized child's parental representation, this trend privileging godmothers appears even stronger. In particular, children who were baptized without a father were far more likely to have a godmother as their sole godparent than for the sample as a whole. Among the sixty-eight children in the sample recorded without fathers, thirty-one (46 percent) had a godmother serving as their sole godparent. Twenty-nine (43 percent) had both a godmother and godfather, while only eight (12 percent) had only a godfather.[25] While one might logically expect godfathers to have taken on a greater importance for children baptized without their birth fathers, in reality the opposite seems to have been true, with sole godmothers serving far more frequently in these instances than they did in others. Like for enslaved children—who were not included in the fatherless sample but were likewise frequently recorded without fathers—it seems possible that godmothers played a more active role in the lives of their godchildren than godfathers did, making their presence more important than that of a godfather. Further, it seems possible as well that a child's birth mother may have taken an active role in the selection of a godmother, while birth fathers may have more frequently chosen the godfather. Thus in the absence of a birth father, godfathers appeared absent as well.

While many baptism arrangements involved godmothers serving for a number of different families, strengthening a broad network of social ties, other cases revealed repeated links between a single set of parents and godparents. In August 1814 Apolonia Cardales was chosen as godmother for Justa Rafina, daughter of Pedro Celestino and Gregoria Marrugo. The godfather was named Julian José Cardales, and although the relationship between Julian and Apolonia remains unclear, they surely shared either a familial or marital relationship. In December 1814 Apolonia was again called to serve as godmother, this time for a child named José Lucio, born to Maria Santos Gusman and Pedro Julian Cardales. This time Apolonia served as *copadrino* with Pedro Pablo Cuello. Two years later, in December 1816, Apolonia Cardales was chosen as godmother for the recently born Manuel Salvador. Like Justa Rafina born two years prior, Manuel Salvador was the son of Gregoria Marrugo and, like his sister, had Apolonia and Julian Cardales as his godparents. Their families already linked, Gregoria Marrugo seems to have opted to strengthen their existing ties rather than further expand her social circle. Apolonia was also selected that month to serve as godparent, along with a Gregorio Cardales, of José de la Concepción, though the relationship between Apolonia and Gregorio is likewise unclear.[26]

The case of Apolonia Cardales is distinct from those of Rafaela Perez and Trinidad Lambi, as it demonstrates how the process of selecting godparents could serve to reinforce and strengthen family ties rather than expand one's social circle. Though the exact relationship between these individuals is unclear, the Cardales clan—Apolonia, Gregorio, Julian José, and Pedro Julian—doubled down on their family links through their role as godparents. The nature of Apolonia's service as godmother reveals situations in which free people of color used godparentage not to expand weak social ties but rather to strengthen existing ones. Nevertheless Apolonia would have served as a link between the children for whom she served as godmother (though two were siblings). Her role as a multiple godmother surely would have boosted her social standing in the parish community, if not more broadly.

In nineteenth-century Cartagena, black and mulatto women served as godparents with greater frequency than men, using these formal church roles to elevate their social standing and strengthen ties throughout their community. For free women of color, these types of opportunities to establish respectable reputations and to gain some level of social distinction through formal affiliations were far fewer than for men, who had access to a much wider range of institutional outlets for building social connections and distinction in Cartagena. While free men of color could secure privileges for themselves and their families not typically afforded to African-descended people and establish strong social ties to prominent members of the community and state bureaucracy through their involvement with institutions such as the colonial militia and other forms of voluntary association, such outlets were closed to women of African descent. Thus the church represented one of the few ways free women of color could serve in formal, public roles and gain the same status distinctions more frequently open to their male counterparts.

The selection of free women of color as godmothers signaled to the broader community their status as dependable, trustworthy, and respectable members of the parish. Though godmotherhood perhaps came with greater responsibilities than godfatherhood, women's greater representation among godparents suggests that the benefits of serving in such a role made those commitments worthwhile. Further, that free women of color served with even greater frequency as godmothers for enslaved and fatherless children suggests, perhaps, that the kind of social distinction afforded by godmotherhood was even greater under circumstances where the newly baptized child had a greater need for outside assistance.

The ritual of selecting and serving as godparent served social functions far beyond its more immediate ecclesiastical definitions. By establishing ties to prominent godparents, children and parents developed durable social links to other members of the church and city community. Godparents, for their part, served as the hub of broad networks of social relations and fictive kinship. Those who served as godparents for multiple children in particular were positioned at the center of networks that connected people of African descent both free and enslaved across status lines and generations. As we saw with the case of Rafaela Perez and others, godparents often found themselves at the center of kinship networks that connected children, parents, godparents, and sometimes enslavers to one another. Godparents, particularly godmothers, raised their social profile by serving in positions of relative distinction within the parish community. Children, parents, and godparents alike expanded their networks of social relations through these ties of fictive kinship.

ST. PHILIP'S EPISCOPAL CHURCH, CHARLESTON

On January 4, 1812, Grace Clark and her husband, William, welcomed the birth of a child named Hannah Mackenzie; they baptized Hannah that March. The Clarks selected as her baptismal sponsors Thomas Inglis, a hairdresser; Abigail Jones, free woman of color and wife of prominent tailor and hotel proprietor Jehu Jones; and Hannah McKenzie, a free black woman. The Inglis, Clark, and Jones families were some of the city's most prominent free people of color. Clark already had several degrees of connection to the Inglis and Jones families, connections he formalized through baptism. William Clark, Inglis, and Abigail Jones's husband, Jehu, were all members of the Brown

Fellowship Society: Jones joined in 1798, Clark in 1804, and Inglis in 1807. Additionally Jones and Inglis were neighbors, and it seems at plausible that Clark may have lived near them as well, adding yet another level of connection between the father and his daughter's baptismal sponsors. Though he was already a co-parishioner, associational member, neighbor, and perhaps professional colleague, Clark cemented his link to Inglis and Jones by selecting them as baptismal sponsors—a perfect example of how free people of color strengthened horizontal ties through the choice of baptismal sponsors. Though less is known about their daughter's third sponsors, Hannah McKenzie, her inclusion among the prominent Jones and Inglis families, along with the Clarks' decision to name their daughter after her, suggests she held a place of equal social prominence. Through their decisions about baptismal sponsorship, the Clarks ensured their child, Hannah Mackenzie, would always be connected to the elite of free colored Charleston.[27]

The Clarks attended Charleston's St. Philip's Episcopal Church. Unlike Cartagena's Catholic Iglesia de la Santísima Trinidad, which served the city's African-descended popular classes almost exclusively, St. Philip's was the parish of choice for many of Charleston's wealthiest residents, both black and white. Like many southern churches during this era, St. Philip's was an interracial congregation. Though they did not commingle during services, the comembership of both black and white congregants at St. Philip's brought people of different racial backgrounds and statuses into one another's social spheres, and the church recorded their baptisms in a single registry. For both infants and adults, free and enslaved, baptized into St. Philip's, the selection of baptismal sponsors served a crucial social function, offering an opportunity to distinguish oneself among the church community and to establish, strengthen, and formalize social links to prominent members of the city's free black and colored elite. Through participation in church rites and by serving as baptismal sponsors, free and enslaved black members of St. Philip's facilitated the development of a black community in Charleston.

In William Clark's case, he continued to expand his family's social network by serving as a baptismal sponsor himself. Between 1811 and 1815, Clark served as baptismal sponsor for eight different people. He sponsored the baptism of four enslaved people and four free people of color; three were adults, and five were children. He gained ties to five different parents and three different slave owners. He served as cosponsor with ten different individuals, one of whom was white. Through his role as a baptismal sponsor and active member of the church, Clark positioned himself at the center of a social network that expanded considerably over a relatively short period of time.

In 1811 Clark first served as the baptismal sponsor for William Mushington—an adult and free man of color. Along with Clark, John Martin and Ann Snelling served as cosponsors for Mushington. In 1812 Clark served as the baptismal sponsor for two free black children, Tobias and Charles. Tobias was born to Stephen and Thyara Mansfield, and Clark's cosponsor for Tobias was William Eden, another of St. Philip's most prominent free black congregants. Charles was born to William Friday and Letitia Friday, and Clark's cosponsors were William Friday Sr., likely Charles's grandfather, and Martha Cannon. In 1813 Clark sponsored the baptism of a free black woman named Ann Snelling, along with cosponsors Martha Moulton and Susannah Hibben. These baptisms reflected a crucial trend: all of Clark's cosponsors were fellow free people of color.[28]

The example of someone like William Clark allows us to view in microcosm the social components of church involvement for free blacks in early nineteenth-century Charleston. His case reveals how, by carefully selecting baptismal sponsors and serving as a sponsor several times, Clark cultivated social ties with dozens of different people, both black and white, free and enslaved. For some of these individuals, particularly the enslaved, affiliation with Clark would have boosted their social profile and allowed them to include a prominent free person in their network of fictive kin. Clark, in turn, gained the distinction of being a well-respected member of the church's black community and gained a social link to prominent slave owning whites. Links with whites could come in handy, even for someone as prominent as Clark, particularly as the antebellum period wore on. Further Clark strengthened his ties to other free black members of St. Philip's, many of whom seem to have matched his social, complexional, and associational status. By establishing and maintaining links between free families of color, baptism and church involvement served as a way to develop a smaller, more close-knit free black community within a single parish.

Free people of African descent baptized at St. Philip's almost never chose whites as baptismal sponsors. They chose prominent people free people of color instead. Although historians of the antebellum South generally and South Carolina in particular have long argued that free blacks, under increasing social and legal pressure over the course of the nineteenth century, needed to cultivate relationships with prominent white patrons to protect themselves from discrimination and violence, people of African descent at St. Philip's almost never elected to use baptismal sponsorship to serve that purpose.[29] Between 1811 and 1815, 75 men and 74 women sponsored 99 baptisms for free people of color at St. Philip's. Within that group fully 86 percent of the men and 80 percent of the women were fellow free people of color (see table 5.3).

TABLE 5.3 **Baptismal sponsors of Charleston free people of color by race and gender**

Male Sponsor (74)					
Free Person of Color		White		Unknown	
Number	Percent	Number	Percent	Number	Percent
64	86%	6	8%	4	5%

Female Sponsor (76)					
Free Person of Color		White		Unknown	
Number	Percent	Number	Percent	Number	Percent
60	81%	9	12%	3	4%

SOURCE: "Register, St. Philip's Episcopal Church, 1810–1822," South Caroliniana Library, University of South Carolina.

Additionally, unlike in Cartagena men and women served as sponsors with roughly equal frequency. Among ninety-nine free people of color baptized at St. Philip's between 1811 and 1815, 71 percent had both a male and female sponsor, while 4 percent had a male sponsor only and 3 percent had a female sponsor only (see table 5.4).

TABLE 5.4 **Baptismal sponsors of Charleston free people of color by gender**

	Only Male Sponsor		Only Female Sponsor		Both Male and Female Sponsor		No Sponsor Listed	
	Number	Percent	Number	Percent	Number	Percent	Number	Percent
Free People of Color (99)	4	4%	3	3%	70	71%	22	22%

SOURCE: "Register, St. Philip's Episcopal Church, 1810–1822," South Caroliniana Library, University of South Carolina.

Enslaved people as well chose free people of color as their baptismal sponsors, as they did in Cartagena, establishing vertical social links across lines of status and class—relationships free people of color tended to avoid in other contexts. In 1812 Clark was the baptismal sponsor for an enslaved woman named Susy, owned by a Mrs. McCredie. In this instance, in an exception to more general trends, he served alongside Mrs. Christian Logan, a white woman. Clark, along with his wife, Grace, sponsored the baptisms of other enslaved people owned by McCredie as well: on September 9, 1814, he sponsored an enslaved child named Richard Peter, born to a woman named Atkins, while Grace Clark sponsored Susanna Eden, another of Atkins's children. In addition to the Clarks, Harry Edwards, and Nancy Peyton, and William Eden and his wife, all free people of color, served as cosponsors. Clark also served as sponsor, along with free black woman Fanny Williams, for enslaved children Jane and Elizabeth, both owned by Sarah Mitchell.[30]

Other free people of color sponsored the baptisms of enslaved people as well. In 1812 Abraham and Maria, both enslaved people, baptized their two children, Maria and Tibb, aged four and one, respectively. Though owned by different people—Abraham by a Dr. Bradley, Maria by a Mrs. Russell— Abraham and Maria chose neither to serve as baptismal sponsor, instead selecting a free black woman named Rose White. Although they were enslaved by different individuals, siblings Maria and Tibb remained linked through their shared free godmother. The parents of other enslaved people, though their names are not recorded in the baptismal register, seem to have adopted similar strategies. Certain free people of color were particularly prominent in the church and served as baptismal sponsors to enslaved people time and again. William Eden, William Clark, Ratcliffe Smith, Peter Glen, Rose Smith, and Martha Stewart all served as baptismal sponsors for enslaved people multiple times between 1811 and 1815.[31]

Like for the baptisms of free people of color, enslaved people most frequently had both a male and female sponsor, though their baptisms exhibited a higher likelihood they would have only a female sponsor (see table 5.5). Likewise it was far more common for enslaved people to have white baptismal sponsors than for free people of color. Between 1811 and 1815, eighty-two enslaved people had at least once male baptismal sponsor; just over half of those sponsors were white. Among the female sponsors for ninety-nine enslaved people during the same era, fully 70 percent were white (see table 5.6). This pattern was particularly evident for enslaved people who lived in plantations outside the city, as slave owners there held a substantial presence as baptismal sponsors.[32]

TABLE 5.5 Baptismal sponsors for Charleston
enslaved people by gender

	Only Male Sponsor		Only Female Sponsor		Both Male and Female Sponsor		No Sponsor Listed	
	Number	Percent	Number	Percent	Number	Percent	Number	Percent
Enslaved People (128)	5	4%	16	12%	79	61%	28	22%

SOURCE: "Register, St. Philip's Episcopal Church, 1810–1822,"
South Caroliniana Library, University of South Carolina.

TABLE 5.6 Baptismal sponsors for Charleston
enslaved people by race and status

Male Sponsor (82)				Female Sponsor (99)			
Black		White		Black		White	
Number	Percent	Number	Percent	Number	Percent	Number	Percent
39	48%	43	52%	30	30%	69	70%

SOURCE: "Register, St. Philip's Episcopal Church, 1810–1822,"
South Caroliniana Library, University of South Carolina.

And yet about 40 percent of all enslaved people baptized during this era selected a person of African descent as sponsor. That so many chose other people of African descent seems to suggest that many enslaved people in Charleston used the selection of baptismal sponsors to cement and formalize a network of fictive kinship for their children. Through baptism enslaved people forged stronger links to prominent free people of African descent, people from whom they could marshal support in times of distress or need. That enslaved people regularly chose free people of color (and occasionally other enslaved people) as baptismal sponsors also suggests that religious rites could function as another facet of autonomy among urban enslaved people, with enslaved people themselves exercising agency in the selection of sponsors.

In addition to the selection of particular individuals, naming practices also served as a means by which free and enslaved people of color could strengthen social links with their baptismal sponsors. In a number of cases, both free and enslaved people of color seem to have named their children after their baptismal sponsors. Often this involved using the surname of a baptismal sponsor as their child's middle name, but other times the child seems to have been named entirely after a particularly prominent baptismal sponsor. For example in 1811 John Francis, a free black barber in Charleston, baptized his son James Mitchell, naming him after one of his baptismal sponsors. James Mitchell the elder was one of the most prominent free blacks in the city, a tailor by trade and a founding member of the elite Brown Fellowship Society. John and Abigail Jones named their son Edwin Livingston, seemingly taking the surname of his baptismal sponsor John Livingston, who served alongside John Francis in that role. In 1812 William and Grace Clark gave their daughter Hannah Mackenzie the full name of one of her baptismal sponsors. Likewise in 1815 Peter and Clarissa Desverneys named their daughter Sarah Simons after one of her baptismal sponsors. Ratcliffe and Mary Smith, two more very active church members, did the same for their child James, selecting for him the middle name Salters, the surname of his baptismal sponsor Paris Salters. Such a strategy was not confined to the free class, as enslaved people appear to have named their children after the prominent free blacks they chose as sponsors. For example an enslaved woman named Atkins named her daughter Susannah Eden, as she had selected William Eden and his wife to serve as baptismal sponsors.[33]

These naming conventions likely served as an additional way that free black and enslaved parents could attempt to bestow social advantages to their children through the church. In addition to expanding social networks, naming their children after prominent black baptismal sponsors likely functioned as a way to strengthen the link between child and sponsor. Even in instances where the parents themselves were fairly prominent figures among the church's black congregants, as in the case of William and Grace Clark, it seems that these naming conventions offered an additional way to strengthen bonds of fictive kinship. In a city with a relatively small population of free people of color, these naming patterns may have afforded people of African descent a degree of social capital with their white neighbors, particularly with those they did not know personally. Free people of color like James Mitchell and Susannah Eden would have been known widely in the city, so naming one's children after them would have been a way for free people of color to endow their children with an obvious connection to the city's free colored elite. In this way naming their child at least in part after a baptismal sponsor also may have served as a way of exporting the link between the two out into the Charleston community outside St. Philip's. While

one's relationship with a baptismal sponsor may not have been widely evident to the members of other congregations, a shared name could function
as a marker of social distinction.

The distinction of serving as a baptismal sponsor at St. Philip's sometimes
became connected to other markers of distinction for free people of color
elsewhere in the city. For example because St. Philip's was home to many
Brown Fellowship Society members, serving as sponsor could facilitate entry
into that association, while other members chose fellow members to serve
as baptismal sponsors. For example Charles Le Mar selected as a baptismal
sponsor for his daughter Hager Susannah tailor and Brown Fellowship
Society member Joseph Humphries. For his son John, four years younger
than Hager but baptized the same day, Le Mar chose shoemaker and Brown
Fellowship Society member William Cooper and his wife to serve as sponsors. Three years later, in 1816, Le Mar gained entry to the Brown Fellowship
Society as well. Similarly William Mushington, who gained Brown Fellowship entry in 1814, selected James Campbell to be baptismal sponsor for his
daughter Clodia Ann in 1815; Campbell entered the organization the following year. When Henry Chatter (a Brown Fellowship member since 1803)
baptized his son Daniel Cooper in 1810, he also chose Brown Fellowship
member William Cooper (a naming convention discussed above) as well as
Robert Grant, one of the originators of the Brown Fellowship Society. For
parishioners at St. Philip's, baptism could both establish and reinforce social
links that proved useful even outside the church community.[34]

Through their involvement in baptisms, free people of color developed
and strengthened social links to one another and likely bolstered their reputations as respectable people of social distinction. By selecting and serving
as baptismal sponsors—and sometimes naming their children after those
sponsors—free people of color expanded and strengthened their social networks within the city, formalizing relationships with other people of African
descent (as well as some prominent whites). It established new patterns of social relations and reinforced existing ones. The frequency with which Brown
Fellowship Society members chose one another to serve as baptismal sponsors, for example, reveals how this process could serve to strengthen horizontal ties and reinforce reputations as a distinct class within the Charleston
community. Enslaved people, for their part, also developed durable social ties
to free people of color, bringing themselves and their children into networks
of fictive kinship. Taken together, these links that connected congregants of
African descent at St. Philip's facilitated the development of what seems to
have been a closer-knit racial community, one that crossed the line between
slavery and freedom.

CONCLUSION

In Cartagena and Charleston, free and enslaved people of African descent chose free people of color to serve as their baptismal sponsors, developing broad networks of fictive kinship for both themselves and for their children. As means of cultivating or formalizing social ties to prominent free people of color, the church generally and the process of selecting baptismal sponsors specifically served to expand one's social network in the nineteenth-century Atlantic world. Whether through expanding and strengthening a social network through horizontal ties or by seeking advantage through vertical links to godparents of higher status, baptism served crucial social functions for people of African descent throughout the Americas and Caribbean. As scholars have shown for other areas of Spanish America and the United States, the act of serving as baptismal sponsor afforded free people of color a degree of respectability and social distinction within their local communities. While in Cartagena women of African descent took advantage of this possibility more frequently than men, in both Charleston and Cartagena free people of color served frequently as baptismal sponsors for fellow people of African descent, gaining a degree of social prominence in the process. Finally that whites so rarely served as baptismal sponsors for free people of color suggests that throughout the urban Atlantic world, the church served as a key site for the formation of a more close-knit sense of racial community than was possible in cities more broadly. By taking on roles within the church, free people of color gained social distinction and respectability in ways that undermined the racial ideologies that underpinned much of the urban Americas.

CONCLUSION

Throughout the urban Americas, people of African descent creatively and persistently attempted to improve their lives through any means available. Enslaved people sought routes to freedom, alternately leveraging and skirting legal codes as needed. In freedom they engaged the intellectual and cultural currents of the Atlantic world, not just informing themselves about such events as the Haitian Revolution but also deeply considering how revolutionary Atlantic movements might impact their daily lives. They also looked closer to home for opportunities to improve their individual circumstances. Free people of color used their skill, thrift, and industry to gain economic stability for themselves and their families and to craft reputations as useful and respectable. They also cultivated social networks that included fellow artisans of color and prominent whites, people capable of supporting them in times of need. They founded and joined a wide variety of voluntary organizations, using their affiliation with elite groups to gain a measure of social distinction within their local community. And they took on leadership roles in their local churches, serving as baptismal sponsors for people of African descent both free and enslaved, establishing themselves as respectable individuals within their church community and beyond. Through these efforts free people of color gained opportunities to achieve social prestige, distinguishing themselves from enslaved people as well as the popular classes of African descent. Yet even as they worked to improve their individual circumstances, free people of color engaged white elites and state authorities in ways that challenged the logic of American racial hierarchies. Through their social striving and efforts to achieve respectability, free people of color cultivated identities and carried themselves in ways that undermined the ideological foundations of white authority in the early modern Atlantic world.

Despite these broad parallels in the social and cultural worlds of free people of color, the lived experience of freedom for African-descended people could differ in crucial ways between Spanish America and the United States. Although hurdles to achieving freedom existed both in Charleston and in Cartagena, white racial anxieties were predicated on fundamentally different views of slave emancipation. While whites in Cartagena sought to restrict manumission as a way of ending slavery under carefully controlled circumstances—and worried about the preparedness for freedom of the formerly enslaved—authorities in Charleston attempted to curtail manumission, because they viewed it as a threat to slavery, an institution they believed would, and must, survive in perpetuity. Likewise, although free people of color throughout the Americas looked to artisan trades and skilled occupations for opportunities to improve their economic fortunes and social standing, demographic realities shaped those opportunities in significant ways. Artisans of color in Charleston faced regular competition both from whites and from enslaved people in ways their counterparts in Cartagena never did.

Perhaps the most important difference between Spanish America and the United States in the efforts of free people of color to achieve social distinction is the role of the state and access to public institutions. In Cartagena and throughout Spanish America, a public, institutional aspect of respectability existed for free people of color that simply did not for their counterparts in Charleston. Free people of color in Cartagena joined the voluntary militia, a crucial public institution, formally obtaining access to expanded rights and benefits not available to others of African descent. Through their affiliation with an elite, corporately ordered institution, free people of color fought for special legal considerations and gained access to local and royal officials from whom they won a wide variety of concessions. Even outside militia membership, free people of color petitioned the Crown to receive a number of social privileges not normally afforded to people of African descent—sometimes even including exemptions from their racial ancestry altogether.

In the United States, and in Charleston in particular, free people of color cultivated a far more private respectability than their counterparts in Spanish America, lacking access to public institutions free people of color in Cartagena enjoyed. Consequently free people of color in Charleston founded private organizations and carefully cultivated personal relationships to support their efforts to achieve social distinction in the city. Many of these organizations attempted to cultivate, at times explicitly, the kinds of personal and moral habits among its members that could counter whites' more general expectations for how people of African descent would act in freedom. By demonstrating their commitment to shared cultural values with whites—characteristics such as sobriety, thrift, industriousness, and piety—free people of color established themselves as distinguished, respectable members of the local community. Even outside these private social organizations, free people of color cultivated social ties with prominent whites through their work, worship, and everyday lives as a means of gaining the types of privileges, advantages, and distinctions they were barred from obtaining from the state.

Yet although the nature of respectability between the Americas at times differed, examining the worlds of free people of color reveals the many ways they sought to improve their lives in the face of persistent racial discrimination. Free people of color appealed to the Crown, petitioned the state legislature, cultivated social ties with other prominent community members, and in myriad other ways attempted to improve their individual circumstances and those of their families, striving to achieve social distinction throughout the urban Americas. Through these efforts to overcome racism and gain social prestige, free people of color challenged the very nature of white authority in the Atlantic world. By fighting for rights and privileges not normally afforded to African-descended people, establishing respectable reputations for themselves and their families, and carving out social distinction throughout the urban Americas—in short by living in ways that ran counter to whites' expectations of African-descended people—free people of color confronted the basis of racial discrimination and undermined the logic supporting racial hierarchies foundational to American societies. By expanding the cracks in that foundation and creating new ones, free people of color in the African Americas contributed to a long struggle for recognition, civil rights, and justice that still continues today.

Notes

INTRODUCTION

1. "Relación que manifiesta los Artesanos que existen en el Barrio de Santo Thorivio el presente año de 1780," Archivo General de la Nación (Colombia), Section Colónia, Fondo Miscelánea, tomo 31, 149v.

2. "Manumission of Jehu Jones," South Carolina Department of Archives and History, Miscellaneous Records, vol. HHH, pp. 442–43; "Rules and Regulations of the Brown Fellowship Society" (Charleston: J.B. Nixon, 1844), in "Brown Fellowship Society Records, 1794–1990," AMN 1005, box 1, Avery Research Center, Charleston, S.C.; Goldsmith, *Directory and Stranger's Guide.* See also Johnson and Romero, "Jehu Jones."

3. I am using *American* here to describe collectively North America, South America, and the Caribbean.

4. Taking a top-down approach focused primarily on legal codes of the United States and Latin America, scholars such as Frank Tannenbaum argued beginning in the 1940s that the milder slavery and continued recognition of the personhood of African-descended people in Latin America largely explained the lack of contemporary racism there, particularly as compared to the United States. This image of racial democracy in Latin America, and this approach to comparative scholarship, has largely been replaced by more recent work that takes local dynamics and evidence more seriously. Yet the conclusions of scholars such as Tannenbaum have proved remarkably, and frustratingly, durable, as scholars' broad comparative gestures are often still informed in some way by this work. Tannenbaum, *Slave and Citizen;* Elkins, *Slavery;* Klein, *Slavery in the Americas;* Degler, *Neither White nor Black.*

5. De la Fuente and Gross, "Slaves, Free Blacks, and Race"; de la Fuente and Gross, "Comparative Studies of Law, Slavery, and Race"; de la Fuente, "From Slaves to Citizens?"; Dantas, *Black Townsmen;* Dunn, *Tale of Two Plantations;* Landers, *Against the Odds.*

6. Dantas, *Black Townsmen.* For another comparative study focused more specifically on economic culture, see Townsend, *Tales of Two Cities.*

7. Dantas, *Black Townsmen,* 4.

8. Berlin, *Slaves without Masters.* The recent literature on free blacks in the United States is too voluminous to offer anything more than a partial list here. For the early national and antebellum South, see Buchanan, *Black Life on the Mississippi;* Curry, *Free Black in Urban America;* Ely, *Israel on the Appomattox;* Hanger, *Bounded Lives, Bounded Places;* Marks, "Community Bonds in the Bayou City"; Lebsock, *Free Women of Petersburg;* Rockman, *Scraping By;* Schafer, *Becoming Free, Remaining Free;* Sidbury,

Ploughshares into Swords; and von Daacke, *Freedom Has a Face.* On the early national and antebellum North, see Gronnigsater, "Delivering Freedom"; L. M. Harris, *In the Shadow of Slavery;* Hodges, *Root and Branch;* Horton and Horton, *In Hope of Liberty;* Polgar, "Standard Bearers of Liberty and Equality"; Rael, *Black Identity and Black Protest.*

9. Bolster, *Black Jacks;* Cañizares-Esguerra, Childs, and Sidbury, *Black Urban Atlantic;* Geggus, *Impact of the Haitian Revolution;* Gilroy, *Black Atlantic;* Landers, *Atlantic Creoles in the Age of Revolutions;* Scott and Hébrard, *Freedom Papers;* Sidbury, *Becoming African in America.*

10. Wikramanayake, *World in Shadow;* Johnson and Roark, *Black Masters;* Powers, *Black Charlestonians;* Myers, *Forging Freedom.*

11. For depictions of slavery and race relations as milder in Latin America, see Tannenbaum, *Slave and Citizen;* Elkins, *Slavery;* Freyre, *Masters and the Slaves.* For literature transforming that narrative, see Butler, *Freedoms Given, Freedoms Won;* Childs, *1812 Aponte Rebellion;* McGraw, *Work of Recognition;* Reid-Vazquez, *Year of the Lash.*

12. Andrews, *Afro-Argentines of Buenos Aires;* Andrews, *Blackness in the White Nation;* Díaz, *Virgin, the King, and the Royal Slaves of El Cobre;* Ferrer, *Freedom's Mirror;* Frank, *Dutra's World;* Hünefeldt, *Paying the Price of Freedom;* Kinsbruner, *Not of Pure Blood;* La Rosa Corzo, *Runaway Slave Settlements in Cuba;* Schmidt-Nowara, *Slavery, Freedom, and Abolition;* Sweet, *Domingos Álvares;* Vinson, *Bearing Arms for His Majesty.*

13. See, for example, Bennett, *Colonial Blackness;* Restall, *Black Middle.*

14. P. F. Gómez, "Bodies of Encounter"; Landers, "African Landscape of Seventeenth-Century Cartagena and Its Hinterlands"; Wheat, "Afro-Portuguese Maritime World"; Wheat, *Atlantic Africa.*

15. Helg, *Liberty and Equality;* Lasso, *Myths of Harmony;* McGraw, *Work of Recognition;* Sanders, *Contentious Republicans.*

16. Múnera, *El fracaso de la nación;* Múnera, *Fronteras imaginadas.*

17. Chaves, "Honor y libertad"; Chaves and Anrup, "La 'plebe' en una socieda"; Maya Restrepo, *Brujería y reconstrucción de identidades;* Maya Restrepo, "Racismo institucional"; Sanchez Mejia, "De esclavos a campesinos"; Solano D., "Pedro Romero"; Solano D. and Flórez Bolívar, "'Artilleros pardos.'"

18. I owe a significant intellectual debt to Ann Twinam's *Purchasing Whiteness* for the way it shifted my thinking about the impact of African-descended people's efforts to achieve social distinction, particularly her characterization of the *pardos* and mulattoes who attempted to purchase whiteness in colonial Spanish America as "unheralded civil rights pioneers"; see Twinam, *Purchasing Whiteness,* xvi. My methodological approach has been informed and inspired in large part by two articles: Putnam, "To Study the Fragments/Whole," quote on 615; R. J. Scott, "Small-Scale Dynamics of Large-Scale Processes."

19. McNeil, *Mosquito Empires,* 145.

20. Wheat, *Atlantic Africa,* 3–19.

21. Ibid., 278.

22. Wheat, "First Great Waves," 2.

23. Wood, *Black Majority,* 3.

24. Ibid., 6.

25. Ibid., 25.

26. Dusinberre, *Them Dark Days*, 7.

27. Wood, *Black Majority*, xviii.

28. Ibid., xiv.

29. Quintana, *Making a Slave State*, 2.

30. Dusinberre, *Them Dark Days*, ix.

CHAPTER ONE

1. Rensselaer Van Rensselaer to his father, January 1, 1829, in Van Rensselaer Bonney, *Legacy of Historical Gleanings*, 446–47.

2. Tannenbaum, *Slave and Citizen*, 53.

3. Twinam, *Purchasing Whiteness*, 86.

4. Ibid.

5. de la Fuente, "Slaves and the Creation of Legal Rights in Cuba," 663.

6. "La Carta de Jamaica," September 6, 1816, AGN, http://www.archivogeneral.gov
.co/sites/default/files/NoticiasAdjuntos/Carta%20de%20Jamaica.pdf.

7. "Sobre Libertad de Esclavos," June 2, 1816, AGN, "Negros y Esclavos" Online Portal, Legislación, http://negrosyesclavos.archivogeneral.gov.co.

8. "Bolívar llama a armas a 5,000 esclavos y les ofrece la libertad," 1820, AGN, "Negros y Esclavos" Online Portal, Legislación, http://negrosyesclavos.archivogeneral
.gov.co.

9. For discussion of the link between racial equality and patriotism in New Granada, see Lasso, *Myths of Harmony*.

10. "Sobre la Libertad de Esclavos," Jan 22, 1820, AGN, "Negros y Esclavos" Online Portal, Legislación, http://negrosyesclavos.archivogeneral.gov.co.

11. "Ley 19 de Julio de 1821," AGN, "Negros y Esclavos" Online Portal, Legislación, http://negrosyesclavos.archivogeneral.gov.co.

12. Ibid.

13. McGraw, *Work of Recognition*, 20–50.

14. This decline of slavery was roughly similar, both in process and in timing, to gradual emancipation in the U.S. North. See, for example, Melish, *Disowning Slavery;* White, *Somewhat More Independent.*

15. "Decreto sobre censo de esclavos," April 12, 1842, AGN, "Negros y Esclavos" Online Portal, Legislación, http://negrosyesclavos.archivogeneral.gov.co.

16. Ibid. For further reading on apprenticeship in the British Caribbean, see Holt, *Problem of Freedom;* Heuman, "Apprenticeship and Emancipation in the Caribbean."

17. "Ley de 29 de Mayo de 1842, Adicional a la de Manumisión," AGN, "Negros y Esclavos" Online Portal, Legislación, http://negrosyesclavos.archivogeneral.gov.co. Original held in AGN, Sección República, Fondo Libros Manuscritos y Leyes Originales de la República, libro 120.

18. Barragan, "To the Mine I Will Not Go"; see chap. 4.

19. McGraw, *Work of Recognition*, 23.

20. Berlin, *Generations of Captivity.*

21. Wood, *Black Majority*, 102–3.

22. These manumissions (along with most later ones) appear periodically in the "Miscellaneous Records" series of the South Carolina Department of Archives and History (hereafter SCDAH).

23. The full title of the law is "An Act Respecting Slaves, Free Negroes, Mulattoes, and Mestizoes; For Enforcing a More Punctual Performance of Patrol Duty; And to Impose Certain Restrictions on the Emancipation of Slaves."

24. "An Act Respecting Slaves, Free Negroes, Mulattoes, and Mestizoes," December 20, 1800, in McCord, *Statutes at Large of South Carolina*.

25. December 27, 1805, SCDAH, Miscellaneous Records, vol. 3V, 354.

26. March 10, 1801, SCDAH, Miscellaneous Records, vol. 3O, 427.

27. Historical Census Browser, University of Virginia, Geospatial Statistical and Data Center: http://mapserver.lib.virginia.edu. Such rapid growth in the free black population remains a mystery, especially in light of the fact that it does not appear to have been driven by new manumissions. The borders of the Charleston District also shrank slightly in the years after 1800, so it is not a matter of an increased population on paper only. It seems possible that slave owners alive in the Revolutionary era who arranged to free slaves in their last will and testament may have begun dying in the 1810s, leading to the emancipation of slaves not just in Charleston or in South Carolina but across the South. Given the economic possibilities of Charleston and the number of free blacks from outside of Charleston who registered their freedom in the city in the years following 1800, it seems possible that many of these formerly enslaved people migrated to Charleston. Coupled with the arrival of foreign free blacks and the existing free black population's natural increase, it seems this type of growth could at least have been plausible. It seems unlikely that natural increase was primarily responsible for this increase in the free black population. Though the federal census did not break down the free black population by age groups prior to 1820, in that year 35.6 percent of the free black population was under the age of fourteen. In the same year, 40.4 percent of the white population was under the age of the fifteen. Meanwhile the free black population increased by more than 200 percent from 1810, while the white population only increased by about 20 percent. In 1830, though the numbers declined slightly (to 3,594), they did not return to pre-1820 levels.

28. McCord, *Statutes at Large of South Carolina*, 459–60.

29. "William N. Mitchell, petition asking permission to emancipate a boy slave according to the wishes of his deceased father, who was a free black man," November 10, 1823, SCDAH, Legislative Papers, Petitions to the General Assembly, roll 1347, no. 129, 607–11.

30. "Report on the petition of William B. Harris, John Ryan, and William N. Mitchell," December 6, 1823, SCDAH, Legislative Papers, Committee Reports, No. 228.

31. "Petition of Irvin Moses," November 14, 1836, SCDAH, Petitions to the General Assembly, roll 1355, no. 40, 773–783. Irvin refers simply to serving "General Marion." This was almost certainly South Carolina native Francis Marion, who served the Continental Army as brigadier general and lieutenant colonel during the Revolution.

32. "Petition of Irvin Moses," November 14, 1836, SCDAH, Petitions to the General Assembly, roll 1355, no. 40, 773–783.

33. Committee Report on Petition of Moses Irvin, December 4, 1836, SCDAH, Legislative Papers, Committee Reports, no. 63.

34. April 3, 1827, SCDAH, Miscellaneous Records, vol. 5D, 435.

35. For a broader discussion of manumission in Colombia, see Helg, *Liberty and Equality in Caribbean Colombia*, 111–13, 169–70, 217–18; Lasso, *Myths of Harmony*, 58–60, 65–66; McGraw, *Work of Recognition*, 22–24; and Barragan, "To the Mine I Will Not Go."

36. Through the nineteenth century, Santa Marta was, along with Barranquilla, one of the few cities along Colombia's Caribbean coast that could rival Cartagena in size and importance. Santa Marta was likewise a commercial entrepôt and shipping port, and African-descended people constituted a similar proportion of the population there as they did in Cartagena.

37. Helg, *Liberty and Equality*, 111.

38. See, for example, Hünefeldt, *Paying the Price of Freedom*.

39. Helg, *Liberty and Equality*, 112–13.

40. AGN, Sección Colonia, Fondo Negros y Esclavos, Bolívar, t. 10, ff. 927–85.

41. AGN, República, Manumisión, t. 1, ff. 140–52.

42. Ibid., t. 1, ff. 282–98.

43. Ibid., t. 1, ff. 441–45.

44. For discussion of other such autonomous runaway communities, see La Rosa Corzo, *Runaway Slave Settlements in Cuba;* Price, *Alabi's World;* Price, *Maroon Societies;* Price, *First-Time*.

45. "Visita de la Santa Iglesia Catedral de esta ciudad de Cartagena a sus respectivos parroquias," January 13, 1781, Archivo General de Indias (hereafter AGI), Fondo Santa Fé, Legajo 1171. For additional discussion of palenques in Caribbean Colombia, see, for example, Landers, "African Landscape of Seventeenth-Century Cartagena."

46. In the 1990s Colombia's national government finally acknowledged the land rights of the descendants of these groups in *Ley 7 de Negritudes*.

47. "Sobre lo representado por el virrey de Santa Fe acerca de abandono en que viven muchas personas y aun familias que habitan en las montañas de la Provincia de Cartagena," December 11, 1790, AGI, Santa Fé, Legajo 997.

48. These calculations come from a thorough and systematic analysis of the Miscellaneous Records series of the SCDAH.

49. June 13, 1776, SCDAH, Miscellaneous Records, vol. SS, 234, 248.

50. July 14, 1784, SCDAH, Miscellaneous Records, vol. 3A, 67.

51. February 17, 1790, SCDAH, Miscellaneous Records, vol. YY, 216–17.

52. February 18, 1796, SCDAH, Miscellaneous Records, vol. 3G, 132–34.

53. August 18, 1792, SCDAH, Miscellaneous Records, vol. 3D, 5.

54. September 17, 1800, SCDAH, Miscellaneous Records, vol. 3Q, 143.

55. March 30, 1798, SCDAH, Miscellaneous Records, vol. 3O, 156

56. January 23, 1799, SCDAH, Miscellaneous Records, vol. 3M, 24.

57. November 15, 1800, SCDAH, Miscellaneous Records, vol. 3Q, 189.

58. I derived this figure through an analysis of all manumissions in the Miscellaneous Records series at the SCDAH, filed between 1776 and 1800.

59. Manumission of Diana, April 16, 1777, SCDAH, Miscellaneous Records, vol. SS, 49.

60. May 27, 1777, SCDAH, Miscellaneous Records, vol. SS, 136.

61. December 4, 1779, SCDAH, Miscellaneous Records, Vol. SS, 316.

62. June 1, 1796, SCDAH, Miscellaneous Records, vol. 3G, 253–54

63. June 6, 1796, SCDAH, Miscellaneous Records, vol. 3G, 265.

64. June 30, 1796, SCDAH, Miscellaneous Records, vol. 3G, 281–82.

65. January 22, 1798, SCDAH, Miscellaneous Records, vol. 3H, 442–43.

66. June 26, 1797, SCDAH, Miscellaneous Records, vol. 3I, 313.

67. See for example the manumission of Amey, May 31, 1798, SCDAH, Miscellaneous Records, vol. 3K, 316; and Hannah, August 21, 1798, SCDAH, Miscellaneous Records, vol. 3K, 347.

68. November 9, 1780, SCDAH, Miscellaneous Records, vol. SS, 431.

69. September 23, 1778, SCDAH, Miscellaneous Records, vol. RR, 566.

70. November 15, 1779, SCDAH, Miscellaneous Records, vol. SS, 378–79.

71. November 1, 1787, SCDAH, Miscellaneous Records, vol. XX, 574.

72. December 30, 1800, SCDAH, Miscellaneous Records, vol. 3O, 394.

73. See also the manumission of James via William Anderson, February 26, 1774, SCDAH, Miscellaneous Records, vol. 3D, 76; and that of Charles via Patrick McDonald, April 1, 1799, SCDAH, Miscellaneous Records, vol. 3M, 31.

74. January 19, 1779, SCDAH, Miscellaneous Records, vol. RR, 586.

75. March 16, 1780. SCDAH, Miscellaneous Records, vol. SS, 340–41.

76. June 9, 1795, SCDAH, Miscellaneous Records, vol. 3F, 122.

77. June 2, 1797, SCDAH, Miscellaneous Records, vol. 3I, 297.

78. April 24, 1797, SCDAH, Miscellaneous Records, vol. 3I, 310.

79. November 10, 1797, SCDAH, Miscellaneous Records, vol. 3I, 342–43.

80. September 11, 1798, SCDAH, Miscellaneous Records, vol. 3K, 232.

81. October 24, 1800, SCDAH, Miscellaneous Records, vol. 3Q, 261.

82. For further reading on how enslaved women navigated sexual relationships with white enslavers, see Berry and Harris, *Sexuality and Slavery.* Perhaps the most well-known such example is that of Sally Hemmings and Thomas Jefferson; see Gordon-Reed, *Hemingses of Monticello.*

83. June 6, 1778, SCDAH, Miscellaneous Records, vol. SS, 268.

84. January 25, 1779, SCDAH, Miscellaneous Records, vol. SS, 291.

85. November 9, 1789, SCDAH, Miscellaneous Records, vol. YY, 90.

86. January 20, 1790, SCDAH, Miscellaneous Records, vol. YY, 117.

87. November 30, 1793, SCDAH, Miscellaneous Records, vol. 3D, 316.

88. July 14, 1792, SCDAH, Miscellaneous Records, vol. 3B, 326.

89. March 17, 1796, SCDAH, Miscellaneous Records, vol. 3G, 155.

90. July 27, 1799, SCDAH, Miscellaneous Records, vol. 3M, 282; September 5, 1799, SCDAH, Miscellaneous Records, vol. 3M, 283; September 5, 1799, SCDAH, Miscellaneous Records, vol. 3M, 284.

91. January 25, 1793, SCDAH, Miscellaneous Records, vol. 3C, 147.

92. September 20, 1797, SCDAH, Miscellaneous Records, vol. 3H, 389.

93. May 10, 1797, SCDAH, Miscellaneous Records, vol. 3I, 329.

94. June 2, 1797, SCDAH, Miscellaneous Records, vol. 3I, 294.

CHAPTER TWO

1. J. S. Scott, "Common Wind." Unpublished for nearly three decades, this work was published by Verso Books in 2018.

2. Reading evidence of slave insurrections is, as many historians have noted, a complicated process that necessarily involves a level of speculation that is less than ideal. Throughout the history of the early modern Atlantic World, far more instances of racial violence were alleged, rumored, and "discovered" prior to any concrete actions taking place than there were instances where insurrections actually occurred. Voices of African-descended people are frequently absent from the evidentiary base of these alleged insurrections, and historians are forced to glean meaning from what are essentially white sources: newspaper accounts, correspondence between white citizens and officials, and public statements by white leaders. Some of these alleged conspiracies strain credulity, particularly in cases where the source base is particularly thin—a single newspaper account, for example. Yet when multiple sources speak specifically to rumors of racial violence that had been thwarted, at the same time and with the same details, I believe we can begin to use this evidence to speak to the lives of African-descended people even though their voices are absent in any kind of direct way. Throughout this chapter I discuss incidents of insurrection and racial violence that never occurred and attempt to make clear my assessment of the veracity of the whites' claims about alleged conspiracies. I also try to read more deeply into these insurrection rumors to discuss what I believe they reveal about the intellectual worlds of free and enslaved people of African descent during this era and the way they conceived of their individual and collective identities. Even if the details of some of these alleged conspiracies aren't entirely accurate, I believe that the instances I have chosen to discuss in this chapter were in some way grounded in reality and offer insight into black lives in a way that would otherwise be entirely absent. For further reading on the problems of using slave conspiracy evidence, see "The Making of a Slave Conspiracy," a forum in the *William and Mary Quarterly* 58, no. 4 (2001): 913–76 and 59, no. 1 (2002): 135–202. In particular see Sidbury, "Plausible Stories and Varnished Truths"; and M. Johnson, "Reading Evidence." See also Jordan, *Tumult and Silence at Second Creek.*

3. Both Julius Scott and W. Jeffrey Bolster have demonstrated the frequency and effectiveness of communication between black sailors and the residents of port cities. See Scott, "Common Wind"; and Bolster, *Black Jacks.* More broadly other scholars have explored the impact news of the Haitian Revolution had on local communities throughout the Atlantic. See Geggus, *Impact of the Haitian Revolution in the Atlantic World.*

4. Ship logs and advertisements appeared regularly in Charleston's newspapers throughout the era of the Haitian Revolution. For mention of ships arriving or departing for ports in Saint Domingue, see, for example, *Charleston City Gazette & Daily Advertiser* [hereafter *City Gazette*], March 8, 1793, 3; May 12, 1794, 3; June 15, 1795, 3; May 5, 1796, 1; January 24, 1798, 3. For just a few examples of the advertisement of goods from Saint Domingue, see *City Gazette*, p. 309, n. 5: February 8, 1793, 1; March 8, 1793, 3; March 12, 1793, 4; April 12, 1793, 3; April 30, 1793, 1; *Columbian (S.C.) Herald*, May 9, 1793, 3. Sasportas was almost surely a relative of Isaac Sasportas, the French agent in

Charleston who was executed in 1799 in Jamaica for his attempt to incite the slaves there to insurrection. See Sidbury, "Saint Domingue in Virginia," 542.

5. *City Gazette*, June 8, 1798, 3.

6. *City Gazette*, December 19, 1798, 2.

7. *City Gazette*, January 25, 1799, 3.

8. *City Gazette*, June 19, 1799, 3.

9. Even for the many nonliterate people of color in Charleston, black communication networks seem to have functioned in such a way that only a few members of a community needed to have literacy in order for printed notices to gain purchase in the wider community relatively quickly.

10. "Fresh Disturbances in St. Domingo," *Carolina State Gazette*, August 4, 1791.

11. *City Gazette*, September 12, 1791.

12. *City Gazette*, January 10, 1792.

13. *Carolina State Gazette*, June 10, 1793, 2.

14. *City Gazette*, June 21, 1793, 2.

15. *State Gazette of South Carolina*, July 1, 1793, 2.

16. *State Gazette of South Carolina*, July 2, 1793, 2.

17. *City Gazette*, August 13, 1793, 2.

18. *City Gazette*, October 3, 1793, 2; description of Saint Domingue as "wretched" in *State Gazette*, October 5, 1793, 2.

19. *City Gazette*, November 25, 1793, 2.

20. *City Gazette*, November 26, 1793, 2.

21. *City Gazette*, October 25, 1797, 2.

22. *City Gazette*, July 8, 1797, 3.

23. Lionel H. Kennedy and Thomas Parker, *An Official Report of the Trials of Sundry Negroes*, (Charleston, 1822) in Egerton and Paquette, *Denmark Vesey Affair*, 214.

24. *City Gazette*, September 28, 1793, 3.

25. *City Gazette*, October 3, 1793, 3.

26. *State Gazette of South Carolina*, October 12, 1793, 3; *City Gazette*, November 15, 1793, 2.

27. The first example of this regular notice was published in the *City Gazette*, September 30, 1793, 3.

28. *City Gazette*, November 9, 1793, 2; *Columbian Herald*, November 9, 1793, 3. It seems likely that Vesey's ties to the Caribbean in general and Saint Domingue in particular, as a ship captain and merchant, made him a logical choice to spearhead the distribution of aid to the refugees in the city. These ties have come under scrutiny from historians attempting to unravel the influences and meaning behind Denmark Vesey's alleged 1822 insurrection attempt.

29. *State Gazette of South Carolina*, March 4, 1794, 1.

30. *City Gazette*, January 17, 1795, 3; February 6, 1795, 4.

31. *City Gazette*, November 7, 1793, 3.

32. *City Gazette*, December 30, 1793, 3.

33. *City Gazette*, January 3, 1794, 3.

34. *City Gazette*, August 28, 1794, 3.

35. *City Gazette*, February 23, 1795, 3.

36. *City Gazette*, November 8, 1799, 4.

37. *City Gazette*, September 20, 1803, 3.

38. For charity sermons see *City Gazette*, February 21, 1805, 3; February 25, 1805, 3. For concerts see *City Gazette*, February 24, 1804, 2; March 1, 1804, 3.

39. *City Gazette*, January 6, 1804, 3.

40. *City Gazette*, August 14, 1804, 4.

41. *City Gazette*, February 13, 1805, 3; February 25, 1805, 2. An article published in August 1804 estimated that in the previous eight months, citizens of Charleston and previously displaced French refugees in the city contributed $3,667 to a total of 1,015 refugees. See *City Gazette*, August 25, 1804, 3. The committee responsible for dispensing aid to the "distressed" refugees from Saint Domingue estimated that between December 1803 and January 1805, they purchased 37,035 rations, 100 cords of wood, 100 blankets, 15 mattresses, and 300 yards of flannel. See *City Gazette*, February 25, 1805, 3.

42. *City Gazette*, March 26, 1805, 3.

43. See Alderson, "Charleston's Rumored Slave Revolt of 1793."

44. *City Gazette*, January 9, 1796, 1.

45. *City Gazette*, January 6, 1798, 3.

46. *City Gazette*, October 2, 1800, 4.

47. *City Gazette*, August 7, 1802, 4.

48. *City Gazette*, March 20, 1803, 1.

49. *City Gazette*, February 21, 1805, 3.

50. *City Gazette*, May 1, 1805, 3.

51. In total it seems likely that somewhere around four hundred to five hundred refugees, mostly whites, arrived in Charleston in during the 1790s. See Gilikin, "Saint Domingue Refugees in Charleston."

52. May 28, 1797, South Carolina Department of Archives and History (SCDAH), Miscellaneous Records, vol. 3I, 327. Gaugin carried out the manumission "to recognize the good services rendered to me by my Negresse Eleanore." The original was written in French: "pour reconnaître les bons services que m'a rendue ma *Negresse* Eleanore." Translation by the author.

53. March 28, 1798, SCDAH, Miscellaneous Records, vol. 3K, 234.

54. May 30, 1798, SCDAH, Miscellaneous Records, vol. 3K, 86.

55. July 15, 1798, SCDAH, Miscellaneous Records, vol. 3K, 293–94.

56. June 8, 1811, SCDAH, Miscellaneous Records, vol. 4C, 555.

57. November 1, 1800, SCDAH, Miscellaneous Records, vol. 3Q, 185–86.

58. December 4, 1799, SCDAH, Miscellaneous Records, vol. 3O, 627.

59. September 1, 1800, SCDAH, Miscellaneous Records, vol. 3Q, 131.

60. March 10, 1801, SCDAH, Miscellaneous Records, vol. 3O, 424.

61. "Committee on the presentment of the Grand Jury of Charleston District, concerning the assembling of groups of free blacks and slaves to be introduced to freemasonry, and conceived to be inappropriate by the committee," February 2, 1791, SCDAH, Petitions to the General Assembly, no. 145.

62. Messages to South Carolina governor William Moultrie regarding the Secret Keeper conspiracy, including the letter and materials forwarded by Virginia governor James Woods, can be found in SCDAH, Legislative Papers, Governor's Messages, no.

577. The Secret Keeper conspiracy and its relationship to the Saint Domingue has also been examined by Sidbury, "Saint Domingue in Virginia"; and Alderson, "Charleston's Rumored Slave Revolt of 1793."

63. Sidbury, "Saint Domingue in Virginia," 541.

64. Secret Keeper Messages, SCDAH, Governor's Messages, no. 577, 19.

65. Ibid.

66. *City Gazette*, October 9, 1793, 2.

67. Ibid.

68. *City Gazette*, October 18, 1793, 2.

69. *Columbian Herald*, October 17, 1793, 3.

70. *Columbian Herald*, December 10, 1793, 2.

71. *City Gazette*, May 12, 1794, 2.

72. *City Gazette*, July 9, 1795, 2.

73. *Columbian Herald*, March 31, 1796, 3.

74. *City Gazette*, November 7, 1796, 2.

75. *City Gazette*, November 22, 1797, 3.

76. "Message concerning the rent of the Charleston District Jail," December 6, 1797, SCDAH, Governor's Messages, no. 707.

77. "Petition proposing stiffer regulations on the importation of Negroes," December 11, 1797, SCDAH, Petitions to the General Assembly, roll 1331, no. 117, 331–39; see also no. 87, 282–90.

78. Ibid.

79. Ibid.

80. Message from Governor Pinckney to the House of Representatives, 1798, SCDAH, Governor's Messages, no. 721.

81. *City Gazette*, June 8, 1798, 3.

82. *City Gazette*, April 24, 1799, 3. The article was reprinted in the *Georgetown (S.C.) Gazette*, May 8, 1799, 2.

83. Egerton and Paquette, *Denmark Vesey Affair*, xix–xxiv

84. *City Gazette*, November 9, 1793, 2; *Columbian Herald*, November 9, 1793, 3; Egerton and Paquette, *Denmark Vesey Affair*, 5–7.

85. Evidence of the court proceedings related to the Vesey conspiracy have been the source of considerable controversy among historians. Although the original court records no longer exist, the interrogations of conspirators in Charleston courts during the summer of 1822 produced four distinct documents, each presenting a mostly similar, yet still distinct, summary of the proceedings. Two were trial transcripts prepared at the request of the governor and presented to the South Carolina legislature's house and senate, respectively; the senate version is the more complete and more frequently cited one. In addition participants in the proceedings also published two lengthy accounts of the trial, including the official report prepared by attorneys Lionel Henry Kennedy and Thomas Parker Jr. The official report was published in large measure to help assuage white fears of racial violence in the months following the episode. These accounts differ from one another in some important ways but, I believe, can still offer insight into the intellectual and cultural worlds of African-descended people in Charleston during the early 1820s.

86. *Official Report* in Egerton and Paquette, *Denmark Vesey Affair,* 163.

87. Ibid., 182.

88. "Senate Report," in ibid., 283.

89. *Official Report,* in ibid., 178.

90. Ibid., 191. This claim about the letter was repeated in several additional confessions and testimonies, but the nature of the record leaves unclear whether they divulged this information independently or if they were asked about letters to Boyer specifically.

91. For examples from newspaper accounts and correspondence, see Egerton and Paquette, *Denmark Vesey Affair,* 376, 386, 398, 450–51.

92. Ibid., 553. See also Schoeppner, "Navigating the Dangerous Atlantic."

93. Egerton and Paquette, *Denmark Vesey Affair,* 640–41.

94. Sidbury, "Plausible Stories and Varnished Truths," 182.

95. Though Cartagena is surprisingly absent in Scott's "Common Wind," Caracas played a major role. Given the strong military, administrative, and commercial links between Caracas and Cartagena de Indias, information about the revolution in Saint Domingue likely arrived in Cartagena with similar frequency, either directly or by way of Caracas.

96. Julius Scott and Jeffrey Bolster have both extensively documented the effectiveness of black communication networks in Atlantic port cities. Pablo Gomez has also demonstrated the breadth of interaction and the cosmopolitan nature of seventeenth-century Cartagena. See Gómez, "Bodies of Encounter."

97. Archivo General de Indias [hereafter AGI], Fondo Estado, Legajo 58, n. 4; Scott, "Common Wind," 248–55.

98. Lasso, *Myths of Harmony,* 28; Helg, "Fragmented Majority," 157.

99. Lasso, *Myths of Harmony,* 28.

100. Ibid., 32.

101. "Comisionados Franceses de Martinica: Informe del gobernador de Cartagena sobre haber izado ellos la bandera de su nación en la casa en que estaban alojados," May 1803, AGN, Sección Colonia, Fondo Milicias y Marina, tomo 113, 76–87.

102. "Sobre conspiración de negros esclavos franceses," AGI, Estado, Legajo 52, n. 76; AGI, Legajo 53, n. 77.

103. "Sublevación de negros corsarios franceses," May 25, 1799, AGN, Colónia, Fondo Milicias y Marina, tomo 15, 583–87.

104. "Sobre sublevación en Maracaibo de negros y mulatos franceses," AGI, Estado, Legajo 52, n. 81.

105. "Sublevación de negros corsarios franceses," May 25, 1799, AGN, Colónia, Fondo Milicias y Marina, tomo 15, 583–87.

106. AGI, Estado, Legajo 71, n. 3.

107. Pedro Mendinueta to Josef Antonio Caballero, November 19, 1800, AGI, Estado, Legajo 52, n. 102.

108. Helg, *Liberty and Equality in Caribbean Colombia,* 104.

109. Lasso, *Myths of Harmony,* 79.

110. Ibid., 113. For a full discussion of the Remigio Marquez conflict, see 108–15.

111. See, for example, Childs, *1812 Aponte Rebellion;* Reid-Vazquez, *Year of the Lash.*

112. Aline Helg has argued that the fact that 1799 was the only time enslaved people acted collectively is evidence of the barriers to collective racial identification. She contends that class, color, and status divisions, along with the outlets of Cartagena's urban slave system—the possibility of self-purchase, ability to live separately from one's master, to hire out one's own time—reduced the possibility that slaves would attempt to overthrow white rule. Yet those same divisions and release valves were facets of life in cities throughout the greater Caribbean and Atlantic worlds, in places where slave revolts *did* happen. Indeed successful or attempted slave revolts seem a high bar by which to measure the presence of racial consciousness or identity. The conspiracies and rumors that emerged during the era of the Haitian Revolution certainly seem to suggest that blacks of different origins, complexions, classes, and statuses at least began to consider collective action at various points.

113. See Landers, *Atlantic Creoles in the Age of Revolutions;* Jones, "Seaman and Citizen."

CHAPTER THREE

1. Curry, *Free Black in Urban America,* 25.

2. Ibid., 24.

3. Rael, *Black Identity and Black Protest,* 25.

4. Rael, *Black Identity and Black Protest,* 24.

5. Berlin, *Slaves without Masters,* 233.

6. Barnes, *Artisan Workers in the Upper South,* 132.

7. Ibid., 141.

8. Klein and Vinson, *African Slavery in Latin America and the Caribbean,* 221.

9. For additional discussion of the experiences of free people of color in urban Latin America, see Andrews, *Afro-Argentines of Buenos Aires;* Bernand, *Negros esclavos y libres en las ciudades hispanoamericanas;* King, *Blue Coat or Powdered Wig;* Kinsbruner, *Not of Pure Blood;* Schmidt-Nowara, *Slavery, Freedom, and Abolition in Latin America and the Atlantic World;* Vinson, *Bearing Arms for His Majesty.*

10. Twinam, *Purchasing Whiteness,* 63.

11. Reid-Vazquez, *Year of the Lash,* 30.

12. Reid-Vazquez, *Year of the Lash,* 33.

13. Carvalho Soares, "African Barbeiros in Brazilian Slave Ports," 218–19.

14. Unfortunately the federal decennial census did not record specific occupational information until 1850, after the period under study here. Nevertheless the 1850 returns, along with data culled from other sources such as city directories, allow for the development of a statistical and demographic sketch of Charleston during the first half of the nineteenth century. Leonard Curry observed a similar difficulty in his impressive statistical analysis of urban America and noted that, through a combination of other sources, he could conclude that patterns of black occupations in 1850 "prevailed throughout the entire period." He argued that in Charleston, along with Boston and Baltimore, "there was no appreciable shift in the patterns of occupational opportunity for free persons of color" between 1800 and 1850. See Curry, *Free Black in Urban America,* 30–31.

15. "Manumission of Jehu Jones," January 22, 1798, SCDAH, Miscellaneous Records, vol. 3H, 442–43.

16. Nell, *Colored Patriots of the American Revolution*, 244.

17. "Manumission of Jehu Jones," January 22, 1798, SCDAH, Miscellaneous Records, vol. 3H, 442–43; "Rules and Regulations of the Brown Fellowship Society" (Charleston: J. B. Nixon, 1844), in "Brown Fellowship Society Records, 1794–1990," Avery Research Center (Charleston, S.C.), box 1, AMN 1005; Goldsmith, *Directory and Stranger's Guide*. See also Johnson and Romero, "Jehu Jones"; Johnson and Roark, *Black Masters*, 252; Powers, *Black Charlestonians*, 43–47, 57; Wikramanayake, *World in Shadow*, 110–11.

18. "Petition of John L. Wilson, Guardian of Jehu Jones," ca. 1823, SCDAH, Petitions to the General Assembly, no. 1871, 322–24; "Report of the Special Committee for the Petition of John L. Wilson, Guardian of Jehu Jones a colored man," ca. 1823, SCDAH, Petitions to the General Assembly, no. 1302A; Petition on behalf of Jehu and Abigail Jones, November 6, 1827, SCDAH, Petitions to the General Assembly, no. 102, 810–15.

19. "Lista de los artesanos que comprehende el padrón general del barrio de Santa Cathalina año de 1780," AGN, Censos Redimibles, Varios Departamentos, tomo 6, 618v [hereinafter cited as "1780 Artisan Census, Santa Catalina"]; Helg, *Liberty and Equality*, 81, 122. Unfortunately the returns from the 1777 census for the barrio of Santa Catalina are missing, as are the notarial and parish records with which the listing in the artisan census could be complemented.

20. José Ignacio de Pombo, "El informe de la Junta Suprema de Cartagena de Indias de 1810," in Múnera, *Ensayos Costeños*, 130.

21. Helg, *Liberty and Equality*, 122. Ann Twinam has dealt extensively with attempts by people of African descent to purchase whiteness through the process of acquiring *gracias al sacar* from the Spanish Crown. One of the primary reasons people of African descent attempted to acquire whiteness, she has found, was for the privilege of attending university. See Twinam, *Purchasing Whiteness*.

22. Lasso, *Myths of Harmony*.

23. While the 1830 federal census for Charleston County recorded 3,594 free colored persons—1,554 men and 2,040 women—the city's 1831 directory listed only about 100 (and only 82 with occupations).

24. Goldsmith, *Directory and Stranger's Guide*, 120–28.

25. Historical Census Data Browser, University of Virginia, Geospatial and Statistical Data Center, http://mapserver.lib.virginia.edu.

26. The directory recorded thirteen barbers, twelve tailors, and nine carpenters.

27. Goldsmith, *Directory and Stranger's Guide*, 120–28.

28. *Census of the City of Charleston*, 29–35.

29. Ibid., 27–35.

30. For more on African Americans and barbering, see Bristol, *Knights of the Razor*.

31. Curry, *Free Black in Urban America*, 266.

32. Berlin, *Slaves without Masters*, 221.

33. Curry, *Free Black in Urban America*, 33, 260.

34. "Thomas Cole and Other Free Blacks, Petition asking that they may be exempt from the Negro Act of 1740 and enjoy the rights and privileges of free citizens," January 13, 1791, SCDAH, Petitions to the General Assembly, roll 1326, no. 81, 189–92.

35. White objections to competing with African Americans in skilled trades emerged throughout the South, as various white workers' groups urged local and state

bodies to enact penalties and prohibitions on enslaved and free blacks to prevent them from engaging in artisan work. See Berlin, *Slaves without Masters*, 230; Curry, *Free Black in Urban America*, 17.

36. Bricklayer and carpenter were two of the jobs particularly dominated by free blacks in early Charleston. See "Bricklayers and carpenters of Charleston, petition concerning Negroes who are underpricing them for work, asking the honorable House to stop such practices," July 19, 1783, SCDAH, Petitions to the General Assembly, roll AD1321, no. 159, 647–51. Philip D. Morgan has argued that such a labor dynamic existed in Charleston for much of the colonial era as well. See Morgan, "Work and Culture."

37. "Sundry Mechanics of Charleston, Petition to form the Charleston Mechanics Association and for Legislative Relief from Colored Mechanics and Tradesmen," SC-DAH, Petitions to the General Assembly, roll 1287, no. 48, 142–45. This petition is dated 1811 in the SCDAH's records, but given the reference made to the law passed in 1822 prohibiting enslaved people from hiring out their own time, the petition is likely from 1823 or 1824. Given this timing, it seems possible that these mechanics were attempting to capitalize on the fears of racial violence that arose in the wake of Denmark Vesey affair for their own gain.

38. Berlin, *Slaves without Masters*, 235.

39. "South Carolina Mechanics Association, Petition to indict the hirer and owner of a slave hiring out his own time and that a tax or other remedy be placed on free blacks to insure more equitable competition for jobs," November 16, 1858, SCDAH, Petitions to the General Assembly, roll 1374, no. 25, 285–88.

40. SCDAH, Petitions to the General Assembly, roll ND1304, no. 2801, 895–99.

41. "South Carolina Mechanics Association, Petition," November 16, 1858, SCDAH, Petitions to the General Assembly, roll 1374, no. 25, 285–88.

42. Meisel Roca and Aguilera Díaz, "Cartagena de Indias en 1777," 233.

43. Ibid., 264–71.

44. Ibid., 271–75.

45. "Padrón del barrio de Sto. Thoribio, año de 1777," AGN, Colonia, Fondo Miscelánea, tomo 41, 1004–79 [hereinafter cited as "1777 Census, Santo Toribio"]; "Padrón que comprehende el barrio de Nra. Sa. de la Merced, y su vecindario, formado en el año de 1777, por su comisario Dn. Francisco Pero Vidal, Capitan de Milicias de Blancos," AGN, Colonia, Censos Redimibles, Varios Departamentos, tomo 8, 132v–64v [hereinafter cited as "1777 Census, Las Mercedes"]; "Barrio de San Sebastián, Año de 1777," AGN, Colonia, Miscelánea, tomo 44, 945–58 [hereinafter cited as "1777 Census, San Sebastián"]; "Padrón general ejecutado por Dn. Mariano José de Valverde, regidor interino de M.Y.C.J. y Regimiento de esta ciudad de Cartagena de Indias en el ella comisario del Barrio de la Santísima Trinidad de Getsemaní en el presente año de 1777," AGN, Censos Redimibles, Varios Departamentos, tomo 8, 75–133 [hereinafter cited as "1777 Census, Getsemaní"].

46. Given the popularity of barbering as an occupation among people of African descent throughout the urban Americas, it is at least somewhat surprising that even this many whites engaged in the trade.

47. "Relación que manifiesta los Artesanos que existen en el Barrio de Santo Thorivio el presente año de 1780," AGN, Colonia, Miscelánea, tomo 31, 148–55 [hereinafter cited as "1780 Artisan Census, Santo Toribio"];

48. "Lista de los Artesanos que comprehende el Barrio de Nra. Sra. de las Mercedes, en sus Manzanas, Calles, y Casas," AGN, Censos Redimibles, Varios Departamentos, tomo 6, 259–60 [hereinafter cited as "1780 Artisan Census, Las Mercedes"]; 1777 Census, Las Mercedes, 132v–64.

49. Aside from *pulperos*, whites were distributed fairly evenly across other occupations. The five occupations presented above were the most popular occupations in Santa Catalina (discounting *pulpero*) in addition to being the most popular in most other neighborhoods. 1780 Artisan Census, Santa Catalina, 615–19.

50. Census, Getsemaní, 75–133.

51. Artisan Census, Santo Toribio; 1780 Artisan Census, Santa Catalina; 1780 Artisan Census, Las Mercedes; 1777 Census, Getsemaní.

52. Telles, *Pigmentocracies.*

53. Vinson, *Bearing Arms for His Majesty,* 107.

54. Reid-Vazquez, *Year of the Lash,* 30.

55. Artisan Census, Santo Toribio; 1780 Artisan Census, Santa Catalina; 1780 Artisan Census, Las Mercedes; 1777 Census, Getsemaní.

56. In this regard it is crucial to note that Charleston was not strictly segregated. Leonard Curry, using the index of dissimilarity (a common measure, particularly among social scientists, for determining neighborhood segregation), determined that Charleston had "insignificant residential concentration by race," even after 1850 when the city incorporated Charleston Neck into its limits. See Curry, *Free Black in Urban America,* 56. For use of index of the dissimilarity as a measure of segregation in the social sciences, see Massey and Denton, *American Apartheid,* 21, 74.

57. For examples of the necessity of white patrons for southern free blacks, see Johnson and Roark, *Black Masters;* Berlin, *Slaves without Masters.*

58. Goldsmith, *Directory and Stranger's Guide,* 120–28.

59. *Census of the City of Charleston,* 2–3.

60. In the city 3.67 percent of free people of color engaged in mercantile trades, compared with 1.71 percent in Charleston Neck.

61. The categories for these occupations are borrowed from Curry, *Free Black in Urban America.* Additionally the percentages listed for barber, carpenter, shoe/boot maker, and tailor are of the free black *male* population listed with occupations in the 1850 census (because no women were represented in those trades); the percentages for the subsequent occupations and categories are for the total free black population listed with occupations, to account for the presence of women in some of the trades.

62. Michael P. Johnson and James L. Roark in particular have demonstrated how a free man of color, William Ellison, could use a carefully crafted combination of slave ownership, skills, and social contacts to enter into the elite planter class in the state. Walter Johnson has argued for the social benefits one could acquire through the buying and selling of enslaved people. See Johnson and Roark, *Black Masters;* W. Johnson, *Soul by Soul.*

63. Fifth Census of the United States, 1830, Charleston District. National Archives Records Administration, Washington, D.C.

64. Woodson, *Free Negro Owners of Slaves,* 27–31. Woodson compiled the names of slave owners and their households. I calculated the statistics using his data.

65. In 1850 the average slaveholding size in the city was 4.5, while it was 3.5 in the neck. Twenty years earlier those numbers were 4.5 and 7, respectively.

66. In the city the average enslaved person owned by a free person of color was twenty-seven years old, whereas in the neck they were twenty-nine years old. The female-to-male ratio in the city was nearly even at 1.1, while it was 1.32 in the neck.

67. Among free blacks listed in the 1850 census with occupations, slave owners constituted 20 percent in the city, compared with 17 percent in the neck. For the free black population as a whole, 3.5 percent owned slaves in the city, while a slightly lower 2.7 percent did in the neck.

68. Free blacks comprised 2.2 percent of all slave owners in the city in 1850, while they comprised just 1.2 percent in the neck. The figures in this paragraph are drawn from my own calculations, using the free schedule and the slave schedule of the 1850 federal census, which I used to create a database that could provide me with summary statistics. Unlike the 1830 census, which provides the name of the head of household and the number of people within the household, both free and enslaved, the 1850 separates out free individuals from enslaved ones. The slave schedule (schedule II), which identifies slave owners and the age, race, and sex of the enslaved people they owned, did not identify the race of the slave owner. This required me to create and manipulate a database to create the statistics I could compare with 1830. First, I created a database of the entire slave schedule for 1850 in the parishes of St. Philip's and St. Michael's, being the parishes that included the four wards of the city and Charleston Neck. Then I used various functions in Microsoft Excel to compare this list to the list of free blacks listed in the 1850 free schedule with occupations. I first compared the lists using the concatenate function, taking just the first three letters of the name and surname so as to avoid false negatives (i.e., so that "Edwd Lee" and "Edward Lee" could be identified as the same person). I then went through these matches manually, to eliminate resultant false positives. This allowed me to identify all of the free black slave owners for each of the city wards and for the neck. While this method surely misses many free black slave owners (particularly free black women slave owners, who were the majority of slave owners in 1830 but were far less likely to be listed with occupations in the 1850 census), I feel these omissions are reasonably likely to be evenly spread across the city's neighborhoods, thus rendering the statistics still valid. See Seventh Census of the United States (1850), Schedule I, Free Inhabitants; and Schedule II, Slave Schedule; both for Parishes of St. Philip's and St. Michael's, Charleston District, South Carolina.

69. It seems like Maria Petrona may have been employed by the Marquecho family as a live-in domestic worker of some kind.

70. Census, Santo Toribio, 1029r. For whatever reason Ynitola is not listed in Santo Toribio's 1780 census of artisans.

71. Artisan Census, Santo Toribio, 149v; 1777 Census, Santo Toribio, 1015r–17r.

72. Artisan Census, Santo Toribio, 150; 1777 Census, Santo Toribio, 1033v–34r.

73. For more on race and residential patterns elsewhere in Spanish America, see Kinsbruner, *Not of Pure Blood*.

CHAPTER FOUR

1. Deal, "Middle-Class Benevolent Societies," 84.

2. E. Horace Fitchett, in his seminal work on Charleston's free people of color, argued that the free mulatto elite's ability to establish something akin to a tripartite system in the city, as evidenced by the Brown Fellowship Society, "seemed to protect them from some of the most oppressive techniques of control" exercised by the city's white elite. See Fitchett, "Free Negro in Charleston," 2. Marina Wikramanayake argues not only that a lighter complexion allowed a segment of Charleston's free blacks to interact more easily with the city's whites but also that free people of color in Charleston explicitly modeled racial and complexional divisions after the class boundaries of white society. See Wikramanayake, *World in Shadow,* 78–83. Michael Johnson and James Roark as well view the Brown Fellowship Society's restriction of membership to mulattoes as evidence of their desire to establish themselves as "an intermediate class between slavery and freedom and between blacks and whites." See Johnson and Roark, *Black Masters,* 215.

3. There are at least some links between the Ekpe Society of Calabar and African American organizations in Charleston, though any direct links are necessarily speculative. See Hackett, *Religion in Calabar,* 34–37. Edmund L. Drago makes a similar argument in *Charleston's Avery Center,* 34–38. The presence of free Africans in eighteenth- and nineteenth-century Charleston likewise would have provided free people of color in the city with at some knowledge and understanding of slave traders' private societies in West Africa as well. See Sparks, *Africans in the Old South,* 17–56.

4. "Rules and Regulations of the Brown Fellowship Society" (Charleston: J. B. Nixon, 1844), "Brown Fellowship Society Records, 1794–1990," AMN 1005, box 1, Avery Research Center, Charleston, S.C. In their constitution the society stated that it was the duty of the organization's stewards to "call on the sick, examine their circumstances, and finding he is in need of assistance from the society," the individual or family in question would be eligible to receive at least $1.50 per week from the society's funds. If a member or one of their family members died but was unable to afford a funeral, those costs were also to be paid by the organization.

5. "Rules and Regulations of the Brown Fellowship Society"; Johnson and Roark, *Black Masters,* 227; R. L. Harris, "Charleston's Free Afro-American Elite," 292. Finding space to bury free people of color in the growing city was not easy. The opportunity to receive a proper burial for one's self and family seems not to have been trivial. In 1817, for example, a petition by a group of free blacks to purchase two plots of land to be used as cemeteries was turned down by a legislative committee. SCDAH, Legislative Papers, Committee Reports, no. 119. A group calling themselves the Brotherly Association of Charleston petitioned the legislature for similar purposes in November 1856. See SCDAH, Petitions to the General Assembly, no. 13, 108–12.

6. Like in Cartagena, it seems possible that these public displays of mourning were a means of achieving a degree of visual distinction within the city. Mourning the death of a member in such a way would create an additional level of separation between Brown Fellowship members and the free black poor and enslaved populations of the city. Additionally this emphasis on funerals, burials, and mourning suggests at least a tenuous link with an African cultural heritage, as some West African mutual aid societies similarly emphasized funerary practices. See Drago, *Charleston's Avery Center,* 35. See also Brown, *Reaper's Garden;* Hackett, *Religion in Calabar,* 34–37. It is perhaps

likewise plausible that this emphasis on funerary practices had a European origin as well, passed through white voluntary organizations in the city.

7. "Rules and Regulations of the Brown Fellowship Society," 11.

8. Ibid., 21.

9. Ibid., 12.

10. Johnson and Roark, *Black Masters*, 227.

11. Though not stated explicitly in the rules and regulations, membership rolls seem to indicate that the Brown Fellowship Society was open only to men of mixed racial ancestry—a distinction that has long captivated the interests of historians of Charleston. While the Brown Fellowship Society was only open to people of lighter complexion, it also seems that individuals of mixed racial ancestry were not just more likely to become free, they were more likely to have the kinds of skills that would allow for them to attain a measure of economic standing. Further the relative wealth of free artisans of color in the city probably made census takers more likely to view them as mulattoes, irrespective of their complexion. See Berlin, *Slaves without Masters*, 57–58, 312–13; Fitchett, "Free Negro in Charleston," 121; R. L. Harris, "Charleston's Free Afro-American Elite," 289–90; Johnson and Roark, *Black Masters*, 215; Wikramanayake, *World in Shadow*, 78–83.

12. "Holloway Family Scrapbook," Avery Research Center, AMN 1065, College of Charleston. Accessed through the Lowcountry Digital Library, http://lcdl.library.cofc .edu.

13. Ibid.

14. Ibid., note dated November 3, 1821.

15. Ibid., receipt; W. L. King, *Newspaper Press of Charleston*, 169.

16. Letter to Elizabeth Holloway, June 29, 1845, "Holloway Family Scrapbook." See also Bowler and Drago, "Free Black Benevolence in Antebellum Charleston," 394–98.

17. "Committee Report . . . concerning the assembling of groups of free blacks and slaves to be introduced to Freemasonry," February 4, 1791, SCDAH, Petitions to the General Assembly, no. 145.

18. A December 1791 newspaper report, for example, discusses the meeting of these organizations in the city. Ample newspaper accounts and other evidence reveal the existence of white Masonic lodges in Charleston. See *City Gazette*, December 30, 1791, 2. While there are some parallels between the Brown Fellowship Society and the secret societies such as the Ekpe of the West African slaving coast (its function as a source of both distinction and social cohesion), it seems far more likely that the operative referent for these black Charlestonians was the Masonic lodges found in South Carolina and throughout the United States.

19. Hinks, "John Marrant and the Meaning of Early Black Freemasonry."

20. Ibid., 115–16.

21. For further discussion of black Freemasonry in the Atlantic world, see Hinks and Kantrowitz, *All Men Free and Brethren*.

22. "Rules and Regulations of the Brown Fellowship Society."

23. Ibid.; Powers, *Black Charlestonians*, 51–52; R. L. Harris, "Charleston's Free Afro-American Elite," 291.

24. Payne, *Recollections of Seventy Years*, 14; R. L. Harris, "Charleston's Free Afro-American Elite," 295; Drago, *Charleston's Avery Center*, 34.

25. Records for the Friendly Union Society were compiled by Susan M. Bowler and Edmund L. Drago, in their unpublished manuscript "Free Black Benevolence in Antebellum Charleston," 364–90.

26. As John G. Deal has observed for white, middle-class benevolent societies in antebellum Norfolk, these antebellum organizations concerned themselves with "not only the improvement of the physical well-being of the individual, but also the moral and spiritual elevation of the person's character." Thus these later voluntary organizations are not just within the mainstream of free black thought in the United States but also of southern middle-class values more broadly. Deal, "Middle-Class Benevolent Societies," 84.

27. Bowler and Drago, "Free Black Benevolence in Antebellum Charleston," 302.

28. Ibid., 306.

29. "Proceedings of the Friendly Moralist Society," May 13, 1844, in Bowler and Drago, "Free Black Benevolence in Antebellum Charleston," 57.

30. Ibid., 118.

31. Ibid., 119–20.

32. Ibid., 121.

33. Ibid.,121–22.

34. Ibid., 122; see also Johnson and Roark, *Black Masters*, 215–18.

35. Payne, *Recollections of Seventy Years*, 14; R. L. Harris, "Charleston's Free Afro-American Elite," 295.

36. Eggart's ideas about moral improvement and education dovetail neatly with Patrick Rael's discussion of black identity in the antebellum North, where free black leaders emphasized the need for respectability in order to change white minds about black capacity for freedom. In so doing, Rael argues, free blacks helped fabricate the meaning of middle-class virtue and respectability. See Rael, *Black Identity and Black Protest*.

37. "Constitution and Rules of Humane Brotherhood, Organized June 19th, 1943," Special Collections, Langston Hughes Memorial Library, Lincoln University, Penn.; R. L. Harris, "Charleston's Free Afro-American Elite," 296.

38. "Constitution and Rules of Humane Brotherhood," 34.

39. R. L. Harris, "Charleston's Free Afro-American Elite," 298–99; Bowler and Drago, "Free Black Benevolence in Antebellum Charleston."

40. R. L. Harris, "Charleston's Free Afro-American Elite," 304.

41. The group presumably took its name from Clio, the Greek muse of history.

42. Drago, *Charleston's Avery Center*, 35–38.

43. "Minutes of the Clionian Debating Society, 1847–1851," Charleston Library Society, Charleston, S.C. Accessed on microfilm through Fondren Library, Rice University, Houston, Tex.; Bowler and Drago, "Free Black Benevolence in Antebellum Charleston."

44. Wikramanayake, *World in Shadow*, 2

45. Ibid., 83.

46. Rael, *Black Identity and Black Protest*, 10.

47. Nicole von Germeten, "Black Brotherhoods in Mexico City," in Cañizares-Esguerra, Childs, and Sidbury, *Black Urban Atlantic*, 250.

48. Ibid., 252.

49. Ibid., 247. For more on *cabildos* and black associational life in Mexico City, see von Germeten, *Black Blood Brothers.*

50. Matt D. Childs, "Re-creating African Ethnic Identities in Cuba," in Cañizares-Esguerra, Childs, and Sidbury, eds., *Black Urban Atlantic*, 86.

51. Ibid., 87.

52. Ibid., 89.

53. See, for example, P. Gómez, *Experiential Caribbean;* P. F. Gómez, "Bodies of Encounter"; Landers, "African Landscape of Seventeenth-Century Cartagena"; Maya Restrepo, *Brujería y reconstrucción de identidades;* Wheat, "First Great Waves"; Wheat, *Atlantic Africa and the Spanish Caribbean.*

54. Landers, "African Landscape of Seventeenth-Century Cartagena," 149.

55. It seems at least somewhat significant that these cabildo houses were located inside the walled city rather than in Getsemaní, where a larger population of both enslaved people and Africans resided. It seems likely the cabildo houses had historically been located closer to centers of church activity inside the walled city. As Childs shows, Havana's urban code forced cabildo houses there to relocate outside the walled city in 1792, offering them greater independence from church supervision. See Childs, "Re-creating African Ethnic Identities," 91.

56. Census, Santo Toribio.

57. Ibid., 1055r.

58. Ibid., 1063v, 1070v–71v.

59. Ibid., 1058v–59r.

60. Eltis and Richardson, *Atlas of the Trans-Atlantic Slave Trade.* Greater detail and more precise numbers can be gathered from Voyages: The Transatlantic Slave Trade Database, http://www.slavevoyages.org.

61. P. F. Gómez, "Bodies of Encounter"; Landers, "African Landscape of Seventeenth-Century Cartagena"; Wheat, "First Great Waves," 1–22.

62. Helg, *Liberty and Equality,* 97; Helg, "Limits of Equality," 10–13.

63. Ultimately the question of African ethnic identity and cultural survival in Cartagena is a subject for more detailed consideration outside of this book.

64. Several studies in recent years have discussed this phenomenon throughout Spanish America and the Caribbean. See Belmonte, "El Color de los Fusiles"; Contreras, "Artesanos mulatos y soldados beneméritos"; King, *Blue Coat or Powdered Wig;* Vinson, *Bearing Arms for His Majesty.*

65. Vinson, *Bearing Arms for his Majesty,* 2.

66. Helg, *Liberty and Equality;* Lasso, *Myths of Harmony;* Kuethe, "Status of the Free Pardo"; Kuethe, "Flexibilidad racial en las milicias disciplinadas de Cartagena de Indias"; Solano and Flórez Bolívar, "'Artilleros pardos y morenos artistas.'"

67. Kuethe, "Status of the Free Pardo"; Kuethe, "Flexibilidad racial en las milicias disciplinadas de Cartagena de Indias"; Helg, *Liberty and Equality,* 100–103.

68. Helg, *Liberty and Equality,* 102.

69. Ibid., 100–105

70. The distinguishing mark of militia membership was by no means exclusive to Cartagena. Throughout Spanish America and beyond, free people of color used military participation to gain social recognition and a variety of privileges not afforded to members of the popular classes. In prerevolutionary Saint Domingue, like in Cartagena, for example, members of the free colored militia dominated the local artisan community and used their military contacts to cultivate their social networks. Militia membership was used as a "significant route for social advancement and financial gain in colored society." See King, *Blue Coat or Powdered Wig*, xiii.

71. "Domingo Esquiaqui, su comunicación sobre goce del fuero militar," AGN, Colonia, Fondo Milicias y Marina, tomo 30, 199–201; Solano D. and Flórez Bolívar, "'Artilleros Pardos y morenos artistas.'"

72. Colombia AGN, Colonia, Milicias y Marina, tomo 46, no. 32, 492–505.

73. Helg, *Liberty and Equality*, 104.

74. "Felix Martinez Malo, comandante de milicias de Panamá; su acusación por violación de los reglamentos militares," AGN, Colonia, Fondo Milicias y Marina, tomo 40, 668–87.

75. "Honores fúnebres," AGN, Colonia, Fondo Milicias y Marina, tomo 2, 234–35.

76. AGN, Colonia, Fondo Policía, tomo 2, 516–39.

77. For further reading on the ways free and enslaved people of African descent used militia service in the urban Atlantic world, see Blanchard, *Under the Flags of Freedom*; King, *Blue Coat or Powdered Wig*.

CHAPTER FIVE

1. For further reading on baptism and godparentage, see Gudeman and Schwartz, "Cleansing Original Sin"; Higgins, *"Licentious Liberty"*; Metcalf, *Family and Frontier*; Stark, "Ties That Bind"; Casares and Delaigue, "Evangelization of Freed and Slave Black Africans"; Shaw, "Birth and Initiation on the Peers Plantation"; Abel, Tyson, and Palsson, "From Enslavement to Emancipation"; Carvalho Soares, "Heathens among the Flock."

2. See, for example, Desmangles, *Faces of the Gods;* Griffith and Savage, *Women and Religion in the African Diaspora;* Fernández Olmos and Paravisini-Gebert, *Sacred Possessions;* Sweet, *Recreating Africa;* Sweet, *Domingos Álvares;* Mintz and Price, *Birth of African-American Culture;* Paton, *Obeah and Other Powers;* Pulis, *Religion, Diaspora, and Cultural Identity;* Thornton, "Development of an African Catholic Church"; Weaver, *Medical Revolutionaries;* Wedel, *Santería Healing;* Wirtz, *Ritual, Discourse, and Community in Cuban Santería.*

3. Schmidt-Nowara, *Slavery, Freedom, and Abolition*, 60; Klein and Vinson, *African Slavery*, 161.

4. Sweet, *Recreating Africa*, 7.

5. P. F. Gómez, "Bodies of Encounter"; Maya Restrepo, *Brujería y reconstrucción de identidades.*

6. Frey and Wood, *Come Shouting to Zion;* Genovese, *Roll Jordan Roll;* M. Gomez, *Exchanging Our Country Marks;* Joyner, *Down by the Riverside;* Hall, *Africans in Colonial Louisiana;* Raboteau, *Slave Religion;* Sobel, *Trabelin' On.*

7. Sobel, *World They Made Together.*

8. Young, *Rituals of Resistance.*

9. Archivo de la Parroquia de la Santísima Trinidad, Getsemaní, Cartagena, "Libro de Bautismos de Pardos y Morenos, 1812." I accessed digital images of this baptismal register electronically thanks to Jane G. Landers and the Ecclesiastical Sources for Slave Societies Project. Thanks also to Dale Poulter at Vanderbilt University for facilitating my access to these records. Throughout Latin America enslavers rarely served as baptismal sponsors for the children of their enslaved people. See Gudeman and Schwartz, "Cleansing Original Sin"; Higgins, *"Licentious Liberty,"* 143–44; Metcalf, *Family and Frontier,* 188; Stark, "Ties That Bind," 86.

10. Gudeman and Schwartz would argue that this relationship is typical, as across cultures "godparents are almost always of a status equal to, or higher than, that of their godchildren." See "Cleansing Original Sin," 45.

11. "Libro de Bautismos de Pardos y Morenos, 1812."

12. Ibid.

13. Granovetter, "Strength of Weak Ties."

14. Gudeman and Schwartz, "Cleansing Original Sin"; Higgins, *"Licentious Liberty,"* 143–44; Metcalf, *Family and Frontier,* 188; Stark, "Ties That Bind."

15. Stark, "Ties That Bind," 86.

16. Ibid., 89.

17. "Libro de Bautismos de Pardos y Morenos, 1812."

18. Unlike the more general trends, this preference for godmothers over godfathers is very different than what Stark has found for Arecibo, Puerto Rico, where nearly every baptism included a godfather. See Stark, "Ties That Bind," 90.

19. After determining that no identifiable trends existed in baptism practices by month, I analyzed the baptismal information for three months of each year for 1811 through 1816, inclusive. This has left me with a database that includes a 25 percent sample of baptisms conducted during those years, allowing me to identify key trends.

20. "Libro de Bautismos de Pardos y Morenos, 1812."

21. Twinam, *Public Lives, Private Secrets,* 128.

22. "Libro de Bautismos de Pardos y Morenos, 1812."

23. Ibid.

24. See, for example, Stark, "Rescued from Their Invisibility."

25. "Libro de Bautismos de Pardos y Morenos, 1812."

26. Ibid.

27. The bulk of this section is drawn from an analysis of the baptismal record for St. Philip's Protestant Episcopal Church for the years 1811 through 1815. Like for my analysis of Cartagena's baptismal records, I have put these records into a database, where I could manipulate the data to analyze it based on race, status, and other factors. The database consists of nearly 230 individual records, each record representing a baptism that occurred during these years. "Register, St. Philip's Episcopal Church, 1810–1822," South Caroliniana Library, University of South Carolina.

28. Ann Snelling's name is rendered as "Snellen" and Martha Moulton's name is rendered as "Molton" in the original source. "Register, St. Philip's Episcopal Church, 1810–1822."

29. See, for example, Berlin, *Slaves without Masters*. Likewise historians point to the church as a site of interracial interaction in the South and at times a source of social control. See Boles, *Masters and Slaves in the House of the Lord*; Irons, *Origins of Proslavery Christianity*.

30. "Register, St. Philip's Episcopal Church, 1810–1822."

31. Ibid.

32. Ibid.

33. The surname "Desverneys" is rendered "Devernier" in the original source. "Register, St. Philip's Episcopal Church, 1810–1822."

34. "Rules and Regulations of the Brown Fellowship Society" (Charleston: J. B. Nixon, 1844), in "Brown Fellowship Society Records, 1794–1990," AMN 1005, box 1, Avery Research Center, Charleston, S.C.; "Register, St. Philip's Episcopal Church, 1810–1822."

Bibliography

ARCHIVAL SOURCES

Archivo de la Parroquia de la Santísima Trinidad. Cartagena, Colombia.
Archivo General de Indias. Seville, Spain.
    Santa Fé
    Estado
Archivo General de la Nación. Bogotá, Colombia.
    Sección Colonia
        Negros y Esclavos
        Milicias y Marina
        Censos Redimibles
        Miscelánea
        Policía
    Sección República
        Libros Manuscritos y Leyes Originales
        Manumisión
Archivo Histórico de Cartagena. Cartagena, Colombia.
Avery Research Center for African American History and Culture, College of Charleston. Charleston, South Carolina.
Charleston Library Society. Charleston, South Carolina.
South Carolina Department of Archives and History. Columbia, South Carolina.
    Miscellaneous Records
    Legislative Papers, 1782–1866
        Petitions to the General Assembly (Series S165015)
        Committee Report (Series S165005)
        Governor's Messages (Series S165009)
South Caroliniana Library, University of South Carolina. Columbia, South Carolina.
South Carolina Historical Society. Charleston, South Carolina.
Special Collections, Langston Hughes Memorial Library. Lincoln University. Lincoln University, Pennsylvania.

NEWSPAPERS

Charleston (S.C.) City Gazette and Daily Advertiser
Charleston Carolina State Gazette
Charleston Columbian Herald
Charleston State Gazette of South Carolina
Georgetown (S.C.) Gazette

PUBLISHED PRIMARY SOURCES

Census of the City of Charleston, South Carolina, for the year 1848, exhibiting the condition and prospects of the city. Charleston: J. B. Nixon, 1849.

Fifth Census of the United States. 1830. National Archives Records Administration. Washington, D.C.

Goldsmith, Morris. *Directory and Stranger's Guide for the City of Charleston and Its Vicinity, from the Fifth Census of the United States.* Charleston, 1831.

King, William L. *The Newspaper Press of Charleston, S.C.: A Chronological and Biographical History, Embracing a Period of One Hundred and Forty Years.* Charleston: Edward Perry (Book Press), 1872.

McCord, David J., ed. *The Statutes at Large of South Carolina: Acts relating to Charleston, Courts, Slaves, and Rivers.* Columbia: A.S. Johnston, 1840.

Múnera, Alfonso, comp. *Ensayos Costeños, de la Colonia a la República, 1770–1890.* Bogotá: Colcoturra, 2004.

Nell, William C. *The Colored Patriots of the American Revolution: With Sketches of Several Distinguished Colored Persons, to Which Is Added a Brief Survey of the Condition and Prospects of Americans.* Boston: Robert F. Wallcut, 1855.

Payne, Daniel Alexander. *Recollections of Seventy Years.* Nashville: Publishing House of the A.M.E. Sunday School Union, 1888.

Seventh Census of the United States. 1850. National Archives Records Administration. Washington, D.C.

Van Rensselaer Bonney, Catharina. *A Legacy of Historical Gleanings, Vol. I.* Albany, N.Y.: J. Munsell, 1875.

DIGITAL SOURCES

Historical Census Browser. Geospatial Statistical and Data Center. University of Virginia. Charlottesville, Virginia. http://mapserver.lib.virginia.edu.

"Negros y Esclavos" Online Portal. Archivo General de la Nación. Bogotá, Colombia.

Voyages: The Transatlantic Slave Trade Database. http://www.slavevoyages.org.

SECONDARY SOURCES

Abel, Sarah, George F. Tyson, and Gisli Palsson. "From Enslavement to Emancipation: Naming Practices in the Danish West Indies." *Comparative Studies in Society and History* 61, no. 2 (2019): 332–65.

Alderson, Robert. "Charleston's Rumored Slave Revolt of 1793." In Geggus, *Impact of the Haitian Revolution*, 93–111.

Andrews, George Reid. *The Afro-Argentines of Buenos Aires, 1800–1900.* Madison: University of Wisconsin Press, 1980.

——. *Blackness in the White Nation: A History of Afro-Uruguay.* Chapel Hill: University of North Carolina Press, 2010.

Barnes, L. Diane. *Artisan Workers in the Upper South: Petersburg, Virginia, 1820–1865.* Baton Rouge: Louisiana State University Press, 2008.

Barragan, Yesenia. "To the Mine I Will Not Go: Freedom and Emancipation on the Colombian Pacific, 1821–1852." Ph.D. diss., Columbia University, 2016.

Belmonte, José. "El Color de los Fusiles. Las milicias de pardos en Santiago de Cuba en los albores de la Revolución Hatiana." In *Las armas de la nación. Independencia y ciudadanía en Hispanoamérica (1750–1850)*, edited by Manuel Chust and Juan Marchena, 37–51. Madrid: Iberoamericana/Vervuert, 2007.

Berlin, Ira. *Generations of Captivity: A History of African-American Slaves*. Cambridge, Mass.: Belknap, 2004.

——. *Slaves without Masters: The Free Negro in the Antebellum South*. New York: Pantheon Books, 1974.

Bennett, Herman L. *Colonial Blackness: A History of Afro-Mexico*. Bloomington: Indiana University Press, 2011.

Bernand, Carmen. *Negros esclavos y libres an las ciudades hispanoamericanas*. Madrid: Fundación Histórica Tavera, 2001.

Berry, Daina Ramey, and Leslie M. Harris. *Sexuality and Slavery: Reclaiming Intimate Histories in the Americas*. Athens: University of Georgia Press, 2018.

Blanchard, Peter. *Under the Flags of Freedom: Slave Soldiers and the Wars of Independence in Spanish South America*. Pittsburgh: University of Pittsburgh Press, 2008.

Boles, John B., ed., *Masters and Slaves in the House of the Lord: Race and Religion in the American South, 1740–1870*. Lexington: University of Kentucky Press, 1990.

Bolster, W. Jeffrey. *Black Jacks: African American Seamen in the Age of Sail*. Cambridge, Mass.: Harvard University Press, 1997.

Bowler, Susan M., and Edmund L. Drago, eds. "Free Black Benevolence in Antebellum Charleston: The Proceedings of the Friendly Moralist Society with Supporting Documents." Unpublished manuscript, Avery Research Center.

Bristol, Douglas Walter, Jr. *Knights of the Razor: Black Barbers in Slavery and Freedom*. Baltimore: Johns Hopkins University Press, 2015.

Brown, Vincent. *The Reaper's Garden: Death and Power in the World of Atlantic Slavery*. Cambridge, Mass.: Harvard University Press, 2010.

Buchanan, Thomas C. *Black Life on the Mississippi: Slaves, Free Blacks, and the Western Steamboat World*. Chapel Hill: University of North Carolina Press, 2004.

Butler, Kim D. *Freedoms Given, Freedoms Won: Afro-Brazilians in Post-abolition São Paulo and Salvador*. New Brunswick, N.J.: Rutgers University Press, 1998.

Cañizares-Esguerra, Jorge, Matt D. Childs, and James Sidbury, eds. *The Black Urban Atlantic in the Era of the Slave Trade*. Philadelphia: University of Pennsylvania Press, 2013.

Carvalho Soares, Mariza de. "African Barbeiros in Brazilian Slave Ports." In Cañizares-Esguerra, Childs, and Sidbury, *Black Urban Atlantic*, 207–30.

——. "Heathens among the Flock: Converting African-Born Slaves in Eighteenth-Century Rio de Janeiro." *Slavery and Abolition* 36, no. 3 (2015): 478–94.

Casares, Aurelia Martin, and Christine Delaigue. "The Evangelization of Freed and Slave Black Africans in Renaissance Spain: Baptism, Marriage, and Ethnic Brotherhoods." *History of Religions* 52, no. 3 (2013): 214–35.

Chaves, Maria Eugenia. "Honor y libertad: Discursos y recursos en la estrategia de libertad de una mujer esclava (Guayaquil a fines del periodo colonial)." Ph.D. diss., University of Gothenburg, 2001.

Chaves, Maria Eugenia, and Roland Anrup. "La 'plebe' en una sociedad de 'todos los colores'. La construcción de un imaginario social y político en la colonia tardía en Cartagena y Guayaquil." *Caravelle* 84 (2005): 93–126.

Childs, Matt D. *The 1812 Aponte Rebellion and the Struggle against Atlantic Slavery.* Chapel Hill: University of North Carolina Press, 2006.

Cohen, David W., and Jack P. Greene, eds. *Neither Slave nor Free: The Freedmen in the Slave Societies of the New World.* Baltimore: Johns Hopkins University Press, 1972.

Contreras, Hugo. "Artesanos mulatos y soldados beneméritos. El batallón de infantes de la Patria, en la guerra de independencia de Chile, 1795–1820." *Historia* 44 (2011): 51–89.

Curry, Leonard P. *The Free Black in Urban America, 1800–1850: The Shadow of the Dream.* Chicago: University of Chicago Press, 1981.

Dantas, Mariana L. R. *Black Townsmen: Urban Slavery and Freedom in in the Eighteenth-Century Americas.* New York: Palgrave Macmillan, 2008.

Deal, John G. "Middle-Class Benevolent Societies in Antebellum Norfolk, Virginia." In *The Southern Middle Class in the Long Nineteenth Century,* edited by Jonathan Daniel Wells and Jennifer R. Green, 84–104. Baton Rouge: Louisiana State University Press, 2011.

Degler, Carl N. *Neither White nor Black: Slavery and Race Relations in Brazil and the United States.* New York: Macmillan, 1971.

de la Fuente, Alejandro. "From Slaves to Citizens? Tannenbaum and the Debates on Slavery, Emancipation, and Race Relations in Latin America." *International Labor and Working-Class History* 77 (2010): 154–73.

———. "Slave Law and Claims-Making in Cuba: The Tannenbaum Debate Revisited." *Law and History Review* 22, no. 2 (2004): 339–69.

———. "Slaves and the Creation of Legal Rights in Cuba: Coartación and Papel." *Hispanic American Historical Review* 87 (2007): 659–692.

de la Fuente, Alejandro, and Ariela Gross. "Comparative Studies of Law, Slavery, and Race in the Americas." *Annual Review of Law and Social Science* 6 (2010): 469–85.

———. "Slaves, Free Blacks, and Race in the Legal Regimes of Cuba, Louisiana, and Virginia: A Comparison." *North Carolina Law Review* 91 (2013): 1699–755.

Desmangles, Leslie G. *The Faces of the Gods: Vodou and Roman Catholicism in Haiti.* Chapel Hill: University of North Carolina Press, 1992.

Díaz, Maria Elena. *The Virgin, the King, and the Royal Slaves of El Cobre: Negotiating Freedom in Colonial Cuba, 1670–1780.* Stanford, Calif.: Stanford University Press, 2000.

Drago, Edmund L. *Charleston's Avery Center: From Education and Civil Rights to Preserving the African American Experience.* Charleston, S.C.: History Press, 2006.

Dunn, Richard S. *A Tale of Two Plantations: Slave Life and Labor in Jamaica and Virginia.* Cambridge, Mass.: Harvard University Press, 2014.

Dusinberre, William R. *Them Dark Days: Slavery in the American Rice Swamps.* Athens: University of Georgia Press, 2000.

Egerton, Douglas R., and Robert L. Paquette, eds. *The Denmark Vesey Affair: A Documentary History.* Gainesville: University Press of Florida, 2017.

Elkins, Stanley M. *Slavery: A Problem in American Institutional and Intellectual Life.* Chicago: University of Chicago Press, 1959.

Eltis, David, and David Richardson, eds. *Atlas of the Transatlantic Slave Trade*. New Haven: Yale University Press, 2010.

Ely, Melvin Patrick. *Israel on the Appomattox: A Southern Experiment in Black Freedom from the 1790s through the Civil War*. New York: Knopf, 2004.

Fernández Olmos, Margarite, and Lizabeth Paravisini-Gebert. *Sacred Possessions: Vodou, Santería, Obeah, and the Caribbean*. New Brunswick, N.J.: Rutgers University Press, 1997.

Ferrer, Ada. *Freedom's Mirror: Cuba and Haiti in the Age of Revolution*. New York: Cambridge University Press, 2014.

Fitchett, E. Horace. "The Free Negro in Charleston, South Carolina." Ph.D. diss., University of Chicago, 1950.

Frank, Zephyr L. *Dutra's World: Wealth and Family in Nineteenth-Century Rio de Janeiro*. Albuquerque: University of New Mexico Press, 2004.

Frey, Sylvia R., and Betty Wood. *Come Shouting to Zion: African American Protestantism in the American South and British Caribbean to 1830*. Chapel Hill: University of North Carolina Press, 1998.

Freyre, Gilberto. *The Masters and the Slaves (Casa-Grande and Senzala): A Study in the Development of Brazilian Civilization*. New York: Knopf, 1946.

Geggus, David P., ed. *The Impact of the Haitian Revolution in the Atlantic World*. Columbia: University of South Carolina Press, 2001.

Genovese, Eugene. *Roll Jordan Roll: The World the Slaves Made*. New York: Pantheon Books, 1974.

Gilikin, Margaret Wilson. "Saint Domingue Refugees in Charleston, South Carolina, 1791–1822: Assimilation and Accommodation in a Slave Society." Ph.D. diss., University of South Carolina, 2014.

Gilroy, Paul. *The Black Atlantic: Modernity and Double Consciousness*. Cambridge, Mass.: Harvard University Press, 1993.

Gómez, Fernándo. "Los Censos de Colombia." In *Compendio de estadísticas históricas de Colombia*, edited by Miguel Urrutia and Mario Arrubla, 9–30. Bogotá: Universidad Nacional de Colombia, 1970.

Gomez, Michael. *Exchanging Our Country Marks: The Transformation of African Identity in the Colonial and Antebellum South*. Chapel Hill: University of North Carolina Press, 1998.

Gómez, Pablo F. "Bodies of Encounter: Health, Illness and Death in the Early Modern African-Spanish Caribbean." Ph.D. diss., Vanderbilt University, 2010.

——. *The Experiential Caribbean: Creating Knowledge and Healing in the Early Modern Atlantic*. Chapel Hill: University of North Carolina Press, 2017.

Gordon-Reed, Annette. *The Hemingses of Monticello: An American Family*. New York: Norton, 2009.

Granovetter, Mark S. "The Strength of Weak Ties." *American Journal of Sociology* 78, no. 6 (1973): 1360–80.

Griffith, R. Marie, and Barbara Dianne Savage, eds. *Women and Religion in the African Diaspora: Knowledge, Power, and Performance*. Baltimore: Johns Hopkins University Press, 2006.

Gronnigsater, Sarah L. H. "Delivering Freedom: Gradual Emancipation, Black Legal Culture, and the Origins of Sectional Crisis in New York, 1759–1870." Ph.D. diss., University of Chicago, 2014.

Gudeman, Stephen, and Stuart B. Schwartz. "Cleansing Original Sin: Godparenthood and the Baptism of Slaves in Eighteenth-Century Bahia." In *Kinship Ideology and Practice in Latin America,* edited by Raymond T. Smith, 35–58. Chapel Hill: University of North Carolina Press, 1984.

Hackett, Rosalind I. J. *Religion in Calabar: The Religious Life and History of a Nigerian Town.* New York: de Gruyter, 1988.

Hall, Gwendolyn Midlo. *Africans in Colonial Louisiana: The Development of Afro-Creole Culture in the Eighteenth Century.* Baton Rouge: Louisiana State University Press, 1992.

Hanger, Kimberly S. *Bounded Lives, Bounded Places: Free Black Society in Colonial New Orleans, 1769–1803.* Durham, N.C.: Duke University Press, 1997.

Harris, Leslie M. *In the Shadow of Slavery: African Americans in New York City, 1626–1863.* Chicago: University of Chicago Press, 2003.

Harris, Robert L., Jr. "Charleston's Free Afro-American Elite: The Brown Fellowship Society and Humane Brotherhood." *South Carolina Historical Magazine* 82, no. 4 (1981): 289–310.

Helg, Aline. "A Fragmented Majority: Free 'of All Colors,' Indians, and Slaves in Caribbean Colombia during the Haitian Revolution." In Geggus, *Impact of the Haitian Revolution,* 157–75.

——. *Liberty and Equality in Caribbean Colombia, 1770–1835.* Chapel Hill: University of North Carolina Press, 2004.

——. "The Limits of Equality: Free People of Color and Slaves during the First Independence of Cartagena, Colombia, 1810–1815." *Slavery and Abolition* 20, no. 2 (1999): 1–30.

Heuman, Gad. "Apprenticeship and Emancipation in the Caribbean: The Seeds of Citizenship." In *Race and Nation in the Age of Emancipations: An Atlantic World Anthology,* edited by Whitney Nell Stewart and John Garrison Marks, 107–20. Athens: University of Georgia Press, 2018.

Higgins, Kathleen J. *"Licentious Liberty" in a Brazilian Gold-Mining Region: Slavery, Gender, and Social Control in Eighteenth-Century Sabará, Minas Gerias.* University Park: Pennsylvania State University Press, 1999.

Hinks, Peter P. "John Marrant and the Meaning of Early Black Freemasonry." *William and Mary Quarterly* 64, no. 1 (2007): 105–16.

Hinks, Peter P., and Stephen Kantrowitz, eds. *All Men Free and Brethren: Essays on the History of African American Freemasonry.* Ithaca, N.Y.: Cornell University Press, 2013.

Holt, Thomas C. *The Problem of Freedom: Race, Labor, and Politics in Jamaica and Britain, 1832–1938.* Baltimore: Johns Hopkins University Press, 1992.

Hodges, Graham Russell. *Root and Branch: African Americans in New York and East Jersey, 1613–1863.* Chapel Hill: University of North Carolina Press, 1999.

Horton, James Oliver, and Lois E. Horton. *In Hope of Liberty: Culture, Community, and Protest Among Northern Free Blacks, 1700–1860.* New York: Oxford University Press, 1997.

Hünefeldt, Christine. *Paying the Price of Freedom: Family and Labor among Lima's Slaves, 1800–1854.* Berkeley: University of California Press, 1995.

Irons, Charles F. *The Origins of Proslavery Christianity: White and Black Evangelicals in Colonial and Antebellum Virginia.* Chapel Hill: University of North Carolina Press, 2008.

Johnson, Karl E., Jr., and Joseph A. Romero. "Jehu Jones (1786–1852): The First African American Lutheran Minister." *Lutheran Quarterly* 10, no. 4 (1996): 425–43.

Johnson, Michael. "Reading Evidence." *William and Mary Quarterly* 59, no. 1 (2002): 193–202.

Johnson, Michael P., and James L. Roark. *Black Masters: A Free Family of Color in the Old South.* New York: Norton, 1984.

Johnson, Walter. *Soul by Soul: Life inside the Antebellum Trade Market.* Cambridge, Mass.: Harvard University Press, 1999.

Jones, Martha S. "Seaman and Citizen: Learning the Law of Citizenship, from Baltimore to Valparaiso." In *Race and Nation in the Age of Emancipations: An Atlantic World Anthology,* edited by Whitney Nell Stewart and John Garrison Marks, 89–106. Athens: University of Georgia Press, 2018.

Jordan, Winthrop D. *Tumult and Silence at Second Creek: An Inquiry into a Civil War Slave Conspiracy.* Baton Rouge: Louisiana State University Press, 1996.

Joyner, Charles. *Down by the Riverside: A South Carolina Slave Community.* Urbana: University of Illinois Press, 1984.

King, Stewart R. *Blue Coat or Powdered Wig: Free People of Color in Pre-revolutionary Saint Domingue.* Athens: University of Georgia Press, 2001.

Kinsbruner, Jay. *Not of Pure Blood: The Free People of Color and Racial Prejudice in Nineteenth-Century Puerto Rico.* Durham, N.C.: Duke University Press, 1996.

Klein, Herbert S. *Slavery in the Americas: A Comparative Study of Virginia and Cuba.* Chicago: University of Chicago Press.

Klein, Herbert S., and Ben Vinson III. *African Slavery in Latin America and the Caribbean.* 2nd ed. New York: Oxford University Press, 2007.

Kuethe, Allan J. "Flexibilidad racial en las milicias disciplinadas de Cartagena de Indias." *Historia y Cultura* 2 (1994): 177–92.

———. "The Status of the Free Pardo in the Disciplines Militia of New Granada." *Journal of Negro History* 56, no. 2 (1971): 105–17.

Landers, Jane G. "The African Landscape of Seventeenth-Century Cartagena and Its Hinterlands." In *The Black Urban Atlantic in the Era of the Slave Trade,* edited by Jorge Cañizares-Esguerra, Matt D. Childs, and James Sidbury, 147–62. Philadelphia: University of Pennsylvania Press, 2013.

———, ed. *Against the Odds: Free Blacks in the Slave Societies of the Americas.* New York: Routledge, 1996.

———. *Atlantic Creoles in the Age of Revolutions.* Cambridge, Mass.: Harvard University Press, 2010.

La Rosa Corzo, Gabino. *Runaway Slave Settlements in Cuba: Resistance and Repression.* Chapel Hill: University of North Carolina Press, 1990.

Lasso, Marixa. *Myths of Harmony: Race and Republicanism during the Age of Revolution, Colombia, 1795–1831.* Pittsburgh: University of Pittsburgh Press, 2007.

Lebsock, Suzanne. *The Free Women of Petersburg: Status and Culture in a Southern Town, 1784–1860*. New York: Norton, 1984.

Marks, John Garrison. "Community Bonds in the Bayou City: Free Blacks and Local Reputation in Early Houston." *Southwestern Historical Quarterly* 117, no. 3 (2014): 266–82.

Massey, Douglass S., and Nancy A. Denton. *American Apartheid: Segregation and the Making of the Underclass*. Cambridge, Mass.: Harvard University Press, 1993.

Maya Restrepo, Luz Adriana. *Brujería y reconstrucción de identidades entre los Africanos y sus descendientes en la Nueva Granada, siglo XVII*. Bogotá: Ministerio de Cultura, 2005.

——. "Racismo institucional, violencia, y políticas culturales. Legados coloniales y políticas de la diferencia en Colombia." *Historia Crítica* 43 (2009): 218–45.

McGraw, Jason P. *The Work of Recognition: Caribbean Colombia and the Postemancipation Struggle for Citizenship*. Chapel Hill: University of North Carolina Press, 2014.

McNeil, John R. *Mosquito Empires: Ecology and War in the Greater Caribbean, 1620–1914*. New York: Cambridge University Press, 2010.

Meisel Roca, Adolfo, and María Aguilera Díaz. "Cartagena de Indias en 1777: Un análisis demográfico." In *150 años de la abolición de la esclavización en Colombia: Desde la marginalidad a la construcción de la nación*, 224–89. Bogotá: Ministerio de Cultura, 2003.

Melish, Joanne Pope. *Disowning Slavery: Gradual Emancipation and "Race" in New England, 1780–1860*. Ithaca, N.Y.: Cornell University Press, 2000.

Metcalf, Alida C. *Family and Frontier in Colonial Brazil: Santana de Parnaíba, 1580–1822*. Austin: University of Texas Press, 2005.

Mintz, Sidney W., and Richard Price. *The Birth of African-American Culture: An Anthropological Perspective*. Boston: Beacon, 1992.

Morgan, Philip D. "Work and Culture: The Task System and the World of Lowcountry Blacks, 1700 to 1880." *William and Mary Quarterly* 39, no. 4 (1982): 563–99.

Múnera, Alfonso. *El fracaso de la nación: Region, clase y raza en el Caribe Colombiano, 1717–1821*. Bogotá: Banco de la República, 1998.

——, comp. *Ensayos Costeños: De la Colonia a la República, 1770–1890*. Bogotá: Colcultura, 1994.

——. "Failing to Construct the Colombian Nation: Race and Class in the Andean-Caribbean Conflict, 1717–1816." Ph.D. diss., University of Connecticut, 1995.

——. *Fronteras imaginadas: La construcción de las razas y de la geografía en el siglo XIX colombiano*. Bogotá: Editorial Planeta Colombiana, 2005.

Myers, Amrita Chakrabarti. *Forging Freedom: Black Women and the Pursuit of Liberty in Antebellum Charleston*. Chapel Hill: University of North Carolina Press, 2011.

Paton, Diana. *Obeah and Other Powers: The Politics of Caribbean Religion and Healing*. Durham, N.C.: Duke University Press, 2012.

Polgar, Paul J. "Standard Bearers of Liberty and Equality: Reinterpreting the Origins of American Abolitionism." Ph.D. diss., City University of New York, 2013.

Powers, Bernard L., Jr. *Black Charlestonians: A Social History, 1822–1885*. Fayetteville: University of Arkansas Press, 1999.

Price, Richard. *Alabi's World*. Baltimore: Johns Hopkins University Press, 1990.

———. *First-Time: The Historical Vision of an African American People.* Chicago: University of Chicago Press, 1983.

———. *Maroon Societies: Rebel Slave Communities in the Americas.* Baltimore: Johns Hopkins University Press, 1979.

Pulis, John W., ed. *Religion, Diaspora, and Cultural Identity: A Reader on the Anglophone Caribbean.* New York: Gordon & Breach, 1999.

Putnam, Lara. "To Study the Fragments/Whole: Microhistory and the Atlantic World." *Journal of Social History* 39, no. 3 (2006): 615–30.

Quintana, Ryan A. *Making a Slave State: Political Development in Early South Carolina.* Chapel Hill: University of North Carolina Press, 2018.

Raboteau, Albert J. *Slave Religion: The "Invisible Institutions" in the Antebellum South.* New York: Oxford University Press, 1978.

Rael, Patrick. *Black Identity and Black Protest in the Antebellum North.* Chapel Hill: University of North Carolina Press, 2002.

Reid-Vazquez, Michele. *The Year of the Lash: Free People of Color in Cuba and the Nineteenth-Century Atlantic World.* Athens: University of Georgia Press, 2011.

Restall, Matthew. *The Black Middle: Africans, Mayas, and Spaniards in Colonial Yucatan.* Stanford, Calif.: Stanford University Press, 2013.

Restrepo Tirado, Ernesto, ed. *150 años de la abolición de la esclavización en Colombia: Desde la marginalidad a la construcción de la nación.* Bogotá: Ministerio del Cultura, 2003.

Rockman, Seth. *Scraping By: Wage Labor, Slavery, and Survival in Early Baltimore.* Baltimore: Johns Hopkins University Press, 2009.

Sanchez Mejia, Hugues R. "De esclavos a campesinos, de la 'roza' al mercado: Tierra y producción agropecuaria de los 'libres de todos los colores' en la gobernación de Santa Marta (1740–1810)." *Historia Crítica* 43 (2011): 130–55.

Sanders, James E. *Contentious Republicans: Popular Politics, Race, and Class in Nineteenth-Century Colombia.* Durham, N.C.: Duke University Press, 2004.

Schafer, Judith Kelleher. *Becoming Free, Remaining Free: Manumission and Enslavement in New Orleans, 1846–1862.* Baton Rouge: Louisiana State University Press, 2003.

Schmidt-Nowara, Christopher. *Slavery, Freedom, and Abolition in Latin America and the Atlantic World.* Albuquerque: University of New Mexico Press, 2011.

Schoeppner, Michael Alan. "Navigating the Dangerous Atlantic: Black Sailors, Racial Quarantines, and U.S. Constitutionalism." Ph.D. diss., University of Florida, 2010.

Scott, Julius S. "The Common Wind: Currents of Afro-American Communication in the Era of the Haitian Revolution." Ph.D. diss., Duke University, 1986.

Scott, Rebecca J. "Small-Scale Dynamics of Large-Scale Processes." *American Historical Review* 105, no. 2 (2000): 472–79.

Scott, Rebecca J., and Jean M. Hébrard. *Freedom Papers: An Atlantic Odyssey in the Age of Emancipation.* Cambridge, Mass.: Harvard University Press, 2012.

Shaw, Jenny. "Birth and Initiation on the Peers Plantation: The Problem of Creolization in Seventeenth-Century Barbados." *Slavery and Abolition* 39, no. 2 (2018): 290–314.

Sidbury, James. *Becoming African in America: Race and Nation in the Early Black Atlantic.* New York: Oxford University Press, 2007.

——. "Plausible Stories and Varnished Truths." *William and Mary Quarterly* 59, no. 1 (2002): 179–84.

——. *Ploughshares into Swords: Race, Rebellion, and Identity in Gabriel's Virginia, 1730–1810.* New York: Cambridge University Press, 1997.

——. "Saint Domingue in Virginia: Ideology, Local Meanings, and Resistance to Slavery, 1790–1800." *Journal of Southern History* 63, no. 3 (1997): 531–52.

Sobel, Mechal. *Trabelin' On: The Slave Journey to an Afro-Baptist Faith.* Westport, Conn.: Greenwood, 1979.

——. *The World They Made Together: Black and White Values in Eighteenth-Century Virginia.* Princeton: Princeton University Press, 2003.

Solano D., Sergio Paolo. "Pedro Romero, el artesano: Trabajo, raza, y diferenciación social en Cartagena de Indias a finales del dominio colonial." *Historia Crítica* 61 (2016): 151–70.

Solano D., Sergio Paolo, and Roicer Flórez Bolívar. "'Artilleros pardos y morenos artistas': Artesanos, raza, milicias y reconocimiento social en el Nuevo Reino de Granada, 1770–1812." *Historia Crítica* 48 (2012): 11–37.

Sparks, Randy J. *Africans in the Old South: Mapping Exceptional Lives across the Atlantic World.* Cambridge, Mass.: Harvard University Press, 2016.

Stark, David M. "Rescued from Their Invisibility: The Afro-Puerto Ricans of Seventeenth- and Eighteenth-Century San Mateo de Cangrejos, Puerto Rico." *Americas* 63, no. 4 (2007): 551–86.

——. "Ties That Bind: Baptismal Sponsorship of Slaves in Eighteenth-Century Puerto Rico." *Slavery and Abolition* 36, no 1 (2015): 84–110.

Sweet, James H. *Domingos Álvares, African Healing, and the Intellectual History of the Atlantic World.* Chapel Hill: University of North Carolina Press, 2011.

——. *Recreating Africa: Culture, Kinship, and Religion in the African-Portuguese World.* Chapel Hill: University of North Carolina Press, 2003.

Tannenbaum, Frank. *Slave and Citizen: The Negro in the Americas.* New York: Knopf, 1946.

Telles, Edward, and the Project on Ethnicity and Race in Latin America. *Pigmentocracies: Ethnicity, Race, and Color in Latin America.* Chapel Hill: University of North Carolina Press, 2014.

Thornton, John K. "The Development of an African Catholic Church in the Kingdom of Kongo, 1491–1750." *Journal of African History* 25 (1984): 147–67.

Townsend, Camilla. *Tales of Two Cities: Race and Economic Culture in Early Republican North and South America.* Austin: University of Texas Press, 2000.

Twinam, Ann. *Public Lives, Private Secrets: Gender, Honor, Sexuality, and Illegitimacy in Colonial Spanish America.* Stanford, Calif.: Stanford University Press, 1999.

——. *Purchasing Whiteness: Pardos, Mulattoes, and the Quest for Social Mobility in the Spanish Indies.* Stanford, Calif.: Stanford University Press, 2015.

Vinson, Ben, III. *Bearing Arms for His Majesty: The Free Colored Militia in Colonial Mexico.* Stanford, Calif.: Stanford University Press, 2001.

von Daacke, Kirt. *Freedom Has a Face: Race, Identity, and Community in Jefferson's Virginia.* Charlottesville: University of Virginia Press, 2012.

von Germeten, Nicole. *Black Blood Brothers: Confraternities and Social Mobility for Afro-Mexicans*. Gainesville: University Press of Florida, 2006.

———. "Black Brotherhoods in Mexico City." In Cañizares-Esguerra, Childs, and Sidbury, *Black Urban Atlantic*, 248–68.

Weaver, Karol K. *Medical Revolutionaries: The Enslaved Healers of Eighteenth-Century Saint Domingue*. Urbana: University of Illinois Press, 2006.

Wedel, Johan. *Santería Healing: A Journey into the Afro-Cuban World of Divinities, Spirits, and Sorcery*. Gainesville: University Press of Florida, 2004.

Wheat, David. "The Afro-Portuguese Maritime World and the Foundations of Spanish Caribbean Society, 1570–1640." Ph.D. diss., Vanderbilt University, 2009.

———. *Atlantic Africa and the Spanish Caribbean, 1570–1640*. Chapel Hill: Published for the Omohundro Institute of Early American History and Culture by University of North Carolina Press, 2016.

———. "The First Great Waves: African Provenance Zones for the Transatlantic Slave Trade to Cartagena de Indias, 1570–1640." *Journal of African History* 52, no. 1 (2011): 1–22.

White, Shane. *Somewhat More Independent: The End of Slavery in New York City, 1770–1810*. Athens: University of Georgia Press, 2004.

Wikramanayake, Marina. *A World in Shadow: The Free Black in Antebellum South Carolina*. Columbia: University of South Carolina Press, 1973.

Wirtz, Kristina. *Ritual, Discourse, and Community in Cuban Santería: Speaking a Sacred World*. Gainesville: University Press of Florida, 2007.

Wood, Peter H. *Black Majority: Negroes in Colonial South Carolina from 1670 through the Stono Rebellion*. New York: Norton, 1974.

Woodson, Carter G. *Free Negro Owners of Slaves in the United States in 1830*. Washington D.C.: Association for the Study of Negro Life and History, 1924.

Young, Jeffrey R. *Rituals of Resistance: African Atlantic Religion in the Kongo and Lowcountry South in the Era of Slavery*. Baton Rouge: Louisiana State University Press, 2011.

Index